BYZANTIUM AND ISTANBUL

BYZANTIUM
AND ISTANBUL

by

ROBERT LIDDELL

JONATHAN CAPE
Thirty Bedford Square . London

FIRST PUBLISHED 1956
SECOND IMPRESSION 1958

PRINTED IN GREAT BRITAIN IN THE CITY OF OXFORD
AT THE ALDEN PRESS
ILLUSTRATIONS PRINTED IN PHOTOGRAVURE BY CLARKE & SHERWELL LTD.,
NORTHAMPTON
BOUND BY A. W. BAIN & CO. LTD., LONDON

TO

ALAN BIRD

The last chapter of this book was published in *Encounter* in 1955.

CONTENTS

A MAP OF ISTANBUL appears on the next two pages.

ISTANBUL

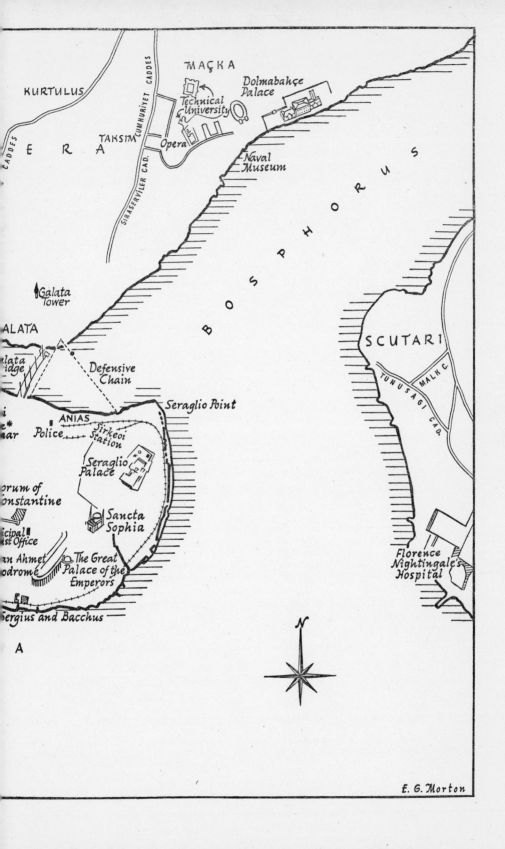

ILLUSTRATIONS

Except where otherwise stated the photographs were provided by the Turkish Embassy in London, by whose courtesy and generosity they are here reproduced.

BYZANTIUM AND ISTANBUL

A NOTE ON TURKISH PRONUNCIATION
AND SPELLING

Turkey adopted a modified Latin alphabet in the place of Arabic script in 1928.

The new orthography is phonetic, though the letters of the alphabet do not all have the same values as in English. There are also a few additional letters (as for example ç and ş) for sounds usually represented by double consonants in English, as well as modified vowels.

The vowels have much the same value as in German. 'A' is pronounced as in 'man', 'e' as in 'set', 'i' as in 'sit', 'o' as in 'top', and 'u' as in 'full'. The modified vowels are: ö, pronounced as in the German 'können' and ü, as in the French 'musée'; 'ı' (without a dot) is pronounced as the 'e' in the second syllable of 'table'. 'Y' is not a vowel.

Consonants have mostly the same values as in English, those which have a different sound being as follows: 'c' is pronounced as the 'j' in 'jam'; 'j' like the 'si' of 'vision'; 'ç' represents the sound of 'ch' in 'child' and ş that of 'sh' in 'shop', hence 'pasha' becomes 'paşa': 'ğ' is unpronounced but usually lengthens the preceding vowel.

Place names have not changed under the Republic but in some cases their Turkish form differs from that traditionally adopted by Western writers. Some of the chief names that differ in this way are as follows: Broussa in Turkish is Bursa, Smyrna is İzmir, Angora is Ankara, the ancient Trabizond is Trabzon.

It should also be noted that the Pera district of Istanbul is, in Turkish, Beyoğlu; Prinkipo is the Turkish Büyükada.

CHAPTER I

FLYING TO BYZANTIUM

ALL approaches to Constantinople are beautiful; so often a lovely city
can only make an unbecoming first appearance, if you go there by
any way you would be likely to take. Oxford and Athens nearly
always begin by disappointing their most eager visitors. But Constantinople lays itself out to please at first sight, and pleases as infallibly as
Jerusalem: it is not always so successful in retaining the visitor's admiration.

The most exciting approach must be that from the north, when the
narrow Bosphorus with its lush-grown hills opens into the wider, airier
Marmara, and Seraglio Point stands out ahead of you, with its trees and
minarets. I first approached Constantinople from the opposite direction,
the Marmara narrowed in front of the ship, the point was turned, and soon
I had to struggle with all the difficulties of landing, amid the hubbub of
Horaçköy. Another arrival was by the Taurus express, travelling from
Egypt to Greece in 1940, when the Mediterranean was better avoided:
we reached the railhead at Haydar Pasha in the middle of the night, and
ferried over in the dark to Galata.

On the present occasion I flew from Cairo. It was five hundred years
after the fall of Byzantium to the Turks. Bells tolled in Greek churches,
and mass was sung for Constantine Dragases, the last emperor — it seemed
to be conveniently forgotten that he had died in communion with Rome.
All Cairo had been talking about a ball given by a Turkish princeling.
Cards had been sent out, with a turban engraved on them: 'La famille
impériale de la Turquie, représentée par le Prince X., vous invite ...'
A Greek couple who had received a card did not wish to offend the
nationalist ideas of their compatriots, still less did they wish to miss the
smartest party of the season; they found a solution worthy of the Duc de
Guermantes: they would go to the ball, indeed, but they would not
arrive till after midnight, when the anniversary was over.

It is always a wrench to leave Egypt; the Delta looks such a vivid green

17

from the air, the desert so golden. And yet, when one returns to them from Europe, too often they seem stifling and parched. The canal, that bone of contention, is exactly the kind of landscape that looks at its best from an aeroplane — golden and blue, and patches of green palm trees.

Cyprus was a preparation for what was to come. It is *de facto* British, and ethnically Greek, but geographically Asiatic. I interested myself in its minor Turkish aspects, because it was to Turkey that I was going. Moreover, it was the feast of Bayram, and the small Turkish minority was particularly noticeable, celebrating the end of Ramazan with illuminations and music and dancing.

It was the first time (for my earlier visits to Constantinople had been hurried) that I had seen churches turned into mosques. One of the Cypriot cathedrals has the prayer-niche and the platform attached to it in the south transept, the other has a niche arranged in the south part of the apse. In either case it is a cruel distortion of the lines of the church. Having seen the greater horror of a Gothic church, all of whose lines flow towards the east, ill-treated in this way, I was prepared for all the Turks could do to Byzantine churches: these do not seem to suffer nearly as much from being re-orientated towards Mecca as the long pier arcades and clerestories of Nicosia or Famagusta.

Unhappy island, with its ugly, broad central plain, and its aguish coasts — I was not very sorry to be leaving it, to fly high over the plateau of Anatolia and its odd, scattered tarns. Ankara, to judge from its airport, must be dry and bracing. Turkish photo-reporters had come out to record the well-known and agreeable smile of Mr. Adlai Stevenson.

The westward journey was over the bare highlands of Anatolia, brown as if seen on a map of their physical geography. Then came a swoop over the Marmara and a distant vision of minarets, and we landed in a dull, flat part of Thrace from which nothing remarkable could be seen.

The drive into the city is a long one, through quiet, southern-English suburban railway country; one should have been sitting in a dining-car, eating placid railway fish cloaked in white paste. There was an enormous number of hoardings along the road, and we even passed a level-crossing. I had not been so far north for several years, and the greenness, the melancholy, long-drawn-out evening, and the apple trees, made me feel myself to be in Kent. Then the road rose, and in front was the superb line of walls that fences in the city on the west, stretching from the Marmara to the Golden Horn. This is so splendid in its preservation, and so tragic in its ruin, that this entry into Constantinople by land is hardly less impressive than an arrival from the sea.

The road ran now between cemeteries, tall, narrow steles standing at different angles to the earth, under groves of cypress trees; then we crossed the fosse, and entered Stamboul by the Adrianople gate. There were the noisy cobbled streets of an oriental town. Lights were coming on in the shops and over the wooden booths of a market. Sometimes two men passed, carrying a kind of bier on which was laid a huge, flat, wooden tray full of white or purple mulberries, decorated here and there by a spray of bougainvillaea or some other flower, and lit by a small oil lamp.

We came to an open space. Was it my first sight of St. Sophia, I wondered, or was I wasting my emotion upon some lesser dome? I cannot be sure. Then my heart sank, for the car went downhill to the Golden Horn, crossed the Galata bridge, and began the ascent of the gloomy hill, where trams grind noisily over the cobbles as they climb steeply up to Pera (the modern Beyoğlu). I was seized again with that peculiar horror that Pera has excited in so many travellers. Unfortunately it is where the foreign visitor is almost compelled to live while he visits the monuments of Stamboul. There can be no other centre of a great city's life and activities that is so unattractive at first sight. The steep, cobbled hills, the grinding trams that threaten to sweep you off the narrow pavements where two people cannot safely pass abreast, the repellent architecture, the glum, ugly faces, all combine in a nightmare vision. Many a visitor, in his expensive, gloomy, noisy, comfortless hotel, must want to cry himself to sleep on his first night in Constantinople. There are few places that make so great and immediate a demand upon one's fortitude.

Yet it would be a pity to follow one's heart and to leave next day. Even a glimpse of Stamboul must convince one that it must be seen, even that it has secrets not likely to be given up to a casual or hurried tourist. Byzantine remains, I knew from experience, must be hunted for; when I had been a hurried tourist, I had not been very successful in finding them. And I knew from Egypt and Syria that mosques lurk shyly down alleys that are not easy to identify. When you get there, they are often locked; you must wait till the hour of prayer, unless someone will produce the

B

key. Everything in an oriental town needs patience. I was to find that
Constantinople requires a Griselda-like patience hardly attainable by me,
trained in waiting though I have been in Egypt, Syria and Greece.

From the heights of Pera I looked across the Golden Horn to Stamboul,
very sparsely lighted at night; there my days would be passed. What
should I make of it? Fallen Byzantium most filled my mind in this year of
anniversary — East Rome, the heiress of Greek and Roman civilization;
often the final outpost of civilization, and sometimes ringed with enemies,
defending Christianity as Alfred defended it on Athelney. 'The political
and administrative centre, the religious and economic centre, the literary
and artistic centre of the monarchy. The Queen city, to which the whole
world looks, the pole of attraction towards which all turn, subjects of the
empire and foreigners alike. She is more than an ordinary town, she is for
the Byzantines "the God-guarded city", or, more simply, "The City";
and when the great cities of the modern west were mostly only poor and
mediocre townships, she was the Queen of elegance, the centre of the
civilized world and (as it has been prettily said) "the Paris of the Middle
Ages". More than once, in the course of her long history, she alone has
been the whole empire!'[1] In the time of Romanus Lecapenus, she was all
the Empire had left of Europe; in the time of the Comnene Emperors, she
was nearly all that was left of Asia. While the city stood, so did the Empire;
in the end she survived the Empire by nearly a century.

For that reason alone, I suppose Byzantium has long haunted the West;
we have seen in it a type and an example of our own struggle and of our
own duty to preserve and hand on our cultural heritage. The city with its
tense, nervous life, generally in danger for its last three hundred and fifty
years, protected by Greek cunning and 'Greek fire', has seemed closer to
our experience than the sweetness and light of Athens. Its formal hieratic
art has been a discovery of this century, admired alike by those who have
seen it as changeless through the centuries, and by those, more far-sighted,
who have seen in it the beginnings of a renaissance which would have
developed parallel with that of the West, 'had Constantinople not fallen
once; had Constantinople not fallen twice'.

Our case may yet be like that of the Byzantine scribes who fled westward — such perhaps is the case of English writers who have already settled
in America — it is like John Servopoulos, for instance, whom we find in

[1] Charles Diehl, *Byzance: grandeur et décadence* (Paris, 1919).

the late fifteenth century copying Greek manuscripts at Reading Abbey. And if we have the kind of mind that is strengthened in adversity by meditating over notable examples of courage, we may add to Regulus returning to Carthage, to Alfred on Athelney, to Saint Thomas More going to his martyrdom, the desperate courage of the last Constantine during the siege of Byzantium, and his death under the walls on 29 May, 1453.

But, as Istanbul, the city has been the capital of another vanished empire, which has left more of its glories behind. The Ottoman civilization means less to us than that of Byzantium, but it is not to be ignored. I had an especial need to struggle against anti-Ottoman prejudice, coming from Egypt where Turkish work is comparatively mean, and where the splendid monuments of Arabian art have been spared by the conquerors, co-religionists of the conquered; the spindly minarets of the Turks look poor beside the great towers which the Mamelukes gave to their mosques in the fourteenth and early fifteenth centuries, or the delicate spires of the Kait Bey period. In a conquered province, already well-equipped with mosques, it is natural that Ottoman work should be unimpressive; it is no preparation at all for the metropolitan mosques – great structures built by emperors, or smaller and even more exquisite works of art erected by their daughters or Grand Viziers. The narrow-minded Byzantinologist, who cares for nothing built after 1453, is as stupid and limited as the classical scholar who, visiting Greece, turns with scorn from every trace of its Roman, Byzantine, Venetian or Turkish past. Such a one, I remember, once told me that Xerxes' canal was the only thing that could interest him on Athos. The Byzantinologist has this much more excuse than the classical scholar: his subject is a comparatively new one, and he may feel he has to struggle for its success. Nevertheless, we must not allow him to waste all our time in the contemplation of crumbling walls where once there were mosaics; it is better to look at walls where there still are tiles.

In these pages, for which no claim to originality can be made, it will be my endeavour to present Constantinople, both Byzantine and Ottoman, with such fairness and fullness as I can, not overvaluing Byzantium for its vanished glories, nor altogether forgetting them in the surviving beauties of Istanbul.

No general survey of Byzantine and Ottoman civilization can be attempted within so narrow a compass; only their metropolitan aspects can be considered, for my emphasis must be upon the city itself. This city, following the general Western tradition, I shall continue to call Constantinople, reserving the name Stamboul for the area bounded by the Golden Horn, the Marmara and the land walls — the old Byzantine and Ottoman capital.

CHAPTER II

EAST ROME

BYZANTIUM is a beautiful and romantic word, and it provides us with an indispensable adjective, 'Byzantine'; but the city was not popularly so called during any period of its greatness. Byzas of Megara founded the first city here, and gave it his name, in 657 B.C. The Delphic oracle told him to choose a site 'opposite the land of the blind'; that is the colony of Chalcedon founded by other Megarians a few years previously, who had neglected the wonderful anchorage of the Golden Horn.

The chequered history of this small Greek colony is of no great interest till its fortunes and its whole nature were transformed by Constantine the Great. He wished to found a great city to be a seat of government in the East. He had considered other sites (Nish, his birthplace, and Alexandria Throas) before his choice fell upon the city of Byzantium, a place, as Gibbon writes, 'formed by nature for the centre and capital of a great monarchy'.

No one has better described its admirable position. 'Situated in the forty-first degree of latitude, the imperial city commanded, from her seven hills, the opposite shores of Europe and Asia; the climate was healthy and temperate, the soil fertile, the harbour secure and capacious, and the approach on the side of the continent was of small extent and easy defence. The Bosphorus and Hellespont may be considered as the two gates of Constantinople, and the prince who possessed these important passages could always shut them against a naval enemy and open them to the fleets of commerce. The preservation of the eastern provinces may, in some degree, be ascribed to the policy of Constantine, as the barbarians of the Euxine, who in the preceding age had poured their armaments into the heart of the Mediterranean, soon desisted from the exercise of piracy, and despaired of forcing this insurmountable barrier. When the gates of the Hellespont and Bosphorus were shut, the capital still enjoyed, within their spacious enclosure, every production which would satisfy the wants, or gratify the luxury, of its numerous inhabitants. The sea-coast of Thrace and Bithynia . . . still exhibits a rich prospect of vineyards, of gardens, and of plentiful harvests; and the Propontis has ever been renowned for an inexhaustible store of the most exquisite fish, that are taken in their stated seasons without skill, and almost without labour. But when the passages of the straits were thrown open for trade, they alternately admitted the natural and artificial riches of the north and south, of the Euxine, and of the Mediterranean. Whatever rude commodities were collected in the forests of Germany and Scythia, as far as the sources of the Tanais and the Borysthenes; whatsoever was manufactured by the skill of Europe or Asia; the corn of Egypt, and the gems and spices of the farthest India; were brought by the varying winds into the port of Constantinople, which for many ages attracted the commerce of the ancient world.'

The end of the promontory, on which the city was built, is strictly a trapezium, but (the fourth side being so short) it is generally spoken of as triangular; a medieval chronicler likened it to a three-cornered sail, blown out by the wind. The northern side overlooked the Golden Horn, that unique natural harbour; one of the two disadvantages of the site (the other was the frequency of earthquakes) was the prevailing north-easterly wind, which often embarrassed the arrival of merchandise in the Golden Horn, but if the point (most famous by its later name of Seraglio Point) could not be rounded in safety, there were smaller harbours on the shores of the Marmara. The Alexandrian grain magazines were in that quarter; therefore the Egyptian corn-ships must have unloaded there as a matter of course.

Constantine modelled his city, so far as he could, upon its mother-city, the greater Rome. He must have been pleased to find that five cross-valleys divided the long ridge, overlooking the Golden Horn, into six hills; a seventh hill, large and isolated, stands in the south-western corner of the trapezium or triangle, divided from the northern ridge by the valley of the Lycus. As in the old Rome, he planned the creation of fourteen 'regions'; the thirteenth, Sycae (now Galata), across the Golden Horn, was to correspond to the quarter of Trastevere. The hippodrome and palace were adjacent, as in Rome; and, like its mother-city with its secret name 'Flora', Constantinople must have a similar secret name, 'Anthusa'. Patrician families were urged to settle in the new city, and other cities of the empire were robbed of art treasures to give it dignity and beauty.

Spear in hand, Constantine is said to have traced out the line of his city walls. When he was asked how far he would go, he replied: 'Until He tarries who now goes before.' The route chosen by Constantine, or chosen for him by his divine guide, cannot now with certainty be mapped out; part, at least, of the fifth, sixth and seventh hills remained extra-mural. The fourteenth region, Blachernae, at or under the sixth hill, seems for a long time to have remained a fortified suburb.

On 11 May, 330, Constantine's city was dedicated, and received the name of New Rome. In one important respect it differed from Rome on the Tiber; pagan associations were left behind. Constantinople was to be a Christian city and, though liberty of opinion was permitted, and pagans were to be found in the university, the celebration of pagan rites was proscribed.

Five years before the dedication of the city, the Catholic faith had been defined by the Council of Nicaea, not far across the Marmara. The heresy of Arius had been condemned, and the second Person of the Trinity had been defined as 'being of one substance with the Father'. The Arians had said 'like substance', *homoiousion* instead of *homoousion*. Carlyle is somewhere very philistine and facetious about people killing one another over the difference of a letter; but, supposing a difference of opinion, or indeed anything whatever, justifies people killing one another, there is as great a difference between the relations of identity and similarity as there is between any two conceptions.

Constantius II reverted to Arianism and 'devoted the leisure of his winter quarters to the amusement or toils of controversy' (it will not be necessary to indicate Gibbon's authorship in further quotations such as this, stamped with his personality). In his day the roads were filled with galloping bishops, going to and from continual Synods. His successor, Julian the Apostate, made a pedantic and less successful attempt to revive paganism; in spite of its failure, it showed the strength of the old religion, and his immediate successors, Jovian and Valens, adopted a cautious religious policy. Theodosius the Great (379-95) ended the toleration of pagans and of Arians alike throughout the Roman empire, of which he was the last sole ruler; the second General Council was held in Constantinople in 381, and reaffirmed the Nicene Creed.

Not only orthodoxy, but also public security, was guaranteed to the city by Theodosius, and its expansion began. 'Should the zeal of the Emperor to adorn the city continue,' said Themistius the orator, 'a wider circuit will be required, and the question will arise whether the city added to Constantinople by Theodosius is not more splendid than the city which Constantine added to Byzantium. No longer is the vacant ground in the city more extensive than that occupied by buildings; nor are we cultivating more territory within our walls than we inhabit; the beauty of the city is not as heretofore scattered over it in patches, but covers the whole area like a robe woven to the very fringe. The city gleams with gold and porphyry ... Were Constantine to see the capital he founded, he would behold a glorious and splendid scene, not a bare and empty void; he would find it fair, not with apparent but with real beauty.'

St. John Chrysostom bears witness to the wealth and luxury of Constantinople in the reign of Arcadius (395-408), the first emperor who reigned in East Rome only. Many nobles had ten or twenty houses, he tells us, and as many baths, and one to two thousand slaves. Doors were often of ivory, ceilings lined with gold, floors covered with mosaic or strewn with rich carpets; walls were of ivory, and beds or couches of ivory or silver or gold or silver-plated wood. He speaks of silks and brocades, of heavy Eastern perfumes, and of cunning oriental cooks, and of lute-girls hired to entertain guests at dinner parties. He complains bitterly of the survival of pagan practices at weddings and at funerals, and of the coquettishness of the deaconesses.

The growing city was extended and splendidly fortified during the reign of Theodosius II (408-50). That prince and his sister, St. Pulcheria, who in 414, at the age of fifteen, was proclaimed Augusta, and made regent for her thirteen-year-old brother, began that tradition of holiness and learning in the court life of Byzantium to which there were so many returns throughout the centuries. St. Pulcheria assisted in her brother's education, and gave him special instruction in deportment; Theodosius took an interest in natural science and astronomy and formed a theological library.

During this reign Anthemius provided the city with its present *enceinte* of walls, beyond which there has never been needed any extension, though in later times Galata and Pera, beyond the Golden Horn, were to increase to an importance altogether unforeseen. The decaying city in 1453 by no means covered the whole area enclosed by the Theodosian walls; it was 'scattered over it in patches', as Constantine's city had once been over a smaller area, and as the decaying city of today is scattered over the larger area.

Constantinople, at the end of the fifth century, had become the heir both of Greece and Rome. Alexandria, till then the centre of Hellenic culture, gave place to Constantinople, the metropolitan city; and Rome, whose last puppet emperor, Romulus Augustulus, was deposed by the barbarians in 476, no longer existed as a seat of government. The barbarian invasions into Balkan countries by-passed Constantinople, and the Arabs had not yet over-run the eastern provinces. East Rome was as rich as it had ever been, and with the collapse of the greater Rome was the seat of the Roman emperor. East Romans called themselves Romans, and their language, though Greek, came to be called Romaic, a name given to modern Greek until today.

And yet Byzantium was not merely the guardian of the two greatest heritages of the ancient world: the culture of Greece and the imperial administration of Rome. The Christian religion had come from Syria (Hellenized though it had been, in Egypt); the diadem, the robes and the worship of the emperor had come from Persia; Syrian rhythms had transformed those of Greece, and the music of the synagogue lived again in the music of the church; eunuchs came from Asia, and the minor arts continued to feel the influence of Persia and, later, of the Arab world. Slavs and Asiatics filled the city and, as often as not, sat upon the imperial throne. The Roman world from which Byzantium inherited was already partly barbarized; and the Greek world from which it inherited was not Periclean Athens, but the orientalized Levantine world left behind by the Ptolemys and the Seleucids. Nor could the Hellenism of the Aegean have remained the same thing, transferred to the damp shores of Thrace. This does not mean that the city remained muddled and cosmopolitan; it had the power of absorption and of transformation, and exerted it over the mixed population that it received. There was such a thing as a Byzantine (though the word was not used), even as America can make Americans, and the Vatican can make a new type of Romans. The 'Romans' of Constantinople had a definite nationality of their own, which must not be denied; but they are not to be called Greeks or Romans.

The city of Constantinople, great and beautiful already in the fifth century, suffered terrible catastrophes: there were violent earthquakes in 478, and on many occasions in the following decade; a great fire raged all over the first hill in 462; three years later another fire lasted seven days and burned eight quarters of the town; in 469 the town burned 'from sea to sea';

seven years later the market and the library were totally destroyed; half the town was destroyed by fire in 491, and there was another severe fire in 498.

An insurrection in the hippodrome in 532, and the consequent destruction, gave rise to the noble restoration of the city by Justinian. The circus factions, Blues, Greens, Whites and Reds, had been brought from the older Rome, though in practice only the plebeian Greens and the more bourgeois Blues were of much importance. On the Ides of January 532, the leaders of the Blues and Greens united to plead for mercy for two culprits in an inter-faction riot who lay under sentence of death. This was refused, and on Tuesday, 13 January, with *Nika* (conquer) for their watchword, the factions made a joint revolt, which began as a protest against unpopular ministers and ended as a general rising against the throne. The palace of the Chalce and St. Sophia were fired, and other buildings near the hippodrome. Justinian was ready for flight, and was only restrained by the courage of his consort, Theodora, who declared that empire was a fine winding-sheet, and that she would sooner die than leave the throne. Justinian's general, Belisarius, attacked the rebels with his Gothic soldiers and about thirty thousand perished.

The restoration of Justinian gave us the Great Church; it was the First Golden Age of Byzantine art. 'Christian art', says Charles Diehl, 'undoubtedly retained many of the customs and traditions of pagan workshops – the secular motives, rustic themes, and mythological subjects dear to Alexandrian art; and from classical tradition it further inherited a feeling for beauty of design, dignity of pose, elegance in drapery, sobriety, and clearness of treatment . . . At this time, with unrivalled skill, use was made of every type of architectural construction . . . Never has Christian art been at one and the same time more varied, more creative, scientific and daring.'[1] The churches of the sixth century in Constantinople – in spite of all they have suffered – and the better preserved churches of Ravenna justify this statement; these monuments and others, and (even more) literature about them caused in Yeats a nostalgia for a Byzantium that never was.

'I think,' he wrote,[2] 'if I could be given a month of Antiquity and leave to spend it where I chose, I would spend it in Byzantium a little before

[1] Art. *Byzantine Art in Byzantium*, ed. Norman H. Baynes and H. St. L. B. Moss (Oxford, 1948).
[2] Cit. T. R. Henn: *The Lonely Tower* (London, 1950).

Justinian opened St. Sophia and closed the Academy of Plato. I think I could find in some little wine-shop some philosophical worker in mosaic who could answer all my questions . . . I think that in early Byzantium, as may be never before or since in recorded history, religious, aesthetic and practical life were one, that architect and artificers — though not, it may be, poets, for language had been the instrument of controversy and must have grown abstract — spoke to the multitude and the few alike. The painter, the mosaic worker, the worker in gold and silver, the illuminator of sacred books, were almost impersonal, almost perhaps without the consciousness of individual design, absorbed in their subject-matter and that the vision of a whole people.'

This vision of Justinian's city inspired those two wonderful poems, 'Sailing to Byzantium' and 'Byzantium', filled with the essence of an ideal Byzantium, and more Byzantine than Byzantium is or ever was. They must be responsible for many people's longing to visit Constantinople. Yeats first sent me to Constantinople, and is largely answerable for my lasting sense of disappointment with 'the Queen of Cities'.

Justinian was the last Roman-minded and Latin-speaking emperor to reign in East Rome, and his other great work, as permanent a monument as the noble edifices built in his reign, was his codification of Roman Law.

The remaining years of the sixth century were those of approaching danger, and of attempts to consolidate the defence of the northern frontiers against the Avars, and of the east against Persia. The seventh century began with a mutiny of the Danubian armies, which was checked only by a reign of terror. No one in 602 could have predicted that Constantinople was to last for another 850 years as a Roman capital.

The reign of Heraclius (610-41) witnessed an almost miraculous recovery. The emperor advanced boldly into Persia, totally defeated the Great King, and regained the True Cross, that had been carried off from Jerusalem by the Persians in 615. He returned in triumph in 629 to Constantinople which, during his absence, had repelled a siege by the Avars in 626, in which the besiegers were aided by Slav contingents and by Persian forces from Chalcedon.

Nevertheless, the city could not long rest in peace; a new danger threatened. Within a few years of the death of Mohammed, the Arabs began to be a world danger. Palestine and Syria fell to them at once; Egypt was theirs by 642, and Cyprus and Rhodes soon followed. Constantinople was subjected to a series of attacks from 673-77, and was only saved by 'Greek fire', with which the enemy ships were burned. Henceforward Constantinople was always on the defensive; the western provinces were now lost, and the empire mainly consisted of Asia Minor – the source of wealth and of man-power – and the hinterland of the city. The Latin language was disappearing from common and official use, and with it most vestiges of Latin culture.

Leo III, the Isaurian, the Asiatic general elected emperor at the end of a period of anarchy, was perhaps a Syrian. In the first year of his reign, between August 717 and 718, he managed to repel Arab attacks by land and sea that threatened the very walls of the capital. The tide turned, and Leo's successor Constantine V, Copronymus, was able to reconquer Cyprus and most of Asia Minor.

Under the Isaurian dynasty Constantinople, once torn by the Arian and the Monophysite heresies, was divided by the iconoclast dispute. In 726 Leo issued an edict against images; several explanations are given of his conduct, and all may be true. Perhaps he was attacking the growing power of monasticism; the monks, custodians of sacred images, were to be struck at through the images themselves. Perhaps he had a sincere desire to repress the idolatry with which many holy icons were worshipped. Moreover he, like all iconoclastic emperors that came after him, was an oriental, and had felt the influence of Islam, with its hatred of representational art; and the armies that supported them had been recruited in Asia.

His successor 'Copronymus', so-called either because of his love for the stables, or from an accident whereby he soiled the water of his baptism, carried the iconoclastic movement further and instituted a real persecution. On 10 February, 753, a packed council of three hundred and thirty-eight bishops at the palace of Hieria, on the Bosphorus, condemned icons and declared Constantine V 'a thirteenth apostle'. Eleven years later his frenzy was at its height: 'all beauty disappeared from the churches', we are told, statues were broken down, pictures were removed, and mosaics were covered with whitewash. Even the private ownership of images was forbidden. The convents were secularized, and monks were forced to file past in the hippodrome, each holding a woman by the hand.

The iconoclastic movement did much to break the unity of the still undivided Church. Pope Gregory II denounced the imperial edict and encouraged the people of Italy to resist its enforcement. He defended images as an aid to devotion; meanwhile, protected by living in a Moslem country, St. John Damascene defended image-worship by claiming that the very incarnation of Christ justified humanity in making images, for God had given an image of Himself in our own likeness.

The wicked Empress Irene, widow of Leo IV and mother of Constantine VI, whom she deposed and blinded, was an iconodule. The Seventh General Council, held at Nicaea in 787, restored images and permitted their worship. Thus peace and union (for Western representatives were present) were restored to the Church by 'the Christ-supporting Empress whose government, like her name, is a symbol of peace'.

She was the first woman to reign alone in the city. 'For five years the Roman world bowed to the government of a female; and, as she moved through the streets of Constantinople, the reins of four milk-white steeds were held by as many patricians, who marched on foot before the golden chariot of their queen.'

One of these patricians, Nicephorus, revolted and made himself emperor. 'His character was stained with the three odious vices of hypocrisy, ingratitude and avarice; his want of virtue was not redeemed by any superior talents nor his want of talents by any pleasing qualifications.' His son Stauracius, and then his son-in-law, Michael I, Rhangabes, composed his ineffective dynasty. Michael was deposed, and the army set Leo V, the Armenian, on the throne. His reign witnessed the defeat of Krum, king of the Bulgarians, who unsuccessfully besieged the city in 813, but succeeded in ravaging the country round. Leo's walls in the quarter of Blachernae are his lasting monument.

Michael the Amorian, Leo's favourite, had been arrested for conspiracy on Christmas Eve, 820. He was sentenced to have an ape tied to him, to be fastened to a pole, and thrown into the furnace which heated the Palace baths. The Empress Theodosia, appalled at this threatened inhumanity, ran barefoot to protest against it. Leo yielded, and delayed the execution of the sentence, though omens and bad dreams made him fear his own death. At night, alarmed by superstitious terrors, he smashed his way through the prison doors to see if the captive was safe. He saw Michael and his keeper asleep, but was himself seen by a young eunuch, hiding under a couch, who recognized the emperor's red boots. Michael and the keeper of the Palace were both afraid, when they heard of Leo's secret

visit; they formed a conspiracy with Michael's servant, Theoctistus, who
was to be sent out to fetch him a confessor. Conspirators mingled with the
choristers, who waited outside the Ivory Gate at dawn on Christmas Day,
before matins in the Palace chapel of St. Stephen. Leo arrived; he and the
priest were wearing felt caps to protect them against the cold. The
emperor was proud of his voice, and took part in the singing of the office;
when he came to a passage of which he was particularly fond, and which
absorbed his attention, the conspirators leapt forth, and he was butchered.

Of all imperial crimes, this murder of Leo most epitomizes the court of
Byzantium; we have here its savagery, its Christian charity and pity, its
piety, its superstition, and its ceremonial. Michael II, the Amorian, who
was dragged from prison to the throne, was proclaimed emperor before
there had been time to strike the fetters off his legs. He was a boorish
barbarian, and he continued the iconoclasm revived by Leo V, in imitation
of Leo the Isaurian. Theophilus, son of Michael II, was, however, a
cultivated prince, and a great builder: in his reign the palace buildings,
inspired by those of the iconoclastic Moslem east, were of great splendour.
Splendid also were his triumphal ceremonies after a victory over the
Saracens. Theophilus sailed up the Golden Horn and disembarked at
Blachernae, whence he rode on horseback to a pavilion in the fields outside the Golden Gate, where captives had been brought from Chrysopolis
to meet him. These captives, trophies and spoils preceded the Emperor,
who rode on a white horse with jewelled harness, wearing a gold-
embroidered tunic, patterned with a design of roses and a bunch of grapes;
a tiara was on his head, and he carried a sceptre. At his side was the Caesar
Alexius, in corslet, sleeves and garters of gold, wearing a helmet with a
golden headband, and holding a golden spear in his hand. At the Porta
Aurea the Emperor received a crown of gold from the magistrates, which
he carried on his right arm. The city had been adorned with hangings in
honour of the procession, and the Mese, the main street of Constantinople
(which led up from the golden milestone, past the column of Constantine,
to the church of the Holy Apostles on the fourth hill) was strewn with
flowers.

It was in this reign that the lovely mechanical toys were introduced into
the palace of Magnaura. A golden plane-tree overshadowed the throne,
and golden birds sang in it. Such birds as Yeats wished to take his 'bodily
form' from:

> Such a form as Grecian goldsmiths make
> Of hammered gold and gold enamelling
> To keep a drowsy Emperor awake:
> Or set upon a golden bough to sing
> To Lords and ladies of Byzantium
> Of what is past, or passing, or to come.

This 'immortal bird', artificial, and outside the changes of nature, superior to the 'dying generations' in the trees:

> Miracle, bird or golden handiwork,
> More miracle than bird or handiwork,
> Planted on the star-lit golden bough,
> Can like the cocks of Hades crow,
> Or, by the moon embittered, scorn aloud
> In glory of changeless metal
> Common bird or petal
> And all complexities of mire or blood.

Gold lions and griffins were at the sides of the throne, and a golden organ played.

The story of Theophilus's marriage is well known. A bride-show was held, and he walked with a golden apple in his hand between two ranks of well-born and beautiful young women. When he stood in front of the poetess Casia, he observed:

> 'A woman was the fount and source of all man's tribulation.'

Quick-wittedly she replied, in the manner of an ancient poet in a verse-contest:

> 'And from a woman sprang the course of man's regeneration.'

She was too witty to be chosen as empress; she became a nun, a composer, and a great poetess.

The golden apple was given to Theodora; she and her mother were secret iconodules, at a time when Theophilus proscribed images in the churches of Constantinople and had image-worshippers scourged. The Palace dwarf once caught Theodora kissing icons in her room: 'They are my pretty dolls, and I love them dearly,' she said, trying to pass it off. 'I was with Nurse,' he told the emperor, Shakesperianly, 'and I saw her take such pretty dolls out of a cushion.' And when Theophilus's daughters went to visit their grandmother, Theoctiste, in her house at the Gastria, little Princess Pulcheria told her father that Theoctiste had taken dolls from a box and pressed them against the children's lips.

At Theophilus's death in 847, Theodora became Regent for her son. She hesitated a little before the open restoration of images, for she feared that Theophilus would be condemned as a heretic. Finally it was decided that Theophilus should be deemed to have repented on his death-bed, and that he should be posthumously absolved. The triumph of the iconodules was kept on 11 March, 843, the first Sunday in Lent, which Sunday is still observed as the 'Feast of Orthodoxy'. Since this date, as a kind of compromise, the Greek Church has forgone the use of sculpture, and has confined itself to painted images; these, however, receive more veneration than any images in the West.

Michael III, Theodora's son, was a drunkard and a clown, given to scurrility and rejoicing in vulgar mockeries of Church ceremonies; a buffoon called 'the Pig', dressed as the Patriarch, performed a travesty of the Eucharist. Michael cared nothing for the lovely things acquired by Theophilus, and melted down the golden plane-tree of Magnaura. In this reign the Russians attacked the city, but their ships were destroyed by a storm; the eastern frontiers were also protected by a victory over the Moslem armies of the Euphrates. The schism between the Eastern and Western Churches widened into the first actual break in 867. Pope Nicholas I condemned the institution of the Patriarch Photius as irregular; Photius retaliated by denouncing practices of the West, such as the celibacy of the clergy, and the introduction into the creed of the *Filioque*, asserting the procession of the Holy Ghost from the Son as well as from the Father. The rift was healed for a time by Pope John VIII, who recognized Photius as Patriarch. But Photius had asserted the independence of Constantinople, and had formulated differences of dogma and practice; henceforward the union of the undivided Church was a frail thing. And from this time onward the cultural split between East and West began to widen; the buffoon Michael III, writing to Nicholas I, calls Latin 'a barbarous and Scythian language'. Byzantium was beginning to think of Latin-speaking people as belonging to a barbarian world.

Basil I, the Macedonian, the murderer of Michael III, is called the founder

Facing, above: ST. SOPHIA FROM THE SOUTH, WITH THE BOSPHORUS BEYOND (EUROPEAN SHORE ON LEFT, ASIATIC ON RIGHT). *below:* ST. SOPHIA, INTERIOR.

RESTORED MOSAIC IN ST. SOPHIA MUSEUM

of a dynasty; he had, however, married Eudocia, the mistress of his predecessor, and it is believed that her son, Leo VI, the Wise, was really the son of Michael and that in him the Amorian dynasty was continued. The Macedonian dynasty, however, is the name given to the emperors of the next ninety years, another Golden Age in the history of Constantinople.

The reigns of Basil I and Leo VI produced the *Basilica*, the last great reconstruction of Roman Law in the Middle Ages, a return to the principles of Justinian. The aims of the Macedonian dynasty were supremacy over church and state, and the protection of the peasantry against the big landowners. It was also a building age; the Nea, the Palace church built by Basil I, was consecrated in 880. The minor arts flourished, and also education and the sciences. At the top of the educational scale, the Patriarch Photius was a man of quite extraordinary attainments; and there was not, as in the west, the illiterate nobleman at the other end of the scale. The western conception of the 'clerk', whose 'clergy' consisted in being able to read and write, was unknown in Constantinople, where laymen also were educated. There were a true survival of classical education and an unbroken tradition of secular learning.

Nor was the profession of scholar unprofitable. We read in a dialogue imitated from Lucian: 'My old father used to say to me: "My son, you learn your letters as well as you can. Look at that man over there, my child; he used to go on foot, but now he has a horse with a double breastplate, and goes about on a fat mule. While he was studying he had no shoes, and now you see him wearing fashionable boots. While he was studying he never combed his hair, and now he is a well-groomed cavalier. While he was studying he did not know the entrance to the baths, and now he has three baths a week." '

Liudprand of Cremona describes his visit to the splendid and civilized court of Constantine VII, Porphyrogenitus (912-59). The golden tree at Magnaura, melted down by Michael III, seems to have been replaced by another of equal beauty. He describes the splendid feasts, the golden table service, the wonderful acrobats who performed in the Palace. Leo VI and Constantine VII were both men of letters; Leo wrote of the military forces of the empire, Constantine of imperial administration and of court ceremonial.

The book of the ceremonies is an astonishing work, revealing the extraordinarily minute regulations that governed the emperor's appearances,

C

whether on religious or secular occasions. A remarkable feature is the use of stylized, panegyric acclamations, with which the imperial family was regularly saluted. 'The task of applause was not abandoned to the rude and spontaneous voices of the crowd. The most convenient stations were occupied by the bands of the Blue and Green factions of the Circus; and their furious conflicts, which had shaken the capital, were insensibly sunk to an emulation of servitude.'

These formulae had been developed from the days of Heraclius onwards; oriental influences were at work, and the two choirs, hidden behind curtains, who saluted the Basileus while he entertained ambassadors in the Chrysotriclinium, resemble the hidden, Persian singers and players who performed at the court of Baghdad.[1]

There were formulae for all occasions, and the fact that in those extant the emperor's name is always left blank indicates that they were not fulsome compliments paid to individual princes, but expressions intended to heighten the dignity of their office. A pleasing example is that which was to be sung when the betrothed bride of an emperor was taken to the palace, with tambourines and cymbals:

'I have taken the flowers of the field and laid them with fervour in the nuptial chamber. I have seen the newly-wed couple like a sun on the couch of precious gold. They embraced each other with loving desire, joy to their beauty, delicious to contemplate, and roses for those who are beautiful as the rose. Joy to the golden pair.'

An extraordinary example is this form of pious cheering during a torch-light race.

> *Cantors.* Holy, thrice Holy, victory to the Blue (the Green).
> *People.* Yes, victory to the Blue (the Green).
> *Cantors.* Lady, Mother of God.
> *People.* Yes, Mother of God, victory to the Blue (the Green).
> *Cantors.* Power of the Cross.
> *People.* Yes, power of the Cross, victory to the Blue (the Green).

There was a kalendar of feasts and station days nearly as elaborate as that still followed in Rome. Christmas was kept by the court at St. Sophia, as also the Epiphany, Easter, Pentecost and the Transfiguration. Easter

---

[1] Egon Wellesz: *A History of Byzantine Music and Hymnography* (Oxford, 1949).

Monday and Low Sunday were kept at the Holy Apostles, with a station
on the way to burn a candle at the Diaconissa, and receptions on the
return journey at St. Polyeucte and St. Euphemia. Easter Tuesday was kept
at St. Sergius and St. Bacchus by the emperor, though the Patriarch went
that day to Blachernae. On Ascension Day the emperor sailed to a wharf
near the Golden Gate, and rode thence to the monastery of Piyi. Palm
Sunday and Maundy Thursday were observed within the Palace, at Our
Lady of the Pharos; and the dedication of Basil I's church was celebrated
in that church on 1 May. The Purification, the Feast of Orthodoxy (first
Sunday in Lent), and Good Friday were observed at Blachernae; the birth
and the annunciation of Our Lady at the Chalcopratia.

These ceremonies in different parts of the city entailed processions, for
which elaborate directions are given. For example, on the return from the
Holy Apostles on Easter Monday, the emperor must put on a short
tunic of purple, with gold thread, enriched with precious stones and pearls.
He holds a golden, jewelled sword. The *praepositus* places on his head a
circle, with a high band of feathers. He leaves the church, preceded by
dignitaries of the bedchamber, and mounts a horse harnessed with gold
and jewels, with silk ribbons on its tail and hoofs; purple-vested dignitaries accompany him on caparisoned horses, and the Master of Ceremonies walks by his side.

Elsewhere we learn the procedure at Constantine's own funeral. At a
signal from the Grand Eunuch, the Master of Ceremonies cried three
times: 'King, enter into thy rest. The King of Kings, the Lord of Lords
calls thee. Lift the crown from thy head.' Thereupon Basil, the Great
Chamberlain, who every night slept at the Emperor's feet, took off the
metal crown, replaced it by a purple diadem, raised the body, and lifted
it into the sarcophagus.

Twenty years after his visit to Constantine Porphyrogenitus, Liudprand
of Cremona returned to Constantinople in 968, as ambassador to Nicephorus II, Phocas, from the Western Emperor, Otto I, to arrange a
dynastic marriage. Nicephorus was an able general, whose conquests of
Crete and Cyprus restored Byzantine supremacy at sea; but he was
unpopular in the capital for his meanness and his debasement of the
coinage. Liudprand comments on his wretched appearance, and on his
sordid entourage, so unlike the court of Constantine VII. Nicephorus was
a fat-headed dwarf, with tiny mole's eyes, a short, thick grizzled beard, a

big belly and a lean behind. 'As Nicephorus, like some crawling monster, walked along, the singers began to cry out in adulation: "Behold the morning star approaches: the day star rises: in his eyes the sun's rays are reflected: Nicephorus our prince, the pale death of the Saracens." (This was, of course, no idle boast, for so he was.) How much more truly might they have sung: "Come, you miserable burnt-out coal, old woman in your walk, wood-devil in your look; clodhopper, haunter of byres, goat-footed, horned, double-limbed; bristly, wild, rough, barbarian, harsh, hairy, a rebel, a Cappadocian!" So, puffed up by these lying ditties, he entered St. Sophia.' Tradesmen with little thin shields and cheap spears lined the route, many of them barefooted; and the nobles wore old tunics, full of holes. The procession was mean and the feast was disgusting: Liudprand was sent a fat goat from the Emperor's table, stuffed with onions, garlic and leeks, and swimming in fish sauce. Liudprand's mission was unsuccessful, he was very badly treated, and he had to listen to a good deal of abuse of his master, whose imperial title Nicephorus, reasonably enough, would not acknowledge. He is a prejudiced witness, no doubt, and Byzantine historians, jealous for the credit of East Rome, do not look upon him with a favourable eye; yet he had admired the city of Constantine VII, though he now found it 'half-starved, perjured, lying, cunning, greedy, rapacious, avaricious, boastful'.

Nicephorus had won the throne, and the guardianship of the youthful Emperors Basil II and Constantine VIII by marriage with their mother, Theophano, widow of Romanus II – a marriage condemned by the Church as incestuous, on account of their spiritual relationship. He failed to keep the empress's favour, and after six years of marriage she had him murdered, on the night of 10-11 December, 969, as he slept, like a hardened soldier, on a tiger-skin on the floor of his apartments. Her accomplice, the Armenian John Zimisces, who had replaced Nicephorus in the empress's affections, an elegant little man of forty-four, was crowned emperor at once, at three or four in the morning of 11 December, in the Chrysotriclinium of the Sacred Palace. His partisans rushed with torches through the snow, proclaiming him and his wards, the two royal children. He submitted humbly to the Church, in return for official recognition, and was crowned again in St. Sophia on Christmas Day. He lost no time in banishing Theophano to Proti, in the Marmara; she escaped thence next year, was caught, and sent into Asia, till she was recalled by her son

Basil II after the death of John Zimisces. John was a great general, and celebrated triumphs over Russia and Armenia; his pious and timely death, just as his wards came to man's estate, was naturally attributed to poison, but may have been due to typhus.

The reign of the great Emperor Basil II, the Bulgar-slayer (976-1025), from the time he assumed active rule, was a splendid period in the life of the City. Foreign conquests extended the empire as far as Armenia and the Duchy of Antioch, and a treaty with the Fatemid Caliph secured peace in the south; the ruin of the Bulgarian empire was achieved by the great victory of 1014, after which 15,000 Bulgarian prisoners were sent home to their country blinded. At home the city was at the height of its wealth and prosperity, the richest, most civilized and probably the most beautiful capital in Europe. The emperor had little taste for learning and, after his youth, was severely simple in his dress and ornaments; but when he was absent at the wars his coadjutor and younger brother, the luxury-loving Constantine VIII, who could not bear the weight of armour or the sound of weapons, represented the imperial power in the capital. The historian Psellus is surprised to record a great literary renaissance during this reign, in spite of Basil's lack of interest. He can only find one astonishing solution; he says: 'The men of those days took to letters for no other end, but simply studied them as an end in themselves.' Constantine VIII, however, as well as being an admirable cook was a polished speaker with a lovely voice. The decorative arts flourished at this time no less than letters, and perhaps it is to this reign that we should assign the great mosaic lunettes over the west door and in the vestibule of St. Sophia.

The most interesting event of the three years of Constantine VIII's sole reign was a treaty between him and the Fatemid Caliph. On the one hand, the mosque in Constantinople was to be restored and to be allowed the privilege of the call to prayer, and the Caliph's name was to be put into the prayers in all mosques in the Byzantine empire; on the other hand, the Caliph was to allow the rebuilding of the church of the Holy Sepulchre and the restoration to the Church of all Christians forced or terrorized into Islam.

Geoffroi de Vinsauf later remarked, after the Fourth Crusade: 'It would have been even right to have razed the city to the ground, for if we believe report, it was polluted by new mosques, which its perfidious emperor allowed to be built, that he might strengthen the league with the

Turks.' Other Christian sects also profited by Byzantine religious toleration; there were Catholic and Armenian churches, and the chief of each
foreign community had his official seat in the great church. Nor were
Jews badly treated, according to Benjamin of Tudela.

The strength of Basil, and the prestige of the Macedonian family, are
proved by the faithfulness of the empire to his nieces, the very eccentric
daughters of Constantine VIII.

On his death-bed, Constantine chose a husband for Zoë, his second
daughter, to be an inheritor of the imperial purple; Romanus III, Argyrus,
on whom the choice fell, was an elderly man, devoted to a very superior
wife. Constantine was dying too fast to have time to search for another
son-in-law; Romanus's wife was tricked into divorcing him to set him
free for Zoë. He had been given till the end of the day to choose between
divorce, Zoë and the succession, or blinding. His wife cut her hair and
took monastic vows to save his eyes.

Zoë, over fifty, was determined to carry on the Macedonian dynasty;
she hung herself over with little amulets and even dropped into herself
pebbles wrapped with charms. Romanus, not behindhand in trying to do
his duty, tried all manner of unctions and frictions. The witch-doctors
gave them hopes of an heir. But he was ten years older than the empress
and, when he saw nothing come of it, he was only too glad to neglect his
conjugal duties; this was to cost him dear. Moreover, he bored her,
talking incessantly about philosophy (in which he was very amateurish) in
his charming voice, and also holding forth on the art of war.

A eunuch in the service of the emperor had introduced his young brother,
Michael, into the palace. 'A finely proportioned young man,' says Psellus,
'with the fair bloom of youth in his face, as fresh as a flower, clear-eyed, and
in very truth "red-cheeked". Her kisses became more passionate, she truly
loving him, he no way desiring her.' Zoë saw him, and fell in love with him.
She made her wishes known, and Michael did his best to comply, out of
ambition, and instructed by his eunuch brother. Soon the violence of her
passion was such that all the palace knew of it; several people had surprised the quinquagenarian empress in bed with the young Paphlagonian.
There is nothing very remarkable, says Psellus, in the fact that she covered
him with rings and jewellery, and clothed him in cloth of gold: 'For what
will an empress in love not offer her lover?' But she played at kings and
queens, making him sit on the throne, turn and turn about with her, and

placing the sceptre in his hand. The chief eunuch of the gynaeceum nearly fainted when he came across them at this game, but Zoë ordered him to attach himself to Michael as his future prince.

Romanus was the last to hear anything about his wife's almost demoniacal passion for Michael and, when he did, he proved a complaisant husband. He was a sick man, whether or not Zoë was slowly poisoning him, and he died in a very mysterious way in his bath; she was, of course, believed to have had a hand in it, but nothing was proved. She promptly placed her lover on the imperial throne, set a crown on his head, and sat beside him in like state, ordering the palace officials to prostrate themselves before them. The Patriarch Alexius was summoned and asked to marry Zoë, now in her fifty-fifth year, widowed only a few hours, and probably by her own contrivance, to a young plebeian thirty years her junior. This he did, that Good Friday night of 1034, and crowned Michael IV, the Paphlagonian, as emperor.

Michael, though an epileptic, without Greek culture, and so oddly brought to the throne, proved one of the better emperors. He made no new innovations, was not dazzled by the eminence to which he was raised, and sincerely tried to do the duties of his position, when his mind was clear. He kept Zoë imprisoned in the gynaeceum, and had conceived a horror for her; it is suggested that this was in part due to shame, for his illness no longer allowed him to live with her as a husband. It is also possible that he had connived at Romanus's death, and felt remorse for his crime – Michael was a pious person, really devout, not a religious amateur like Romanus.

Michael's brother, the eunuch John, persuaded him to make Zoë adopt their nephew Michael, in an attempt to found a dynasty. At Blachernae Zoë adopted Michael Calaphates as her son, and Michael IV raised him to the dignity of Caesar. Meanwhile, Michael's health was deteriorating. He built a very handsome church in honour of the physicians, St. Cosmas and St. Damian, in the suburb of Cosmidion, adorning it with paintings and mosaic. There he frequently went to pray for the cure of his dropsy. Some said that he was also troubled in mind, because spirits had appeared to him in the air, in his youth, promising the empire if he would forgo his salvation. He also sought the company of hermits. 'Which of those who has so lived, has escaped his notice?' asks Psellus. 'What earth has he not sought out, what sea, what clefts in the rocks and what secret caverns of the earth in order to make manifest one of those hidden there?' He also sought out the diseased and ulcerous, embraced them, and placed his face against their sores. He founded a poor-house, and a convent for Magdalens, quickly recruited by a herald from the numerous prostitutes of the city, who were turned to virtue. On 10 December, 1041, Michael IV retired to his monastery of St. Cosmas and St. Damian, and was tonsured as a monk. He did not even say goodbye to Zoë before he went. He died the same evening, and was buried in the church of his foundation.

Michael V, Calaphates, was enthroned. He was full, at first, of grateful and respectful words about Zoë, calling her 'the Empress' and 'my sovereign', but as soon as he could he turned against her. On 18 April, 1042, he had her exiled to Prinkipo. There was an immediate and general rising in her favour. Psellus himself saw women, who had never before been seen outside their gynaeceum, beating their breasts and lamenting for the empress. 'Where is she,' they cried, 'who alone is noble, who alone is beautiful? Where is she who alone among women is free, the sovereign of the whole family, she who legally has the heritage of kingship, whose father was king, and he that begat him, and his father also?' Psellus, the emperor's secretary, was in the inner vestibule, dictating confidential letters, when the mob rushed on the palace; he took horse, and rode through the city, observing the fury of the populace. Young boys and girls were taking part in the riot, and were doing as much damage as anyone. They hauled Theodora, Zoë's younger sister, from her convent on the Golden Horn, put on her a purple robe, dragged her to St. Sophia and proclaimed her empress; and Michael was forced to bring back Zoë. He himself, and his uncle, sailed to the Studium, and took sanctuary in the monastery, but they were forced out, and blinded. The two sisters, who very much disliked each other, now shared the throne.

After a few months of their silly and spendthrift rule, the Empress Zoë took a third husband, and made him emperor as Constantine IX, Monomachus; Constantine introduced his mistress and niece-by-marriage Scleraina into the Palace, and had her made Augusta, and treated her as his legal wife, Zoë making little objection. Zoë was now devoting herself to perfumery and to superstitious private devotions in her over-heated apartments, and was neglecting both her person and her empire. The reign of this very peculiar imperial family was threatened by a Russian attack in 1043, and by two dangerous revolts, that of George

Maniaces and that of Leo Tornikios. The latter laid siege to Constantinople in 1047 and was nearly successful in his assault, but Constantine's military skill won the victory. Although court-life consisted in frivolity and in intrigue to an extent which almost justifies the use of the adjective 'Byzantine' to denote a tangled web of official life, yet Constantine IX was a patron of letters. He refounded the university, which had been abolished by Leo III, and placed Psellus and his brilliant friend Xiphilinus in the chairs of Law and Philosophy; a genuine revival of classical studies followed. Eastern students were attracted to Constantinople. 'If you happen to talk to Persians or Ethiopians,' wrote Psellus to Cerularius, 'they will say that they know and admire me, and have come in pursuit of me; and now one from the borders of Babylon has arrived, with untamed zeal, to drink at my springs.' Court intrigues overthrew Psellus and his friends; they retired into monastic life, and the university was closed again.

When Constantine IX, long a sick man, died in 1055, the aged Theodora, last scion of the house of Basil the Macedonian, emerged from her convent again, and ruled the empire for the last two years of her life, being fortunate in the capacity and honesty of her ministers.

It was now, in the last days of the Macedonian house, that the tragic schism rent the still undivided Church. The violence of Michael Cerularius, the Patriarch of Constantinople, was opposed by the brutal intransigence of Humbert, the Papal Legate. Insolence on both sides, the growing estrangement of Greeks and Latins, and memories of old grievances combined to divide those whom no important dogmatic principle or essential difference of practice need ever have divided. But for the Fourth Crusade, the rent might yet have been mended.

Theodora named the elderly Michael VI, Stratioticus, as her successor. He represented the now important bureaucracy, which aimed at decreasing the power of the army. After a year's rule, he was overthrown in 1057 by the aristocratic military party, who gave the throne to Isaac I, Comnenus, a member of a new but great land-owning family from Cappadocia; but in 1059 Isaac abdicated, and retired as a monk to the Studium, and under his successor, Constantine X, Ducas, the civil servants resumed power. Constantine X, anxious to save money, willingly neglected defence, and only paid the Varangian guard, the emperor's personal guard of Scandinavian soldiers, in which English exiles later found a chief place, after the Norman Conquest. Disaster overtook all the outer fringes of the Byzantine Empire: the Balkan provinces were lost, and Armenia was overrun by the Seljuk Turks. Psellus, however, complacently records the virtues and intelligence of the imperial family, of Constantine X, of his widow Eudocia, Regent for the young Michael VII, and of the latter prince: he is more critical of Eudocia's second husband, associated with her son as Romanus IV, Diogenes, in spite of Romanus's polite attentions to him. He saw him depart on his military campaigns with great misgiving, which was more than justified by the capture of the emperor and the annihilation of his troops by the Turks in the disastrous battle of Manzikert (1071) on the Armenian frontier.

The battle of Manzikert marks the end of the great period. Since the death of Basil II there had been a decline, but the city was still the capital of the greatest state in Europe. After 1071, Asia Minor was soon overrun, and by 1081 the Turks reached the Marmara; a principal source of wealth and man-power was for ever diverted from Byzantium. The brilliant Comnene revival, and the courageous endurance of the last centuries, only held off an almost inevitable fall. And now Byzantium was threatened by a more insidious enemy: it was to be claimed that East Rome had now lost its title as protector of Christendom, and that the West was justified in interference, to keep open the way to the Holy Places.

In the city, the troubled reigns of Michael VII and of Nicephorus III, Botaniates, were followed by a military revolution which placed on the throne a son of the Emperor Isaac I, Alexius I, Comnenus. At last a man of great ability and courage had come to rule the almost ruined empire. Surrounded by rivals and enemies, the heirs or relations of other emperors, he inherited a wasted treasury and an almost desperate military situation. By vigorous taxation, by forced loans, by substituting fines for other punishments, and by selling privileges, Alexius managed to maintain the executive, to rebuild the army till it was strong enough to hold off the Turks, and to impress foreign visitors with a splendid court. His mistake was to give too great commercial advantage to foreign merchants and to debase the coinage, the bezant, which had been the gold standard of Europe since the time of Constantine.

The new enemy now made his way to Byzantium; the city was appointed by Urban II as the gathering-point for the armed forces who should respond to his call for a Crusade, and to the preaching of that sinister demagogue Peter the Hermit. It was assumed that Alexius I, who had been asking for allies, would welcome the crusading hordes; a large assumption, when Alexius would have to feed and house a miscellaneous host over which he had little control. Byzantium learned with considerable alarm, as Alexius's daughter, the learned princess Anna Comnena puts it, that 'all the West and all the barbarian tribes from beyond the Adriatic as far as the Pillars of Hercules were moving in a body through Europe towards Asia, bringing whole families with them'.

First arrived the 'People's Crusade', the disorderly rabble of Peter the Hermit; they were only allowed to infiltrate into Constantinople in small bodies of sightseers, though they pillaged the surroundings. After crossing the Bosphorus they inflicted merciless cruelties and exactions upon the Christian villages of Asia Minor, till they met with merited destruction at the hands of the Turks. The better organized western forces under Godfrey de Bouillon and Hugh de Vermandois were even more uneasy neighbours to Byzantium; relations between them and the emperor were so strained that Godfrey staged an attack on the gate to Blachernae, and Alexius showed he would resist any such attempt to bring pressure on him. The emperor's diplomacy won, and the crusading leaders swore to acknowledge him as their overlord, and to convey to him all of the Byzantine empire that they should recover from the Turks.

Anna Comnena records the oath-taking of the rude, western soldiers: 'This multitude was not, like the Hellenic one of old, to be restrained and governed by the loud voices of nine heralds. They required the constant superintendence of chosen and valiant soldiers to keep them from violating the commands of the Emperor.' She is impressed by their ill-manners. One boorish count seated himself on the emperor's throne and muttered to himself when he was turned off it; when Alexius spoke with him, he boasted of his prowess in single combat. The emperor gently suggested that this would not be much good against the Turks. It was a relief to the Constantinopolitans when the crusading armies were in Asia.

The whole episode further embittered relations between East and West; we have in our own times seen situations that have been almost parallel. Vigorous western armies, from countries with a new and yet crude civilization, were encamped outside an ancient and highly civilized capital. They believed they had come as saviours and expected gratitude, although their intentions in coming had been by no means single-hearted. They were received by the inhabitants with coldness and with well-merited suspicion of their imperialistic aims. The Byzantines regarded the Crusaders as barbarians; the Crusaders, uncomfortably aware of their own cultural inferiority, thought the Byzantines effete and decadent. In the uneasy alliance between Alexius and the western leaders, each was naturally out for himself; as the emperor very properly put first the interests of his own city and empire, and quite correctly thought their safety more vital to Christendom than any activity on the part of the Crusaders, he has neither unnaturally nor quite unjustly been represented as a faithless ally. And he was in many ways more in sympathy with the more civilized rulers of the Islamic states.

The Turks had been driven far back, but the city paid dearly for its alliance with the Crusaders; the continual stream of armed pilgrims passing through the emperor's territories brought ruin with them. Even when encamped under his protection, their capacity for nuisance was very great. In 1101 a detachment of Lombards broke into the courtyard of Blachernae, killed one of the emperor's tame lions, and tried to storm the palace gates. The closing years of Alexius's reign were marked by growing tension between him and the newly founded Latin principalities in Asia.

John II, Comnenus, succeeded, in spite of plots by his sister Anna against his life, to an empire a great deal more prosperous than that which his father had been called to govern; its commercial greatness, however, was on the wane. The Latin kingdoms in the Levant, and the privileged settlements of Italian merchants in Constantinople, were to be the ruination of its trade. 'Feared by his nobles, beloved by his people, John was never reduced to the painful necessity of punishing, or even of pardoning, his enemies. During his government of twenty-five years the penalty of death was abolished in the Roman Empire . . . He despised and moderated the stately magnificence of the Byzantine Court, so oppressive to the people, so contemptible to the eye of reason. Under such a prince innocence had nothing to fear and merit had everything to hope; and without assuming the tyrannic office of a censor he introduced a gradual though visible reformation in the public and private manners of Constantinople.'

Anna Comnena, though a would-be fratricide, is a not unsympathetic figure when we see her in retirement, in her sixties, 'idly moving a pen at the time of the lighting of the lamps' and 'slightly nodding over the writing'. Her history, though a biased panegyric of her father, is yet an invaluable document, and its details of Byzantine court-life are more intimate than anything to be collected from the descriptions of its ceremonial by Constantine Porphyrogenitus. She gives a picture of a strange mixture of pomp and informality: beggars come unchecked to the emperor's door; at night no guards are set; the eunuch attendant of the bedchamber may walk in, even if the sovereigns are asleep, and Alexius's attempted murder by Nicephorus Diogenes was only prevented by the chance presence of a maidservant, fanning away mosquitoes. We find the emperor visiting his subjects, playing chess or polo with his friends, and inviting any person he wishes to honour to his own table; the Empress Irene reads the Fathers at luncheon, and she and her daughters help to nurse the dying Alexius.

Anna and her husband, Nicephorus Bryennius, both such notable historians, are outstanding figures in the intellectual life of the period, when literature again made its way in a society besotted with quail-hunting and with draughts. Anna thinks it worthwhile to praise Bryennius not only for his beauty and intelligence, but also for the accuracy of his speech.

Manuel I, Comnenus, the successor of John II, was a Latinophile prince who aspired to the crown of a reunited empire, and was willing to purchase it from the Pope by a reunion of the Eastern and Western churches; but his ambitions were personal, backed by no public feeling among his subjects, and were predestined to failure. His attitude to the Crusaders was friendly, but an aliveness to the first interests of his empire limited the help he gave them. The cleavage in interests is put most clearly by the most recent authority: 'Was it to the better interest of Christendom that there should be occasional gallant expeditions to the East, led by a mixture of unwise idealists and crude adventurers, to succour an intrusive state there [i.e. the Latin Kingdom of Jerusalem] whose existence depended on Moslem disunity? Or that Byzantium, who had been for so long the guardian of the Eastern frontier, should continue to play her part unembarrassed from the West?' The policies were not compatible. 'When Constantinople itself had fallen and the Turks were thundering at the gates of Vienna, it would be possible to see which policy was right.'[1]

In Manuel's reign the city was still very splendid. 'May God, in His

---

[1] Steven Runciman: *A History of the Crusades*, vol. II (Cambridge, 1952).

grace and generosity, deign to make of it the capital of Islam!' exclaimed an Arabian traveller; while the Spanish Jew, Benjamin of Tudela, wrote: 'Strongholds are filled with garments of silk, purple and gold. Like unto these store-houses and this wealth, there is nothing in the whole world to be found . . . The Greek inhabitants are very rich in gold and precious stones, and they go clothed in garments of silk with gold embroidery, and they ride horses, and look like princes. Indeed, the land is very rich in all cloth stuffs, and in bread, meat and wine. Wealth like that of Constantinople is not to be found in the whole world. Here also are men learned in all the books of the Greeks, and they eat and drink every man under his vine and his fig tree.' In the Hippodrome, 'Lions, bears and leopards were shown, and all nations of the world were represented, together with surprising feats of jugglery'.

Manuel I corresponded, or so he believed, with Prester John; there is no doubt about his correspondence with Henry II of England, who sent him some hounds. The Seljuk Sultan, Kilidj Arslan II, visited him in Constantinople in 1161 and stayed for eighty days; a naval display was held in his honour, and a demonstration of 'Greek fire'. Twice a day food was sent to him in gold and silver vessels, which were never taken back. It is hardly surprising that he was so dazzled by the splendour of the court that he dared not sit at the emperor's side, showing more proper modesty than that of the Frankish knight who tried to sit on the throne of Alexius I. Ten years later, Amaury I, king of Jerusalem, was also the emperor's guest.

But the splendour of the court was maintained by crushing taxation. Manuel's reign ended in the alienation of all his western allies, and a disastrous defeat in Asia at the hands of the Seljuk Turks. And the city itself was rent by Greek and Latin feuds, so many were the 'barbarians' whom Manuel had brought or allowed in from the West. Byzantium was rapidly approaching its first fall.

Alexius II, a child of twelve years old, succeeded his father, Manuel I, as emperor; his mother, Mary of Antioch, was regent. The government relied heavily on the Latin element, which provoked anti-Latin riots. A sinister character, 'the future Richard III of Byzantine history', Andronicus, a cadet of the Comnene family, a wandering exile during most of Manuel's reign, led the anti-Latin section. The Latin quarters were attacked with the utmost savagery; the papl laegate was murdered; houses and churches were pillaged; in one hospital the sick were butchered, and many Latins were sold into Turkish slavery. Andronicus I made himself joint-emperor with Alexius II, and shortly afterwards had the boy strangled.

Andronicus could only keep in power by a reign of terror, and yet he was an able administrator, and the taxpayers felt a considerable relief in his reign. The contemporary historian, Nicetas Choniates, is lyrical: 'Everyone, to quote a prophet, lay quietly in the shade of his trees and having gathered grapes and the fruits of the earth ate them joyfully and slept comfortably, without fearing the tax-collector's menace, without looking askance at the gleaner in his vineyard or being suspicious of the gatherers of corn stalks; but he who rendered unto Caesar those things which are Caesar's, of him no more was required; he was not deprived, as he used to be, of his last garment, and he was not reduced to the point of death, as formerly was often the case.'

What was it really like to live in Byzantium? It is difficult to form a concrete picture of life there. Private lives are generally hidden from us in the Middle Ages; only occasionally does history, biography or hagio-graphy throw some light on the lives of the obscure. Moreover, the historian who gleans and collects over a wide period is apt to forget that life changed in the past from decade to decade, even if changes were less rapid and complete than they are in our own times – hence the falsity of even well-documented historical novels. In *The Cloister and the Hearth*, for instance, Charles Reade drew upon manners and customs belonging to a very much longer space of time than that covered by the action of the book. Such a book, therefore, as that of Professor Koukoules, though he carefully indicates dates and sources, and though it is full of information about Byzantine life through the whole long period, helps us less than we should like to know the feeling of living in Byzantium at any particular time.

An author of a popularized outline of Byzantine life, who ventured in youthful enthusiasm and arrogance to call Gibbon a 'pseudo-historian', has entitled one of his chapters 'The Joyous Life'; and indeed we have seen some of the beauty, the civilization and the intelligence of life in the Queen of Cities. But there are other sides to the picture. During long periods there was a haunting feeling of insecurity, and, though the 'God-defended City' successfully resisted barbarian invasions until the Fourth Crusade, dwellers in outlying parts of it were at many times seized by invaders, and their fate was cruel. The Russians, who came in the reign of Romanus, crucified their captives; the Saracens hanged or stoned them; the Persians gave them to wild beasts; the Scythians offered the most beautiful women they took prisoners as sacrifices to demons; other barbarians grilled their captives. Rape was so much a law of war that the Canons forbade a husband to put away a wife who had been defiled by an enemy. The selling of the captive population into slavery was also a common event, and both the Church and individuals did much charitable work for the redemption of such unfortunate people. Cruel separations between members of a family accompanied each fall of the city, as in mythology they followed the fall of Troy; we are told of two sisters, in 1453, who were fortunate enough to die of broken hearts in their last embrace instead of enduring the long misery of separate captivity.

Though Constantinople was better lighted than most western cities, Odon de Deuil, in the twelfth century, speaks of a perpetual night in many quarters, for the streets were cramped; the dark was full of crimes, in spite of night watchmen and other police. Theft was extremely prevalent. Sometimes recourse was had to astrology, to detect the culprit; sometimes a kind of trial by ordeal was given to suspects. *Pain bénit* was administered to them, with the prayer: 'Lord Jesus Christ, our God, who sent thy holy angel into the den of thy holy prophet Daniel and shut the lions' mouths, O Good Lord, send him to us, to come and bind the mouth of the man who stole this thing, so he may be dumb and speechless till he confess it, to the glory of the Father.' If the ordeal were successful, the thief would be unable to swallow the bread.

Though aqueducts provided the city with an exceptionally good water-supply, though subterranean conduits fed its kitchen gardens, and though drains led directly to the sea, yet Odon de Deuil found the streets disgusting and full of filth. There were violent contrasts. Rich houses might line the foulest streets; everything, he said, was here out of measure. Benjamin of Tudela also was struck by the juxtaposition of misery and splendour; he speaks of tanners throwing out into the street the stinking water they had used in their work.

These observers speak of the city after its great period indeed, but before the Latin conquest. It was sadder and more bedraggled in its last age, when the centre began to empty, when churches and monuments

Facing, above: A MOSAIC IN ST. SOPHIA.
below: MOSAICS IN KARIYE MOSQUE.

were decaying and the Marmara ports were silted up, when the population had dwindled, and when it presented (as the western quarters of
Istanbul present today) the appearance of several villages within the walls,
with empty spaces between them, and when only the quarters by the
Golden Horn were active. It may be doubted if 'the joyous life' is a
very good description for the life of Constantinople at any period,
Byzantine or Ottoman. It has been the destiny of the city to decay and
fall; the melancholy beauty of its situation and the unhappiness of its
climate have always been the same; and cross-currents of influence
between Byzantium and Islam have caused a more fundamental resem-
blance between the life of the city before and after 1453 than is always
taken into account. No one would ever have spoken of 'the joyous life'
of Istanbul.

And yet the city held the affections of its inhabitants; exile, even to a
short distance, was regarded an intolerable evil. This much might perhaps
be said for the superiority of the life of Byzantium over that of Istanbul –
it was not, probably, more 'joyous', but to those above the level of
economic necessity it was continuously interesting. Foreign visitors may
have been unhappy and uncomfortable, but they were seldom bored.

Although corruption was rife in the twelfth century; though one
emperor sent out his tax-gatherers unpaid, free to recoup themselves
upon their victims; though judges bought their offices, and with them the
opportunity to take bribes; though another emperor was accused of
fitting out six vessels to engage in piracy upon his own subjects; though
prisoners were let out of jail to work for the emperor – yet there was a
public opinion which was a force in Byzantium, and could place emperors
on the throne and displace them. This was a different thing from the
indifference of the Ottoman city, where the Osmanli dynasty auto-
matically succeeded, and where individual members were cut off by
palace intrigue or the turbulence of the Janissaries, without the mass of
their subjects taking very much interest. Moreover, there was a respect
for property – Constantinople was the safest place in the Christian East
for investment – and plunder of the individual was resisted, as never in
Ottoman times. When in the late twelfth century a banker called
Kalomodios was seized by some nobles who hoped to exploit him, the
merchants of the city went to the Patriarch and threatened to defenestrate
him if he would not use his influence to obtain the victim's release; the

D

Facing, above: SITE OF THE HIPPODROME.
below: PAMMACARISTOS.

Patriarch gladly intervened, and his intervention was successful. Not only was there a public respect for law, but the Church was the custodian of private and public morality; whereas in Ottoman Constantinople the intervention of the Ulema was almost exclusively destructive, aimed against any liberal reform, and concentrated its powers chiefly upon the enforcement of the more fanatical parts of the Islamic traditions.

The revolution that displaced Andronicus was purely aristocratic, and brought no benefits except to the Byzantine aristocracy, which set on the throne Isaac II, Angelus, a descendant of a daughter of Alexius I. Isaac returned to Manuel's extortionate taxation, without evincing any of his capacity. From time to time revolts broke out during his futile and uneasy reign; one such in 1195 dethroned him and placed his brother Alexius III on the throne. Isaac was blinded and imprisoned. Alexius III was no more competent to rule than his brother, and his short and discreditable reign was marked by lavishness at court, riots in the capital, and street fights between the Venetian and Pisan settlers.

Meanwhile Prince Alexius, son of Isaac II, had escaped to Italy, and thence made his way to Germany, to the court of the King, Philip of Swabia, his brother-in-law. Alexius implored Philip and the Pope to restore the throne to Isaac; he managed to deflect the course of the Fourth Crusade from Egypt to Constantinople, and in 1203 the Crusaders took the city, and restored Isaac II, with his son Alexius IV, as co-emperor. Having accomplished their alleged aim, the Crusaders encamped outside the city to bring pressure on the emperors to fulfil their side of the obligation: that is, to make money payments on a huge scale, to reunite the churches, and for Alexius IV to take the Cross with them.

Discontent inside the capital with the pro-Frankish tendencies of the emperors led to their fall. The nationalistic party set up Alexius V, Ducas, nicknamed 'Murtzuphlus' from his meeting eyebrows. Isaac died in prison, and Alexius IV was strangled. The Crusaders, bound by no promises to Murtzuphlus, were now able to discuss taking the city for themselves. Historians have not yet determined how far this was a long-premeditated crime or how far they allowed themselves to be tempted by developing circumstances. They stormed it by land and sea and, on 13 April, 1204, Constantinople fell, 'assailed by that criminal filibustering expedition, the Fourth Crusade'.[1]

[1] N. H. Baynes: *Byzantine Civilization* (1926).

'You have taken up the Cross,' cried Nicetas Choniates, 'and have sworn on it and on the holy gospels to us that you would pass over the territory of Christians without shedding blood and without turning to the right hand or the left. You told us that you had taken up arms against the Saracens only, and that you would steep them in their blood alone. You promised to keep yourselves chaste while you bore the Cross, as became soldiers enrolled under the banner of Christ. Instead of defending His tomb, you have outraged the faithful who are members of Him. You have used Christians worse than the Arabs used the Latins, for they at least respected women.' And Innocent III, who had at first acquiesced in the fall of Constantinople as a *fait accompli*, raised his voice in protest when he heard of the sacrilege and cruelty that had accompanied the sack of the city.

It was the first time that New Rome, which had successfully repelled Avars, Arabs, Persians, Bulgarians and Russians, fell to a barbarian invader. It was, therefore, still enormously rich, and for three days it was handed over to anarchical plunder. Enormous was the loss of works of art. Bronze figures in plenty were melted down: the Hera of Samos, from the forum of Constantine; the Hercules of Lysippus, from the Hippodrome; Paris giving the apple to Aphrodite, and a statue of Helen ('why could she not soften the barbarians?'). The altars of St. Sophia were broken up for their materials; horses and mules were brought into the Great Church to carry off the swag; a prostitute was put into the patriarchal chair, and danced and sang to amuse the soldiers.

An infinity of relics was carried off by the pious freebooters: in Venice, St. Mark's treasury was filled with reliquaries; Pisa received the head of St. John Chrysostom; Soissons received a head of St. John the Baptist, the head of St. Stephen the protomartyr, and the finger put by St. Thomas into the side of Christ; Halberstadt received a relic of the Precious Blood and the head of St. James, 'the brother of God'; Amiens received another head of St. John the Baptist; Amalfi, the body of St. Andrew; Sens, the crown of thorns; and Bromholm in Norfolk received that substantial relic of the True Cross, venerated as 'the Rood of Bromholm', and mentioned in *Piers Plowman*. And the pillaging of the city continued during the period of the Latin Empire.

Baldwin of Flanders was elected emperor. He was vested in the traditional manner, out of the imperial wardrobe, and, with a jewel of Manuel's at his throat, he was crowned with the Byzantine rites. As he was *de facto* emperor, he was also *de jure* emperor – there was no other – and he was accepted as such with indifference by the mass of the populace, used to emperors from outside. He was lavish of decorations, and black Byzantine eagles appeared on the Crusaders' boots. His own eagles were golden.

Of the Latin empire, an anomalous construction, threatened from the first by Greek states on several sides, little good can be said. Gregorovius summed it up thus: 'A creation of western European crusading knights, of the selfish trade-policy of the Venetians, and of the hierarchic idea of the papacy, it fell after a miserable existence of fifty-seven years, leaving behind it no other trace than destruction and anarchy. That deformed chivalrous feudal state of the Latins belongs to the most worthless phenomena of history.' The only good work done in Constantinople during this period seems to have been the buttressing of St. Sophia; it seems probable that the crusaders did something to preserve the fabric of the Great Church, which they had plundered.

But short-lived as it was, the Latin Empire and its disgraceful beginnings had done harm that was never to be undone. 'The crime of the Fourth Crusade handed over Constantinople and the Balkan peninsula to six centuries of barbarism', said the historian of the city's two conquests,[1] for the second was most surely the consequence of the first.

Greeks, for whom there was no career open in Latin Constantinople, sought Greek-speaking places in Asia Minor; the new state was unable to prevent this departure across the narrow sea, and sometimes was willing to encourage it. The exiles found natural leaders among Greek noblemen, some of whom were allied to the imperial house, and many of whom were landowners in Asia. Theodore Lascaris stood out; he had married a daughter of Alexius III, the widow of Isaac Comnenus, and had received the title of despot from his father-in-law. It is believed that he left the city under promise to secure some parts of Asia for Baldwin – Byzantine political morality would not be too far strained. He went to Nicaea, left his wife and children there as hostages, and set about raising an army and subjugating Bithynia. After resisting a Latin invasion, Theodore took the title of emperor and reigned in Nicaea; John Cameratus, Patriarch of Constantinople, returned from Bulgaria to crown him. Nicaea, that beautiful city, home of the Nicene Creed, now became the centre of the

[1] Sir Edwin Pears.

Greek Church and the Greek State, of which Theodore was seen as the future restorer.

The Byzantine monarchy while in exile across the Marmara was rejuvenated and purified. 'A faithful nobility, active and pious Emperors, had governed and led for half a century a people of shepherds and peasants of simple manners and customs.'[1] The Nicaean Empire followed the plan, later adopted by the Turks, of detaching from the Latin Empire, one by one, all its possessions except Constantinople itself. Nor was the final reconquest of the city a matter of much difficulty; the Latin emperor and Patriarch fled, without offering resistance, and on 15 August, 1261, the usurping emperor of Nicaea, Michael VIII, Palaeologus, entered the Golden Gate in triumph.

He had been staying at Meteoron when his armies first made their entry (according to legend, by a subterraneous passage from Balukli), and was asleep when the news arrived. His sister Irene woke him, saying: 'Up, Emperor, you have got Constantinople!' and she repeated it several times without carrying conviction. Only when she had said: 'Up, Emperor, Christ has given you Constantinople', did he believe her. The learned George Acropolita was at once summoned and spent the following day and night composing thirteen prayers of thanksgiving to be used at the solemn entry into the city.

Michael VIII was probably the ablest sovereign of the restored empire; nevertheless the empire to which he was restored was more like a continuation of Nicaea than of East Rome, a Greek medieval kingdom, and little more – 'a slender, dislocated, miserable body,' wrote Diehl, 'upon which rested an enormous head – Constantinople'.

Yet the death of the Roman Empire, if we may follow those historians who see its end in 1204, left something of great cultural importance in its place. Greek culture had not stood still in Nicaea, and there are eminent names among the scholars patronized by the Lascarid emperors. Now was born a new Hellenic patriotism; many wished the emperor to style himself 'Emperor of the Hellenes', there was a new enthusiasm for the glories of ancient Greece, and the non-Greek parts of the Eastern Roman Empire had fallen away. It is the late, revived empire that is more often brought into the mind of the traveller in Greece today than the more glorious Macedonian epoch.

[1] Cit. A. A. Vasiliev: *History of the Byzantine Empire* (Oxford, 1952).

The city Michael VIII entered was in a sorry state; Blachernae was 'full of Italian smoke and fume', according to a contemporary, George Pachymeris. Michael cleansed it and restored the walls, with special attention to the sea walls, for he feared another Latin invasion. These works were continued during the reign of his worthless son, Andronicus II. It was during that last reign that Theodore Metochites erected the superb mosaics in the narthex and exo-narthex of the church of St. Saviour in Chora, the one important example now surviving in the city of the revival of Byzantine art.

At one time the Byzantine renaissance was connected by scholars, through the Crusaders, with the Italian *trecento*; but it has now been proved that this renaissance began too early to have any such origin, and the influence of Byzantium upon Italy has been more satisfactorily demonstrated than that of Italy upon Byzantium. Nor has the theory that the revival was merely due to the efficient copying of Syrian originals of the fourth to the seventh centuries even so much to commend it; the Byzantine work is far too spirited. The Byzantine renaissance is a genuine renaissance, due to creative and original artists, springing up indeed at the same time as the Italian renaissance, but entirely independent of it. 'The great artistic movement of the fourteenth century', wrote Diehl,[1] 'is no sudden and unexpected phenomenon; it owed its being to the natural evolution of art in conditions particularly favourable and vigorous; and if foreign influences partially contributed to its brilliant flowering, it drew from itself, from the deep roots embedded in the past, its strong and original qualities.' The work of this renaissance is to be seen on Athos and at Mistra, in other parts of Greece, and also in Serbia; it can hardly be doubted that it was also well represented in the capital.

Nevertheless, the city was declining. Early in the fourteenth century the Arab geographer Abulfeda observed: 'Within the city there are sown fields and gardens, and many destroyed houses.' Early in the next century Ruy Gonzales de Clavijo, visiting Constantinople on his way to the court of Tamerlane at Samarcand, said much the same thing: 'The city is not throughout very densely populated. There are within its gates many hills and valleys where cornfields and orchards are found, and among the orchard lands there are hamlets and suburbs, which are all included within the city limits.' The same is true today, when villages surrounded by

[1] *Manuel d'art byzantin.*

orchards or market gardens are to be found within the city walls. He added: 'Everywhere throughout the city there are a great many palaces, churches and monasteries, but most of them are now in ruin. It is, however, plain that in former times when Constantinople was in its pristine state it was one of the noblest capitals of the world.' Already in 1403, fifty years before the fall, Clavijo could only say '*Fuit*' of Byzantium. The Great Palace, as we know from many sources, was ruinous; and Buondelmonti, another fifteenth-century traveller, lets us know that the church of the Holy Apostles, the Westminster Abbey or St. Denis of Constantinople, was in decay. A Spaniard who visited the city in the last two reigns said that the church of Blachernae had gone the way of the churches in the Sacred Palace. 'The city is sparsely populated . . . The inhabitants are not well clad, but sad and poor, showing the hardship of their lot, which is not so bad as they deserve, for they are a vicious people, steeped in sin.' The court was still resplendent: 'The Emperor's state is as splendid as ever, for nothing is omitted from the ancient ceremonies, but, properly regarded, he is like a Bishop without a see.'

The attempts of Michael VIII to reunite the Eastern and Western churches were thwarted, he died excommunicated by Pope and Patriarch alike, and his neglect of Asian defence was to lose the empire the whole of Anatolia. Thus the reign of this able prince, the one powerful emperor of restored Byzantium, opened the road to ruin. His successors were nearly all men of poor abilities. In the mid-fourteenth century, the minority of John V occasioned the usurpation of John VI, Cantacuzene, an able general, and the most far-sighted of the later emperors, for he saw that Byzantium could still remain great through its cultural and spiritual influence, even though it were no longer capital of a great state. His introduction of the Turks into Europe, to support him in his civil wars, lost him his popularity, and has left a blot, that is perhaps undeserved, upon his reputation, as if he were ultimately responsible for the Fall.

Pressure from without, poverty and disruption from within, now doomed Constantinople; all that men of ability could do was to postpone inevitable collapse. Such an able man was Manuel II, who went to the west to beg for aid. Adam of Usk, a contemporary English chronicler, wrote of his visit to London: 'I thought within myself, what a grievous thing it was that this great Christian prince from the farther East, should perforce be driven by unbelievers to visit the distant islands of the West, to seek aid against them. My God! What dost thou, ancient glory of Rome? Shorn is the greatness of thine empire this day; and truly may the words of Jeremy be spoken unto thee: "Princess among the provinces, how is she become tributary (Lament. Li)." Who would ever believe that thou shouldst sink to such depth of misery, although once seated on the throne of majesty thou didst lord it over all the world, now thou hast no power to bring succour to the Christian faith?[1] In Paris, Manuel wrote a pleasant description of a tapestry in the Louvre; neither England nor France gave him serious help.

Michael VIII's attempt at a reunion of the churches, the *sine qua non* of Western support, was repeated by other emperors: John V, Palaeologus, went to Rome and made his personal submission to the Holy See in 1369 – he was arrested in Venice, on his return journey, as an insolvent debtor; Manuel II negotiated with Rome in 1417, and in 1439 at the Council of Florence the schism between the two Churches was officially ended by a decree of union, promulgated in the presence of the Pope, Eugenius IV, and the emperor, John VIII. This union broke down at once, popularly denounced in the East, but it was not altogether without fruit; by this act of union several millions of Eastern Christians are today living in union with Rome. Each of the uniate Churches retains its own liturgy and language and vestments; the marriage of priests is permitted, and the use of leavened bread in the Eucharist; the *Filioque* is not pronounced in the creed.

Meanwhile the Turks were coming closer. In 1356 Süleyman, son of Orchan, took the fort of Tzympe near Gallipoli; this was the first Turkish settlement in Europe. Süleyman was buried by the Hellespont, for a hundred years the only Ottoman prince buried in European earth (except for the convert son of Bayazit, buried in the Studium); he was regarded as lying there in wait for the conquest. Bayazit I, the conqueror of Greece, would have made an attack on the city that might well have been fatal if he had not been obliged to turn eastwards; he fell prisoner to Timur the Tartar. Not till the time of his grandson Murad II was there another attempt upon Constantinople; in 1422 Murad encamped outside the gate of St. Romanus, in the garden of the convent of Our Lady, Source of Life. Murad's cannon was inadequate and, when the Panayia showed herself upon the walls both to besiegers and besieged, the Turks

[1] Cit. A. A. Vasiliev, op. cit.

retreated. The Roman Emperor, however, paid them a tribute, and there can have been little doubt on either side that the fall was only delayed. When Murad died in 1451 and was succeeded by the very able and ambitious young Sultan, Mehmet II, the last struggle of the 'God-defended City' was close at hand.

CHAPTER III

THE CHURCHES

BYZANTIUM is not perhaps the most encouraging place in which to study Byzantine art and architecture; there is nothing here so untouched as the great churches of Ravenna. Even Salonica has more churches in better preservation to show, and the Salonican churches are not outclassed by the better-preserved monuments of another civilization.

Two conquests, the lean years in between them, fires, earthquakes, and five hundred years of Turkish rule, have spared us three major monuments: the great church of St. Sophia, the earlier church of SS. Sergius and Bacchus, and the fourteenth-century mosaics and wall-painting of St. Saviour in Chora (which, of course, had only one conquest to weather). A generous guidebook might bestow one grudging star on the venerable ruin of St. John Baptist of Studion, or on the pretty brick exterior of the Pammacaristos. For the rest, if perseverance or thoroughness have caused us to wade through evil-smelling and muddy side-streets after such insignificant monuments as the Pantocrator, the Pantepoptes or the Panachrantos, St. Theodore or St. Theodosia, virtue will have to be its own reward, for there is no other.

It is no adverse criticism of Byzantine art to say that it does not make good ruins; that, after all, was not the artists' intention. Its greatest effects were obtained by the rich decoration of wall space with marble, mosaic or painting. Architecture was generally accorded less attention: the main walls were built in brick; monolithic marble columns with their bases and their carved capitals were inserted in the proper places; vaults were thrown – an enormous amount of mortar was used – and then the church was left to settle, like a cake, before decoration. The walls and vaults would almost certainly be very irregular. 'In the older churches the exterior seems to have been left in simple masses of brickwork, impressive only by their size and proportion. Probably even this effect was not considered of great importance.'[1] Later some external decoration was

[1] Alexander Van Millingen: *Byzantine Churches in Constantinople* (London, 1912).

attempted, as in the shallow niches on the apses of the Pantocrator and St. Theodosia, or the pretty brickwork of the Pammacaristos; the Panto-crator, indeed, was probably faced without, as within.

Except to a Ruskinian, the beauty of Byzantine art is none the worse for being skin-deep; much human beauty, and all painting, is no deeper. Neither Canterbury nor Sens is more satisfying than San Vitale or Sant' Apollinare Nuovo. But the beautiful bones of a fine Gothic church are lovely even when it is in ruins. There seems, however, little reason why we should persuade ourselves to admire the broken brick shell of a Byzantine church, of which we can see nothing that the architect meant to present to our admiration and nothing that his contemporaries would have admired, with the exception of one or two fine columns and capitals. The proportions, perhaps, remain; but they have almost certainly been altered by a rise in the floor level and by the stripping of the walls. And to visit pitted brick walls where mosaics have been is no more sensible than to visit a daffodil bed in the autumn.

Byzantium, too long neglected and despised, has later suffered from a modish admiration; its minor monuments have been accorded more attention than they deserve, while major achievements of Ottoman art have been neglected. This injustice should be redressed. Moreover, the visitor to Constantinople, whose enthusiasm has been kindled by Ravenna, should be forewarned, so that he is not disappointed. The Byzantium of Yeats is not here; if any of it lingers on earth at all it is to be sought in the 'monuments of unageing intellect' at Ravenna, or in Athos, where the sea is still 'dolphin-torn', still 'gong-tormented'.

The earliest church that survives in Constantinople, and the only true basilica in form, is the venerable ruin of St. John Baptist of Studion (Imrahor Cami), not far from the castle of the Seven Towers and the Golden Gate. It was founded in 463 by a patrician called Studius, who attached to it a community of Akoimetai or Sleepless monks, so named because, in three relays, they kept up perpetual prayer; it does not appear that this community held the monastery for long.

In later times this monastery ranked first in the city, and its reputation was much enhanced by its great abbot, St. Theodore, who reformed the rule, and developed studies and music and calligraphy here and made it 'the Cluny of the East'. He was a staunch iconodule, and died in exile in Prinkipo during the iconoclast persecutions, in 826.

It has been conjectured by his biographer that St. Theodore's calli-graphic reforms played a part in the change over from uncial to minuscule writing, which took place about this time. His rules for scribes are severe: a scribe who broke his pen in a fit of temper must do penance for it by thirty prostrations, and a hundred and thirty prostrations were the punishment for not minding stops, or not keeping manuscripts clean.

Every year on the feast of the decollation of St. John the Baptist (29 August), the emperor came here by boat to hear the liturgy, and after-wards the court lunched in the garden. Leo the Armenian, entering the Golden Gate on 10 July, 813, to receive the crown at St. Sophia, made a station at Studion on the way — soon he was to become the persecutor of the Studite monks. Michael VIII, the returning Greek Emperor, made a station here in like circumstances on 15 August, 1261.

Studion (this is a modern corruption of the name: it was known as 'the monastery of Studius') produced several patriarchs: Antony III (974-79), Alexius (1025-43), Dositheus (1191). Its scribes continued to be energetic; Stephen of Novgorod (c. 1350) tells us that many manuscripts came to Russia from Studion. And it was a place of retirement from the world that attracted even emperors: Isaac I, Comnenus, retired here in 1059, and lived an edifying and humble life as the monastic porter; Michael VII, Ducas, also retired here in 1078; Michael V, Calaphates, in vain attempted to take refuge here with his uncle, when the mob rose against him. Here was buried an Ottoman prince, son of Bayazit I, a hostage at the Byzantine court, and a secret Christian; he was baptized before dying of the plague in 1417. At the conquest, the Studion was turned into a mosque by Elias Bey, the equerry of Bayazit II, from whom it is called 'the Mosque of the Equerry', its present name.

A fire in 1782, an earthquake in 1894, and a fire in 1920 have left but a shell. The basilica form is still apparent — nave, aisles, apse, narthex and atrium. The colonnade of the north aisle is still standing, impressive monoliths of verd-antique. Some capitals have been removed from this church and were placed in the Church of the Wisdom of God at Lower Kingswood in Surrey. There are very considerable remains of the superb mosaic pavement given by Michael VIII, but no trace of the splendid wall mosaics that medieval visitors admired in this church. The colonnade and architrave of the narthex and its fine Corinthian capitals are the most beautiful fragments that remain. The Studium is a quiet, peaceful, creeper-grown place, with a pleasant fountain of ablutions outside it – the greatest possible contrast to the present filth and pandemonium of the Pantocrator.

The church of SS. Sergius and Bacchus, or 'little St. Sophia' (Kuçuk Ayasofya Cami) is rather sadly situated near the sea walls of the Marmara, below the end of the Hippodrome. The exterior is not very prepossessing, and it stands in a melancholy courtyard surrounded by Turkish hovels and mud; between the south side of the church and the sea is a railway embankment – goods trains shunt level with the gallery windows. It is by no means easy to get the key of the church; one may sit for hours in the Turkish portico, waiting for admission to this, the loveliest of Byzantine interiors.

It was erected in 527 by Justinian as a thank-offering to the two soldier saints, who had appeared to the Emperor Anastasius and had interceded for him when he lay under the death-sentence for being implicated in a conspiracy. At the same time Justinian built the now destroyed basilica of SS. Peter and Paul, whose narthex was continuous with that of this church; the two churches shared one atrium.

The plan of the church is most interesting; it is a domed octagon within a rectangle, a narthex being attached on the west. This is very like the ground-plan of San Vitale at Ravenna, which was probably begun in the following year, but there the octagon is enclosed within another octagon. The octagon and the rectangle of SS. Sergius and Bacchus have not exactly the same orientation, and the two eastern piers are slightly wider apart than those that support the rest of the octagon; there is thus a not unpleasing irregularity. The north, west and south openings have two regularly spaced columns between them: in the north-east, south-east, south-west and north-west openings these columns are set back to form semi-circular exedras. The lower colonnade supports a horizontal entablature, the upper columns are bound by small arches; the whole forms, as Van Millingen says, on seven sides of the octagon 'a beautiful open screen of fourteen columns, and as many triple arcades'. The pairs of columns, below and above, are alternately verd-antique and white, red-veined synnada marble. In the lower colonnade there are 'melon' capitals (as in San Vitale, and in St. Theodore in Constantinople); in the centre there were monograms of Justinian and Theodora, most of which have been effaced; in the gallery 'pseudo-Ionic' or cushion capitals carry the impost of the arch — these are a little clumsy and heavy.

The inscription on the entablature is thus rendered by Van Millingen: 'Other sovereigns indeed have honoured dead men whose labour was useless. But our sceptred Justinian, fostering piety, honours with a splendid abode the servant of Christ, Creator of all things, Sergius; whom nor the burning breath of fire, nor the sword, nor other constraints of trials disturbed; but who endured for God Christ to be slain, gaining by his blood heaven as his home. May he in all things guard the rule of the ever vigilant sovereign, and increase the power of the God-crowned Theodora whose mind is bright with piety, whose toil ever is unsparing efforts to nourish the destitute.' Theodora had, indeed, erected an asylum for fallen women, hostels for strangers, hospitals for the sick and homes for the destitute.

The dome does not require pendentives, for it rests directly on the octagon: eight concave alternate with eight flat compartments. This device, often used for decoration in later domes, is here necessary and constructional. It is a pity that the recent stencil decoration (here less obtrusive than in many mosques) should confuse the eye and obscure this construction which it seeks to decorate.

Procopius says of this church that 'by the sheen of its marbles it was more resplendent than the sun, and everywhere it was filled profusely with gold'. None of that splendour remains, only the columns, the capitals and the beautifully carved entablature; but it remains an exquisite and graceful interior, more intimate and lovable than the Great Church, of which it is the prototype.

The church of St. Irene stands in the outer court of the Serail; it was turned into an arsenal at the conquest, and later became a museum. It is almost impossible to gain admittance.

Constantine's church of the Divine Peace, closely associated with his church of the Holy Wisdom, together with the latter formed an establishment known as the 'Great Church', and shared the same clergy. Both churches were burnt in the Nika revolution of 532, and they were both rebuilt by Justinian. St. Irene further suffered from an earthquake in 740, and was restored by Leo the Isaurian. In form it is a basilica, with two domes, its aisles and narthex surmounted by wide galleries; there are three windows in the apse, a feature unknown in Roman basilicas of this date. In the apse there are five rows of seats for the clergy, facing west, an arrangement which no doubt also existed at St. Sophia; behind these seats runs a passage, whose function is to amplify the voice of people sitting there. This church is an interesting stage in the evolution of the Byzantine church from a Roman basilica to a domed, cruciform building, and it is a pity that no one can ever see it. The pink exterior, the trees round it, and the old cannons in its enclosure, have all considerable charm.

Chief of all monuments in Constantinople is the Great Church; changing in function, it has always kept its name. It has been the church of the Holy Wisdom, the Ayasofya mosque, and now it is the Ayasofya museum. Its secularization has robbed it of any warmth or life it may still have possessed; it is a place of tourism and not of prayer. It seems a pity, therefore, that the secularization has not been a little more thorough. No one should wish all traces of Moslem worship to be effaced, they are an integral part of the building's history; and, if it is a religious museum, it need not be devoted exclusively to the Christian religion. The fine imperial tribune ought to remain untouched, and the splendid alabaster urns placed by Murad III for fountains of ablutions by the western door. Even on the impossible supposition of its restoration to Christian worship — and no one who values the peace of Christendom can wish this, since its possession would at once be hotly disputed by two communions, with some justice on both sides — only a vandal would remove the charming Ottoman faience from the two little passages on either side of the apse. Nevertheless, I am afraid that with either communion, Orthodox or Catholic, the faience would stand a very poor chance.

There are, however, things that should go. The gigantic, round, green medallions, inscribed with the names of Allah, of the Prophet, of the first Caliphs and of the two first Imams are fine examples of calligraphy; they should be preserved in the museum of Islamic art, or hung in some mosque (such as that of the Conqueror) where they would do no harm. Here they break the effect of the piers, block the gallery arches, and are an intolerable eyesore. Superstition is said to keep them in place, and fear that, if an earthquake or other disaster follows hard upon their removal, the removers will be blamed for it; and this is a place where earthquakes are never unlikely. It is also important that the little green medallions in the apse should go, for they cover imperial portraits in mosaic.

Some immediate changes could be made without offending superstition: the singer's gallery could go; the floor could be freed from the unpleasant, little metal-fenced platforms that have no function in a mosque where prayer is not made; and an enormous amount of ugly metal-work could be stripped from the galleries — it seems unnecessary to protect with ugly rails places where no one is allowed to go. Above all, the slanting steps of the sanctuary should go, which confuse the eye by directing it towards the *mihrab* and Mecca, instead of permitting it to follow the true orientation of the building.

When these minor nuisances are removed, it will be easier to imagine the lost beauty of the Great Church and to appreciate the beauty that still remains.

The first church on this site, planned by Constantine, was probably executed under Constantius. It was burnt down in the Nika riot of 15 January, 532. Justinian almost at once started to rebuild, with Anthemius of Tralles and Isidore of Miletus for his architects. The work proceeded fast, and on 26 December, 537, a procession went from St. Anastasia's church (where the mosque of Sokullu Mehmet Pasha now stands) to the dedication; Menas, the patriarch, rode in the royal chariot, and Justinian walked among the people. 'Solomon, I have vanquished you!' the emperor is said to have exclaimed, when he saw his completed church. Nemesis followed this boast.

On 7 May, 558, an earthquake brought down part of the dome and the apse. Anthemius was now dead, but Isidore was put in charge of the restoration. The dome was now raised twenty feet and made more secure.

Procopius, in his *Aedifices*, probably wrote before the earthquake, which he does not mention; nevertheless, his description of the church is perhaps as good as any other. And perhaps it is better to begin with him under the great dome, whither the visitor is immediately and inevitably drawn.

'In the midst of the church are four masses of stone called piers, two on the north, and two on the south sides, opposite and alike, having four columns in the space between each pair. These piers are formed of large stones fitted together, the stones being carefully selected, and cleverly jointed into one another by the masons, and reaching to a great height. Looking at them, you would compare them to perpendicular cliffs. Upon them four arches arise over a quadrilateral space.'[1]

---

[1] Cit. W. R. Lethaby and Harold Swainson: *The Church of Sancta Sophia, Constantinople* (London, 1894).

We may interrupt Procopius, who now becomes less explicit, to say that the east and west arches are open, the north and south arches are blind, being filled with huge lunettes of masonry, pierced by many windows. Nor is he very explicit about the pendentives that support the lower circle of the dome.

'A spherical-shaped dome', he then continues, 'standing upon this circle makes it exceedingly beautiful; from the lightness of the building, it does not appear to rest upon a solid foundation, but to cover the place beneath as though it were suspended from heaven by the fabled golden chain. All these parts surprisingly joined to one another in the air, suspended one from another, and resting only on that which is next to them, form the work into one admirably harmonious whole, which spectators do not dwell upon for long in the mass, as each individual part attracts the eye to itself. The sight causes men constantly to change their point of view, and the spectator can nowhere point to any part which he admires more than the rest. Seeing the art which appears everywhere, men contract their eyebrows as they look at each part, and are unable to comprehend such workmanship, but always depart thence, stupefied through their incapacity.'

Procopius speaks very truly, but a more recent critic comes nearer to giving the reason for the peculiar beauty of the dome of this church, the most beautiful, surely, in the world. 'Resting thus everywhere on sharply receding surfaces, and further alleviated by forty windows opened at its base, the lofty dome of St. Sophia has well remained to this day the most successful architectural approach to the airborne vault of the universe.'

Half-cupolas on the east and west extend the vast central space. Procopius seems to have been much afraid of each half-dome, 'for it appears not to rest upon a secure foundation, but to hang dangerously over the heads of those below'. Paul the Silentiary, a court poet writing after the earthquake of 558, had even more cause to voice a terror of the dome, which seems to have been shared by many. The half-domes rest each on two lateral niches or exedras, of which Procopius writes: 'On each side of these parts are columns standing upon the floor, which are not placed in a straight line, but arranged with an inward curve of semicircular shape, one beyond another like the dancers in a chorus. These columns support above them a crescent-shaped structure.'

'Let us now proceed', says Procopius, 'to describe the remaining parts

E

of the church. The entire ceiling is covered with pure gold, which adds
to its glory, though the reflections of the gold upon the marble surpass it
in beauty. There are two aisles one above another on each side, which do
not in any way lessen the size of the church, but add to its width. In
length they reach quite to the end of the building, but in height they fall
short of it; these also have domed ceilings adorned with gold. Of these
porticoes one (ground floor) is set apart for male and the other (upper
floor) for female worshippers; there is no variety in them, nor do they
differ in any respect from one another, but their very equality and
similarity add to the beauty of the church.' Procopius of course means
that the north aisle is exactly like the south aisle; not that the gynaeceum
galleries are exactly like the loftier nave aisles, which would not be true.

'Who could tell', he continues, 'of the beauty of the columns and
marbles with which the church is adorned? One would think that one
had come upon a meadow full of flowers in bloom! Who would not
admire the purple tints of some and the green of others, the glowing red
and the glittering white, and those too, which nature, painter-like, has
marked with the strongest contrasts of colour? Whoever enters there to
worship perceives at once that it is not by any human strength or skill, but
by favour of God, that this work has been perfected; the mind rises
sublime to commune with God, feeling that He cannot be far off, but
must especially love to dwell in the place which He has chosen.'

The columns, indeed, keep their ancient places; on either side of the
great central space four green columns of Molossian marble support the
six columns of the gallery above, which in their turn support the huge,
window-pierced lunette. The eight great green columns come directly
from Thessaly, according to Paul the Silentiary, while other authors
derive them from Ephesus — either from the gymnasium, or from the
temple of Diana itself. The more romantic guidebooks have a pre-
history for every monolithic column in St. Sophia; more sober students
seem to be of the opinion that most, if not all, of them were specially
quarried for the church.

There are eight noble porphyry columns, two each in the lower order
of each exedra, supporting the four-columned exedras of the gynaeceum.
'These columns', says the Silentiary, 'were once brought from the cliffs
of Thebes, which stand like greaved warriors by the banks of Nile';
another author says that they came from the Temple of the Sun at

Baalbek, and were given to Justinian for his church by a Roman lady, Marcia, 'for the good of her soul'.

The columns keep their ancient places, and their elaborately carved capitals still bear monograms of Justinian and Theodora. The marble revetment, of which Procopius speaks with such enthusiasm, still lines the walls. The Silentiary is even more enthusiastic: 'Yet who, even in the measures of Homer, shall sing the marble pastures gathered on the lofty walls and spreading pavement of the mighty church? These the iron with its metal tooth has gnawed – the fresh green from Carystus, and many-coloured marble from the Phrygian range, in which a rosy blush mingles with white, or it shines bright with flowers of deep red and silver. There is a wealth of porphyry too, powdered with bright stars, that has once laden the river boat on the broad Nile. You would see an emerald green from Sparta, and the glittering marble with wavy veins, which the tool has worked in the deep bosom of the Iassian hills, showing slanting streaks blood-red and livid white. From the Lydian creek came the bright stone mingled with streaks of red. Stone too there is that the Lydian sun, warming with his golden light, has nurtured in the deep-bosomed clefts of the hills of the Moors, of crocus colour glittering like gold; and the product of the Celtic crags, a wealth of crystals, like milk poured here and there on a flesh of glittering black. There is the precious onyx, as if gold were shining through it; and the marble that the land of Atrax yields, not from some upland glen, but from the level plains; in parts fresh green as the sea or emerald stone, or again like blue cornflowers in grass, with here and there a drift of fallen snow – a sweet, mingled contrast on the dark shining surface.'[1]

The 'marble pastures' are still on the walls – marble panels cut, and turned outwards, like wood veneer, to form fantastic natural patterns; there are grey and white marble devils and bats that might almost have been designed by Aubrey Beardsley, and strange forms like the 'ghosts' that children make by folding together inky pieces of paper. A zigzag beading encloses the lower panels, and above there are bands of carved border. Nothing has been lost, and yet nothing now shines or glitters or blushes; the dust of centuries has dulled the green, the blue and the porphyry into a sad greyness. No longer are we amid pastures, or flowers that bloom; the bloom is gone, as surely as the Divine Presence that

[1] Cit. Lethaby and Swainson, loc. cit.

seemed to Procopius to be so near, and in this sad, dank museum towards
the end of the afternoon there are moments when one irreverently likens
it to a vast Turkish bath whose furnaces have long, long been cold.

It is difficult now to understand why, to Procopius, this was a place of
light and sunshine. On a bright morning, indeed, sunlight streams into
the church; and standing in the south-east exedra, looking up at the sun-
gilt dome, one can imagine something of the joyful harmony which
Justinian's contemporaries felt in the Great Church. To them it seemed
like a great, permanent canticle of praise, expressed in marble and gold.

But then the warm, golden vaults generated light; now there is only
faded, but very inoffensive, gold paint. A Koranic inscription in the
dome occupies the place once held by the Christ Pantocrator of Basil II.
Faint traces of the prophets, with which the same emperor decorated the
great lunettes, can still be discerned. Only the four seraphs wholly survive,
painted and not in mosaic, on the four pendentives; they seem to bear up
the dome upon their wings. They have survived, perhaps, because they
have no faces; their faces are covered by their wings; only a gold glory
blazed through, shining from their heads. I do not know that anyone has
ever expressed much admiration for them.

What mosaic is hidden under the paint must be still unknown; the
Turks, milder than Byzantine iconoclasts, had been content to paint over
the images of persons or living things, offensive to Islam, but there was no
destruction. Time and damp have from time to time caused many
tesserae to fall from the roof. Lady Mary Wortley Montagu was offered
a handful as a souvenir, and other travellers have recorded the same
experience.

At present the mosaic uncovered in St. Sophia consists of the exquisite
jewelled vault of a small passage near the west door, the vaults and
lunettes of the narthex, and the lunette of the southern vestibule, also the
apse mosaic inside the church, and the mosaics of the gynaeceum, revealed in recent years by the late Professor Whittemore.

In the lunette over the door of the southern vestibule, the present
entrance to the church, Our Lady holds the Holy Child, and is flanked by
the bowing figures of two emperors: Constantine offers his city, and
Justinian his church, crowned by a vast dome. Professor Whittemore[1]
saw Constantine, the saint, as an idealized figure, and Justinian as material-

---

[1] *The Mosaics of St. Sophia at Istanbul* (Oxford, 1933).

ized. He saw a great deal in mosaics that other people cannot see; on the lunettes of the narthex, and on the soffits of the vault he uncovered a number of black crosses, each of which was in fact differently outlined. Nevertheless, his comment is extraordinary: 'They constitute no trivial repetition of a single shape; but each meets the vision as if charioted on a billow of light, each with an appeal as thrilling, and compelling, and personal as it seems possible to experience.' Surely this is the disproportionate enthusiasm of a discoverer and a specialist – and dare we call it American enthusiasm into the bargain?

In the lunette over the great door into the church, Christ, in a chiton of light blue brocade shot with silver, sits on a broad-backed imperial throne. His right hand is raised in blessing, His left hand holds a book inscribed: '✠ Peace be with you. I am the Light of the world.' At His feet kneels a haloed emperor, vested in a chlamys of soft, dull yellow, a tablion of red and gold, and white shoes. He is Leo the Wise, so we are told by Antony of Novgorod (1200), and it is confirmed by his coinage and by descriptions of his robes given by his son, Constantine Porphyrogenitus. Our Lady and the Archangel Gabriel, Leo's patrons, appear in roundels on either side of the seated Christ.

In the apse, in the traditional position, there is a beautiful seated Virgin holding the Holy Child, erected by Basil I; the apostles Peter and Paul who flanked her are gone, and one of the two archangels. The archangel on the right is splendidly vested, like an emperor of Byzantium.

The gynaeceum gallery is approached by a ramp, up which one could ride on horseback. (It is necessary to obtain permission to go upstairs, and this is no easy thing to do, but no effort should be spared. It is from the gallery that the most satisfying view of the dome can be seen.) In the south gallery is the famous 'Deisis', recently uncovered by Professor Whittemore, the most beautiful mosaic in the Great Church. Christ stands between Our Lady and St. John the Baptist; only the upper part of the figures survive, but the work is of extreme fineness.

The imperial portraits on the east wall are coarse work in comparison. In one Our Lady is flanked by John II, Comnenus, and his empress, Irene, with the Duke Alexius at right angles on another wall. The group on the left has been altered. It now shows Christ standing between the Empress Zoë and Constantine IX, Monomachos; at one time it seems to have shown her previous husband, Romanus III, Argyrus.

Various conjectures have been made why the heads of Christ and of the empress should have been changed, not only that of the emperor; Professor Whittemore inclined[1] to the belief that Zoë's images (including this) had all been destroyed when she was indicted for high treason by Michael V, Calaphates, on 18 April, 1042, but he only had two days in which to do this, before his own overthrow.

As well as enjoying a peculiar reverence throughout Christendom, St. Sophia has also been particularly holy in Moslem eyes. The doors, said to be made from wood from the Ark, were venerated, and travellers prayed before them for Noah's soul before embarking on a voyage; the well, covered with a stone from the well of Samaria, was believed to cure palpitations. The Sweating Column was now transferred from St. Gregory and dedicated to Khidr, a vaguely identified character, a kind of Moslem St. George, easily recognized on the many occasions of his apparition by his boneless thumb, and by the fact that no other Islamic saint rides on horseback. He has appeared in St. Sophia as also in the Atik Ali mosque in Stamboul, and the Atik Validé mosque at Scutari.

The Great Church has many moods: there are days when sun streams in, and it seems allied to the elements of air or fire; there are days when floor and columns drip with moisture, and one is ever conscious of the cisterns underneath it. It compels admiration; the ethereal dome is worthy to be classed as one of the wonders of the world. And it compels pity; it is impossible to forget that once the marbles shone and reflected the vanished gold of the roof, that a silver screen enclosed the sanctuary, and that the exquisite ambo, where the emperors were crowned, stood before it. Most honest visitors admit, however, that an overwhelming disappointment is their first impression when they enter the museum of the Holy Wisdom. This must be overcome; it can never be quite overcome. The church will grow on you, but it will never give the spontaneous joy that the Propylaea gives. It can be deeply admired, but surely never loved.

The external grandeur of the Great Church was, perhaps, the last effect aimed at by its architects; it must, however, always have been guaranteed by the wonderful dome, whose gentle, almost natural, gradient makes it more beautiful than any of the more abrupt domes of the Ottomans. Since 1317, when the ugly buttresses were built, any previous harmony the

[1] In *Byzantion*, vol. XVIII.

church had must have vanished: tombs, fountains, minarets and other accretions have now made the exterior muddled and tiresome; only the dome rises, in almost unimpaired dignity, over the confusion below, and the minarets contribute to the view from Scutari or from the Golden Horn. The planned unity of Sultan Ahmed's mosque nearby, a building that has been built and has not merely grown, shows up the muddle of St. Sophia by its contrast, although it has not a central dome of comparable beauty. The traveller Richard Pococke was in the right when he said: 'This mosque makes a much meaner and heavier appearance on the outside than the mosques that are built in imitation of it', a comparison which makes us less ready than some people have been to disparage Turkish originality. The exteriors of the great imperial mosques do not owe so very much to St. Sophia.

The church of St. Saviour in Chora (now the Kariye Cami, but disaffected as a mosque) is not far from the Adrianople Gate. There is some dispute about its name: over the great door is a head of Christ, with the title 'Η ΧѠΡΑ ΤѠΝ ΖѠΝΤѠΝ', 'the land of the living'. To some people this title of Christ seems to be the origin of the name of the church; to others, the name of the church seems to be played upon in this title of Christ. The second view is more plausible; it is the church of St. Saviour in the Fields, or extra muros, and so it was understood by eleventh-century writers before ever this mosaic of Christ was erected.

If Chora indeed means 'in the Fields', then the first foundation of the church must have preceded the building of the Theodosian walls in 413, for they now enclose it. This is not improbable: the relics of St. Babylas and his companions, martyred at Nicomedia in 298, were here in the ninth century; we do not know the date of their translation to Constantinople, but it is not unlikely that they came in the first century of the city and that a church was built to receive them.

The church that Justinian built here was therefore probably not the first, and it was certainly not the last. It was a basilica, and it is not likely that any of it remains in the present church; twice again it was ruinous, after the reign of Constantine Copronymus (when the triumphant iconodules restored it), and at the beginning of the Comnene period. The church was near Blachernae, the favourite residence of Alexius I, and was restored by Maria Ducaena, his mother-in-law, a restoration that may have amounted to rebuilding. To Maria Ducaena are attributed the cruciform hall, the dome (in so far as it has not been subsequently altered by the Turks), and the marble revetment of the walls; it was probably at this time that the church was dedicated to the Saviour, like other Comnene churches.

During the Latin occupation, the church again suffered badly; it was restored yet again by Theodore Metochites, the grand logothete of the Treasury under Andronicus II, Palaeologos. To Theodore are due the present form of the two narthexes and of the large south chapel, and all the superb mosaic and wall painting in them; the over-curious have tried to find in the mosaic of the miracle of Cana a figure which, by a strained interpretation, gives the date 1303 for the mosaics; this is probably only a perverse misunderstanding of a decorative motif.[1]

The form of the Comnene church (which it may be reasonably assumed was the only church on this site that survives in the present building) is thought to have been a domed basilica, like the church of St. Sophia in Salonica; in Theodore's restoration the walls were thickened, the south aisle was suppressed, the narthex was altered, and the south chapel and outer narthex were added. In Turkish times the dome was raised on a drum.

The main body of the church is panelled with marble; above, the walls were, no doubt, covered with mosaic. On the west wall there is a mosaic panel of the Dormition of Our Lady, and mosaics of Our Lord and of Our Lady are on either side of the entrance to the apse. These mosaics have been attributed to the Comnene period, but they have not yet been cleaned and restored; those who are working on the cleaning and restoration of the mosaics in the narthexes cautiously suspend their judgment. The carving in the church is unusually good; a cornice of grey marble runs above the panelling, carved with an upright leaf; there are carved angels in low relief on the frame above the icon of Our Lady; and on the inner side of the central door is a beautiful porphyry cornice, carved with peacocks drinking at fountains.

The mosaics and the wall-paintings of the narthexes and the south chapel are being restored with the utmost learning, care and good taste. Though scaffolding obscures the general effect, there are no mosaics or wall-paintings that can be seen better in detail; on the scaffolding one can get near to any part of the decoration, and there are powerful lamps to

[1] Alexander van Millingen: *Byzantine Churches in Constantinople* (London, 1912).

turn upon it. Nothing can exceed the kindness of the American, English and Greek restorers, when once one has got into the church, unless it be the malignant obstructiveness of the Turkish Department of Antiquities, which does all it can to prevent one getting in.

The outer narthex is covered with mosaic on the vaults, and the lunettes below them; below these there was no doubt a marble revetment, as inside the church. The nativity of Christ, and minor scenes in His life are represented in the lunettes, and then the story is continued on the vault. The story begins with the dream of St. Joseph, and continues with the journey to Bethlehem, and Our Lady and St. Joseph before the Roman procurator, Quirinius (a subject unique in iconography). Over the door the story is interrupted by the great icon of the Saviour, 'the land of the living'; it continues on the south (where the restorers have not yet got to work) where the outer narthex is returned, to meet the south chapel. The vaults, divided east and west, each contain two episodes: for instance, the dome over the door is divided between the feeding of the five thousand and the miracle of Cana — much of the mosaic has perished, but the baskets of loaves remain and, in the Cana miracle, a group of water-pots, and a pleasant irrelevant scene of the killing of an ox for the marriage-feast. The juxtaposition of the two miracles, that of bread and that of wine, has no doubt a reference to the Eucharist.

In the inner narthex are scenes from the life of Our Lady, her story up to the dream of St. Joseph, with which the series in the outer narthex begins. They are the traditional scenes, taken from the Proto-evangelion of St. James the Less. Work is here in progress, and (by the summer of 1953) only the north side, up to and including the door, has as yet been restored. The work is absorbing to watch, and admirable are the tact and taste with which the restorers tint the patches of bare wall that loss of tesserae has here and there left, scrupulously adding nothing original to the design, and yet so covering the exposed plaster that it is unobtrusive, helping the eye to concentrate upon what is left and, as far as possible, to be undistracted by the gaps.

The story is told on the vault, the lunettes and the archivolts. It begins with the prayer of St. Joachim in the desert, while the lunette below shows St. Anne going into the garden and praying under a laurel watched (presumably) by her servant Judith — while St. Anne is praying, a mother-bird comes to feed her two young in a nest in the garden — and the flight of the bird parallels the flight of the angel coming to St. Anne. There follows the tender embrace of St. Anne and St. Joachim at the gate of Jerusalem; the movement of the two figures is very natural and touching, and a faint blush suffuses St. Anne's cheeks. In the second lunette on the east wall is the birth of Our Lady; a cot is prepared, and eight women (hideous and alarming Gamps) attend on the Mother and Child. St. Joachim peeps through the door.

It may be noted that the profiles are never good; they are very crude if compared with those on the Roman pavement of the Great Palace. Nor are full faces always much better; the infant Virgin is in most of the Kariye mosaics represented as almost hydrocephalous. No great originality of design was here possible, for the rules of iconography were rigid. What we can admire is the beauty of colour, of movement, of pattern and of drapery; and in the last category the men's beards may be included. These brilliant mosaics show the life and spirit there were yet in Byzantium, and the capacity of Byzantine artists, had they been left in peace, of possibly generating a renaissance of their own in a place where the Ancient world had never really died. But the mosaics of Kariye had barely been completed when the Turks reached Broussa (now Bursa).

Round the lunette of the birth of Our Lady is a splendid border of red key-pattern, on a gold ground. Above, the infant Virgin is caressed by her parents, flanked by two peacocks. Then follow the Seven Steps: the infant Virgin walks towards St. Anne, and behind her stands an attendant or governess whose scarf, caught by the wind, forms an arc over her head. In the third lunette, Theodore the Logothete, in a wonderful tall head-dress, offers the church to Christ, 'the land of the living'.

On the lunette of the west wall opposite, Our Lady is given the purple thread to weave the temple veil; there follows the prayer of the chief priest over the staves deposited by her suitors; and, in the next lunette, the staff of St. Joseph blossoms; there is then a scene, after their betrothal, in which he reproaches her for being with child.

The greater scenes from the lives of Christ and His Mother were no doubt represented inside the church, where there would have been the regular series of the 'Twelve Feasts'; though it is a little hard to see how there could have been room for this when so much wall space is covered with the marble revetment.

The south chapel (parecclesion) is painted; it has been conjectured that the wall-painting may be by the artist who designed the mosaic. In the apse, on a dark-blue ground, is a noble painting of the Harrowing of Hell. A white-robed Christ, daringly framed in a white *vesica piscis*, vigorously tugs Adam, an old patriarch with a flowing white beard, and Eve from their graves. Bones and broken tombs are under the feet of Christ. Among the risen blessed are Abel, with his shepherd's crook, and David and Solomon; below there is a rank of doctors. On the south the resurrection of Jairus's daughter is represented, and, on the north, that of the widow's son; it has been suggested that this was probably a mortuary chapel, and it contains the tomb of Michael Tornikes, the grand constable and kinsman of Andronicus II. Another noble painting is the Virgin, on the south wall; the yellow step on which she stands has been stained red by candles.

The wall-paintings also are being uncovered by the labours of the Byzantine Institute of Boston — an even more delicate task than the uncovering of mosaic. They are washed with water, scraped with orange sticks, and sometimes dental implements are used for plaster that resists; inch by inch the painting is revealed, and in a state of almost original freshness. It must be the most satisfying form of archaeological work, almost as satisfying as creation, and much more certain of yielding results. The people engaged on it seem to be happy (perhaps the only people in Constantinople who give that impression); it is pleasant to watch them at work, or to picnic with them at luncheon time, outside the Adrianople Gate.

The lesser churches must be approached without great expectations. 'There are many later churches which carry us back to the vigorous age of Byzantine art', says Hutton, but he fails to make out his case. 'The contrast between the monuments of Constantinople,' says a more candid, later writer, 'as described by history and imagination, and their shabby remains, is at first peculiar and sickening. Degradation and death proclaim, not only from the multitude of decrepit graveyards within the boundary walls, but from the crumbling remnants of this ancient bulwark of civilization.'

St. Andrew in Crisei (Mosque of Koca Mustafa Pasha) is in Samatya. The earliest church here was dedicated to St. Andrew the Apostle, but later the dedication was changed to St. Andrew of Crete. That indiscreet person, a fervent iconodule, came from his island to Constantinople on purpose to rebuke Constantine Copronymus for his attack on icons. He obtained, not surprisingly, the crown of martyrdom for his pains, and his body was thrown out to rot with those of malefactors. It was rescued by the pious, and buried in the church of St. Andrew the Apostle, 'in a holy place called Krisis'.

The name of the place means 'judgment', and for centuries a chain hung from an old cypress in the courtyard, which still survives, and had the property of settling disputes. A story is told to its discredit. A Jew had borrowed money from a Moslem, but persisted in denying his debt. One day they both appeared at the cypress to put it to the proof. The Jew first asked the Moslem to hold his stick, then stood beneath the tree, and swore that he had paid his debt. The chain slowly descended in token of confirmation. In fact the stick handed to the Moslem was hollow, and contained the exact amount of the debt in gold.

Krisis is an agreeable place; odd eighteenth- or nineteenth-century buildings surround the courtyard, there is a small Moslem cemetery, and there are some larger tombs. There is a shady café at the gate, the terminus of the 35 bus. The exterior of the church is of no special distinction, but inside there are four verd-antique columns with early Byzantine capitals in the restored south church, and two more in the south aisle of the main church.

Here, after the conquest, were 'discovered' the apocryphal graves of Fatima and Zeinab, daughters of the Imam Hussein, who were said to have been carried off to Constantinople and to have killed themselves to avoid having to marry Christians. Earth from their graves, carried to a sick person, has the property of making him at once better or worse so that, if he has recourse to this heroic expedient, he knows whether it is his destiny to die or to recover.

The church of the monastery of Christ Akataleptos (now Kalender Cami) stands by the aqueduct of Valens, not far from the Mosque of the Shehzade. For a long time it was mistakenly identified with St. Mary Diaconissa, where the emperor always made a station and lit a candle on his processions to the church of the Holy Apostles. This is a ninth-century church, much altered; formerly, perhaps, a nave with double aisles, but now shorn and mutilated into a Greek cross. There is a good deal of marble revetment surviving, though it is much inferior to that of Kariye. The piers at the entrance to the chancel have been adorned by the Turks with admirable fragments from the stone iconostasis. As a mosque, it is a poor sort of place: there is a hideous green *mimber* with an extinguisher roof, and framed inscriptions from the Koran are hung up like 'texts'. There is no minaret; on one visit to the Akataleptos I heard the mid-day Call to Prayer cried by the *muezzin* from a big stone outside the south-west corner of the church.

The church known as St. Theodore (now Kilise Cami) is of doubtful identification; it is near the mosque of Süleyman, on the west slope of the third hill. There is a very fine fourteenth-century western façade, in which sixth-century columns and capitals are incorporated. Like St. Saviour in Chora, it is a more ancient church, remodelled after the Latin occupation, and in the decoration of the west end and of the apse, and in the heightening of the domes, we see the late-Byzantine attention to exterior appearances. But, Van Millingen rather sourly, if justly, reminds us: 'We have not yet reached the animation and grace of a Gothic cathedral, nor the stateliness that crowns an imperial mosque.' Byzantium was never to reach these; and yet, if the city had not fallen, if Sinan (born a Greek and a Christian) had been fated to work for a Greek and Christian prince, in a restored empire, what might not have happened? There is some mosaic in the narthex domes, and very crude it appears, in its present uncared-for state.

The Mirelaion (Bodrum Cami), near the Laleli Mosque, is another pleasant exterior; ruinous after a fire, its pretty brick-work can still be admired, though the lantern is grown over by a creeper. This church (Oil of Myrrh) was part of a convent dispersed by Constantine Coprony-mus, who called the place Psarelaion (Fish Oil) in mockery. It was restored by Romanus Lecapenus, and became his burial place and that of other members of the imperial family.

The church of St. Saviour Pantocrator (Zeyrek Cami) on the fourth hill is now as nasty a place as you can find in a day's walk in Constantinople; there is a wash-place in the outer narthex, unsavoury cooking is usually going on in the inner narthex, the north church is littered with broken biers, and the whole place swarms with singularly nasty little boys, who seem to breed there, for the number increases at each subsequent visit.

Yet it is a church that has had a great history. The popular story of its origin is that it was founded by Irene, daughter of Ladislas, King of

Hungary, and consort of John II, Comnenus; she founded a monastery for seven hundred monks, a hostel, an alms-house, and a hospital. When she found that she could not complete what she had undertaken, she brought the emperor to see the unfinished work, fell at his feet in tears, and begged him to complete it. It appears, however, that the real founder was John II, though Irene was associated in his foundation; an imperial *typicon* or charter made the monastery of the Pantocrator autonomous and tax-free.

When John II died in a hunting accident in Cilicia, Manuel his younger son was chosen as successor; he had Isaac, his elder brother, confined at the Pantocrator. John II was buried here, his body having been sent back by sea; and Manuel I must have put at least the finishing touches to the church of his parents' foundation, for we learn that a mosaic here represented him offering it to Christ.

The present south church was the church begun by John and Irene; Manuel added a chapel on the north, now the middle church (we do not know who built the north church — the Pantocrator is now a muddled congeries of three churches, covering a considerable area). In the middle, funerary chapel, Manuel I buried his first wife, Bertha. Here he placed the porphyry slab where the body of Christ had lain after the deposition from the Cross; when this precious relic arrived from Ephesus, he had carried it uphill on his back from the port of Boucoleon to the chapel of the Great Palace. Beside this slab he was buried in 1180, in a splendid black marble sarcophagus, whose cover was cut in seven protuberances, to represent the seven hills of Constantinople. Later many of the Palaeologi were also to choose the Pantocrator as a burial-place.

Manuel I had brought here the great icon of St. Demetrius from Salonica, compensating that city by the gift of a new one, adorned with gold and silver; during the Latin occupation the church was the temporary home of the great icon of the Panayia Hodighetria, the work of St. Luke the Evangelist, an icon of great virtue which was often taken to menaced parts of the city, and which finally perished in the church of Chora, torn to pieces by the Turks in 1453 and made into amulets. The Hodighetria was taken from the Pantocrator to lead the procession of the returning Greek Emperor, Michael VIII, through the Golden Gate, on 15 August, 1261, when the Latin occupation was over.

The dependencies of the monastery suffered an attack by the Genoese, because it had been occupied by Venetians; and, like other churches, it was sacrilegiously pillaged by the Latins; the Abbot of Péris in Alsace bearing off its relics of the True Cross.

In the later empire the most important event associated with the Pantocrator was the imprisonment here of George Scholarius, by Constantine XI, for his fanatical opposition to the reunion of the churches. After the Fall, he did homage to the Sultan, who established him as the Patriarch Gennadius, in the church of the Holy Apostles.

Richard Pococke, in the early eighteenth century, was still able to report of the Pantocrator: 'The whole is adorned with the figures of the apostles, and of the history of our Saviour in mosaic work, and the subject of each compartment is described in Greek; the Turks have disfigured the faces of all of them.'

Now it is a poor shell of a church; even the exterior is not that which was designed to meet the eye — for Diehl believes there was an exterior revetment of marble. There is, however, some decorative arcading on the apses, and the long line of the western façade is not entirely without charm. Though the mosaic is long since gone, there is some marble facing on the inside of the southern apse, and some Byzantine marble has been used in the pulpit; there are traces of the medieval pavement in the funerary chapel of Manuel, and in the narthexes there are fine red marble doorways. Perhaps the most interesting relic of the past is the big, green sarcophagus in the square outside. It has a hole in the lid, and it is now used as a rubbish dump; it is said to have been the tomb of the foundress, Irene. An early nineteenth-century traveller found the tomb being used as a fountain of ablutions.

Another Comnene church, situated on the edge of the fourth hill, is that of St. Saviour Pantepoptes, the all-seeing Saviour (Eski Imaret Mesjedi). It was founded or restored by Anna Dalassena, the mother of Alexius I, Comnenus, who retired here to end her days in 1100. Alexius V, Murtzuphlus, made his headquarters here during the siege of 1204; he fled in such haste that he left his vermilion tent still standing, and Baldwin of Flanders slept under it. In Frankish times it was in Venetian hands, and belonged to S. Giorgio Maggiore of Venice. After the conquest it was made an *imaret* (refectory) for students and teachers in a school attached to the Conqueror's Mosque, and later was itself turned into a mosque.

It is a lofty, well-proportioned church; there are elegant doors between the outer and inner narthexes, and crosses survive unmutilated upon the lintels. It is, however, hardly worth the trouble to seek out, for this is very considerable; it is half surrounded by houses, and between my first and second visits a new concrete wall had been built to the west, making the neighbourhood even more like a maze. The key is with the grocer at the north-west corner.

The church of St. Mary Pammacaristos, the all-blessed (Fetihye Cami) is also a Comnene foundation. It is splendidly situated on a platform at the edge of the fifth hill, overlooking the Phanar and the Golden Horn. It was founded, or restored, by the curopalates and grand domestic, John Comnenus, and Anna Dalassena his wife, the parents of Alexius I. A further restoration was made in the fourteenth century by Michael Ducas Glabas, the protostrator, and Maria Ducaena Comnena Palaelogina Blachena, his wife. The southern parecclesion was added as his funerary chapel, and on its outside wall his wife placed a touching inscription, part of which reads:

> Therefore I will construct for thee this tomb as a pearl oyster shell,
> Or shell of the purple dye, or bud on a thorny brier.
> O my pearl, my purple, rose of another clime,
> Even though being plucked thou art pressed by the stones
> So as to cause me sheddings of tears. . . .

The Patriarch Gennadius moved here from the Holy Apostles in 1456, and during the next 138 years the Pammacaristos was successively the seat of seventeen patriarchs. During the sixteenth century it was resplendent with icons and imperial portraits, and rich in relics preserved by Gennadius. In 1586, under Murad III, it was turned into a mosque, being coveted because of its fine position; it was given the title of Fethiye, Mosque of the Conquest, on account of the recent conquest of Georgia and Azerbaidjan. The patriarchate then moved downhill to the Phanar, where it has remained ever since.

The tradition that this church was the burial place of Anna Comnena is of little value; it is most probable that she was buried in the Kecharitomeni (St. Mary Full of Grace), a convent now destroyed, whither she had retired. This was a foundation of her mother's, and probably was somewhere near Blachernae.

The exterior of the Pammacaristos is most beautiful, the best Byzantine exterior in the city; the decorative brickwork, the arcading on the south apse (though the central apse has been replaced by the Turks by an ugly triangular projection) and the well-grouped domes are as pleasing as the interior is muddled and confusing. Not that it is an easy matter to get in; a guardian is posted on the roof to keep people out, although the building is securely locked. Bribes are of no avail, for he will be betrayed by the neighbours if he lets you in, and he may be bastinadoed by the orders of the Department of Antiquities; such things have been known to happen. An attempt to get in should, however, be made, for there is an extremely beautiful mosaic dome (Christ, surrounded by twelve prophets) over the chantry of Michael; further discoveries will no doubt be made here, when the Byzantine Institute of Boston gets to work on this church.

St. Theodosia (Gül Cami) is probably the church of St. Euphemia built by Basil I at the end of the ninth century, whose dedication was altered in honour of St. Theodosia, because her extremely thaumaturgic relics were there. This lady had been the proto-martyr of the iconodule faction; in revenge for the death of the soldier who was thrown from a ladder by the angry crowd as he attempted to pull down the picture of Christ from the gate of the Palace, she was dragged to the Forum Bovis (Aksaray) where a ram's horn was driven into her neck. 'The ram's horn' [to quote the office for her feast] 'in killing thee, O Theodosia, appeared to thee a new Horn of Amalthea.'

This was a popular shrine; it was visited on 28 May, 1453, the last day of Constantinople, by Constantine XI, accompanied by the Patriarch and Senate, for that day was the eve of St. Theodosia. Many people spent that night there in prayer, and were thence carried away into captivity by the conquering Turks next day. There is a popular belief that it won its present name, 'The Rose Mosque', because it was garlanded with roses for its feast on the day of the Fall; this is unlikely to be true, for it did not become a mosque until more than a hundred and fifty years later, which is too long a time for such a tradition to survive. The name was probably given as a compliment to the beauty of the building, as Laleli is called 'The Tulip Mosque'.

The east end of the church is indeed beautiful; it is lofty and dignified, and the apses are adorned with decorative niches, but the interior has been totally transformed and could only interest a professional archaeologist.

F

There is no evidence at all to support the legend that the last emperor is buried here.

The church of St. Mary Panachrantos, all-immaculate (Fenere Isa Mesjedi), down in the Lycus valley, may just be worth a visit; it is a congeries of churches like the Pantocrator, and like the Pantocrator it has pretty apses. The history of this church is obscure and its identification is a matter for dispute. The brick walls are bare and pitted, but in the north church there are Byzantine capitals and fragments of a frieze, and in the south church there are vestiges of mosaic on the south wall of the south aisle — that is to say, they are physically there, but too vestigial to be the subject of any aesthetic judgment.

Two ruins are St. John Baptist in Trullo (Ahmed Pasha Mesjedi), on the fifth hill, not far from the Pammacaristos, and the monastery of Gastria (Sandjakdar Mesjedi) in Samatya; the former is a pretty little ruin, part of which is now a private house, and washing was hanging up to dry in the roofless church when I visited it; the latter is a dull, weed-grown, broken shell.

The small chapel of the Gastria was probably a chantry; it is too small to have been a convent church. The convent was probably founded early in the ninth century, either by Euphrosyne, step-mother of the Emperor Theophilus, or by Theoctiste his mother-in-law, an ardent iconodule. Gastria means 'the flower pots', and no doubt potters worked in the neighbourhood; the myth that St. Helena brought here plants that she had potted on Calvary was no doubt invented to fit the name. Its Moslem name means 'The Mosque of the Standard-Bearer'. Hayreddin, the standard-bearer of Mehmet II, turned it into a mosque and is buried there.

St. John Baptist in Trullo is chiefly noteworthy because the Concilium Trullanum of 692 was not held here, though some authors have been under that erroneous impression; it was held in a domed hall of the Great Palace, which gave it its name. This little church is unique in Constantinople in having an apse that is semi-circular exteriorly, not framed in the usual half-hexagon.

Two churches in the Phanar deserve to be visited out of piety or sentiment, though their artistic value is small. St. Mary of the Mongols, or the Mouchliotissa, a little church with crinkly yellow walls, stands like dignity beside the impudence of the hideous, red-brick Greek school, whose lantern is the one serious blot on the skyline seen from the Golden

Horn. It is the one church that has remained uninterruptedly in Christian hands. It is believed that the foundress was Maria Palaeologina, natural daughter of Michael VIII, who in 1265 went to the Mongol court to marry Holagu, Khan of the Mongols, with a big retinue conducted by Theodosius de Villehardouin, Abbot of the Pantocrator. When they reached Caesarea, they learnt that Holagu was dead; nevertheless, they continued their journey, and Maria was married to Abaga, his son. When Abaga was poisoned by his brother in 1281, she returned to Constantinople. This princess may have made gifts to this church and convent, but the founder appears to have been Isaac Ducas, her father's uncle. At the conquest, this church is said to have been given by Mehmet II to Christodoulos, his Christian architect.

The plan of the church, much obscured by later additions, is interesting; the central dome rests on four half-cupolas, a miniature anticipation of the plan, adapted from that of St. Sophia, that Sinan was to carry out so much more grandly in the Mosque of the Shehzade. It is a melancholy fact that this venerable church has, in Christian hands, suffered quite as much from careless rebuilding and tasteless decoration as any church that has been turned into a mosque.

The patriarchal church in the Phanar is a dull, eighteenth-century structure, with a very conspicuous and ugly pulpit, decorated with mother-of-pearl. There are two mosaic icons: the Pammacaristos, in the iconostasis, and St. John the Divine, on the south wall. These are said to come from the former patriarchal church, the Pammacaristos, and very likely they do; they are framed, portable icons, and of inferior work. The Phanar is a homely place; there is here none of the silver and the eunuchs of St. Sophia, nor the splendour of a modern papal ceremony; yet the office is decent and reverent, and the gigantic figure of the Œcumenical Patriarch, though more approachable than that of the Pope, has its own awe.

CHAPTER IV

BYZANTINE SECULAR MONUMENTS

The Hippodrome and the Palace

THE Hippodrome, the great centre of Byzantine life, was begun by Septimius Severus in 203: he had ruined three-quarters of the city to punish it for a revolt, and now gave it a circus in order to regain the goodwill of the citizens, for he had realized the great advantages of its geographical position. He built half the seats, and erected images of Castor and Pollux, to whom he dedicated his hippodrome; then he was recalled to Italy by Gallic invasions, and left the work unfinished.

Constantine enlarged the plan and finished the work, and the inauguration of his hippodrome took place at the same time as that of his city, on 11 May, 330.

The plan was that of every ancient stadium, a long rectangle with a semi-circular end, and tiers of seats rising all round: in the early thirteenth century Robert of Clari saw thirty or forty rows. There was a double course, separated by what was elsewhere called the *spina* or backbone, but here was known as the *euripus*. Three monuments now mark this line, but Gyllius saw seven towards the middle of the sixteenth century; the *spina* was probably a low wall on which these monuments were set. Round the course were barriers on which the spectators leaned, and there was a promenade above the seats, ornamented with statues; here, most probably, were the famous bronze horses of Lysippus, now in Venice, though they may have adorned the Kathisma, or imperial seat. Theodosius II brought them here from Chios; Henry Dandolo sent them to Venice, after the fall of Constantinople to the Crusaders; Napoleon, in his turn, took them to Paris, whence they returned to St. Mark's in 1815. No other work of art from the hippodrome survives.

At the top of the seats there were columns, perhaps a colonnade over the walks. When Gyllius was first in Constantinople, seventeen columns stood on the side facing the Marmara; they were taken by Süleyman to build a hospital and, to Gyllius's grief, many Byzantine columns appropriated by the Turks at this time were not taken for use as columns, but were broken up as building material. The hemicycle at the end, the *sphendone*, had thirty-seven columns; it rested on a brick substructure, because of the declivity of the soil. A high wall enclosed the whole hippodrome, shutting it off from the city.

The Blues, bourgeois and Orthodox, occupied the right side, and were responsible for the end of the course near the entrance; at this *meta* stood their silver organ. The Greens, lower-class and Monophysite, were responsible for the other *meta*, and occupied the left side of the hippodrome. On their side was the Kathisma, or the imperial box, supported by twenty-four marble columns; there was here a suite of rooms, where the emperor could eat, rest and change his robes, and from these apartments he could directly reach the palace without entering the hippodrome – a wise precaution when the course was so often the scene of riot and uproar. The day before the races a great silken veil was hung in front of the imperial box to keep it cool; this was the official announcement of the games. Chariot races were at first the rule; they took place at Christmastide and in the octave of Easter, on the birthdays of the city and of the emperor, on the occasion of imperial weddings or of the reception of ambassadors. The drivers were regarded as *inhonestae personae*, and were frequently Jews; it was disgraceful to keep company with them. Nevertheless, the Byzantines were passionately interested in every detail they could learn about drivers and horses, and were violent partisans. The games lasted from morning to night, and few would leave during the luncheon interval, from fear of losing their places. It was a sport calculated to rouse the passions, for there was no idea of fair play; every driver tried to trip and unseat his rivals, and it was the greatest triumph to perform this feat opposite the imperial Kathisma. Magic was also resorted to, to win victory and to defeat others, though the practice was illegal. The mania for racing often called forth ecclesiastical disapproval, and St. John Chrysostom called the hippodrome 'Satanodrome'.

Later, mimes and wild beast shows were introduced, and the knights who brought Joanna of Savoy as a bride for Andronicus III in 1326 introduced jousts and tourneys, and thereafter this western form of entertainment replaced all others. The hippodrome was disaffected after the Fall, ruined, pulled down, and built over. It had been much neglected since palace life moved to Blachernae.

A great part of the site is now clear; it has been made into a long, pleasant public garden with pollarded acacias. Much of it is covered by the courtyards of the mosque of Sultan Ahmed, in which some building material from the hippodrome is incorporated. Archaeologists have been at work on the site, and a good deal of the substructure of the *sphendone* can be made out, and its cistern; but to the ordinary visitor the only satisfaction is to know that he is in a spot where so much has happened. I have often sat in a café on the right-hand side, as if I were a rather privileged Blue, with paper lanterns (left over from Bayram) in the chestnut trees above me, and lime-flowers falling on me from some invisible tree, watching children playing in the gardens, or flat-capped Turkish sailors strolling about. The only ancient thing to see is the monuments of the *spina*.

Nearest to St. Sophia is the hideous and sumptuous fountain given by the last German Emperor to the Sultan Abdul Hamid II. Ernest Mamboury says truly, in his indispensable guidebook,[1] that 'the fine marbles and rich mosaics make a remarkable effect in the sun'. Its donor could easily be guessed, even if all records and oral traditions had perished.

The obelisk of Theodosius I, originally erected at Karnak by Tuthmes III (*c.* 1471 B.C.) was, after some unsuccessful attempts, or so it would appear, raised on four cubes of bronze, which rest on a most interesting sculptured base. On each of the four sides the imperial family is shown in the Kathisma; on one side they watch a chariot-race; on another, crowns are awarded to the victors, and a dance is going on; on the third side they watch the erection of the obelisk; and on the last they receive the homage of vanquished chieftains. These reliefs are in a very good state of preservation and are most valuable evidence of the dress and manners of the time.

Here, as in the next monument, the Serpent Column, one can see how the level of the soil has risen; the *spina*, if it ever were a wall supporting these columns, is now deeply buried. The Serpent Column was brought here by Constantine from Delphi. It was an offering to Apollo from the thirty-one Greek cities who had fought at Salamis and Plataea, and was made with bronze melted down from the booty taken in those battles; originally it terminated in three serpents' heads, and supported a golden tripod which, in its turn, upheld a golden vase. Now there is nothing but the very splendid green coil of bronze. A fifteenth-century Russian pilgrim, the deacon Zosimus, says that a touch of this column cured snake-bite.

[1] *Istanbul touristique:* by far the most useful book on Constantinople.

The last monument, a constructed obelisk, is called the Colossus of Constantine Porphyrogenitus, by whom it was restored; it was at one time covered with plates of bronze, of which it was stripped by the rapacity of the Crusaders. Gyllius says of this monument: 'One Day, being the Festival of the Circumcision of the Prince of *Boldania*, I saw an ingenious Fellow of a Mountebank climb to the Top of it, and come down safe. The same Attempt was immediately made by another, who made a shift to reach the Top of it, but the Height so dazzled and confounded him, that, despairing of getting down without Hurt, he threw himself, with all his Might, as far as he could from the *Colossus*, to avoid the Danger of being dash'd to pieces upon the Foundation; so that falling down right upon his Feet, he stuck deep in the Earth, and dy'd upon the Spot.'

The Great Palace was on the Marmara side of the hippodrome, connected with the Kathisma, from which the emperor watched the games; it covered some hundred thousand square metres and was, like the Turkish Serail, a complicated arrangement of courts, gardens and buildings, rather than a coherent palace, such as Versailles. Work was still done upon it till the tenth century when, during the reign of Constantine Porphyrogenitus, it was at its greatest glory. The Comnene emperors, who much preferred Blachernae as a residence, allowed the Great Palace to decay and, though it was still used for official ceremonies in the fourteenth century, Buondelmonti found little left when he visited the city in 1422. 'The spider has wove his web in the imperial palace,' said the Conqueror, when he entered it, 'and the owl hath sung her watchsong on the towers of Afrasiab.' It was not the Turks who had destroyed it; Byzantine neglect, Latin pillage, and the poverty of Baldwin II, who used its lead roof for coinage and its timbers for firing – these were the causes that brought it so low.

Archaeologists have attempted several reconstructions of the plan for, though hardly anything remains, the Book of Ceremonies by Constantine Porphyrogenitus describes the processional routes followed on several ceremonial occasions.

The gate-building facing the hippodrome was called Chalce, from its great bronze doors, or perhaps from bronze tiles on the roof; it had been rebuilt by Justinian after the Nika riots, and was restored in the ninth century by Basil the Macedonian. Over the door was that icon of Christ that was pulled down by the iconoclasts, the episode that ended in the martyrdom of St. Theodosia. Here was a vestibule, with statues, and a reception room. Within were the quarters of the palace guard.

Farther in was the Triclinium, a banqueting-chamber with nineteen beds where three hundred guests could recline and eat; and, beyond, a palace called the Daphne, from a statue of that nymph, a construction begun by Constantine, and haphazardly added on to at different times. Beyond this was the Sacred Palace, containing the emperor's private apartments, and the Chrysotriclinium, a superb octagonal room built by Justin II. There were also the palace of Magnaura, on the south-east of St. Sophia, and the seaside palaces of Boucoleon, the lower part nearest the sea built by Theodosius II, and the upper part built by Nicephorus Phocas, and inhabited by Alexius Comnenus; they were named from a sculptural group of a bull assaulted by a lion. Somewhere (its position is most uncertain) was the Porphyra, the porphyry-lined chamber set apart for the empresses' lying-in; those born in this chamber were called Porphyrogeniti, 'born in the purple'.

Though there was no plan, and no architectural unity about these palaces, many of the buildings must have been of great beauty and splendour.

Procopius (thus rendered by the translator of Gyllius) speaks of a court built by Justinian 'which was encompassed with so calm a sea, that when you walk'd in the Galleries, you might discourse audibly with the sailors. It made a very beautiful, a very delightful, and most magnificent Prospect. It was fann'd with gentle breezes, supported with lofty Columns, and laid with the most curious Marble, which like the Sun, reflected a most amazing Lustre'.

The buildings erected in the reign of Theophilus (829-42), stimulated by reports of the palace of the Caliphs at Baghdad, must also have been exquisite. Then the Trikonchos was built, with shell-like apses on three sides, and a roof upheld by fifteen columns of many-tinted marble; on the north side was the *mysterion*, a sort of whispering gallery. In the court of the secret fountain, there was a bronze fountain with a silver rim, and a golden pine cone in the middle. There was the hall of Pearl, and gardens and 'sunneries' were added; in one room there were green mosaic trees against a golden sky, for Theophilus's iconoclasm had brought a new naturalism into the art of his time.

Magnaura, where the emperor received ambassadors, was full of beautiful and fantastic mechanical toys. When Liudprand of Cremona was sent as Berengar's envoy to Constantine Porphyrogenitus, he observed that 'before the Emperor's seat stood a tree, made of bronze gilded over, whose branches were filled with birds, also made of gilded bronze, which uttered different cries, each according to its varying species'. The throne was 'guarded by lions, made either of bronze or of wood covered over with gold, who beat the ground with their tails, and gave a dreadful roar with open mouth and quivering tongue'. Suddenly, to Liudprand's amazement, the emperor was shot up to the ceiling by some mechanical device.[1]

Many were the palace churches and oratories, rich in treasure and relics. At St. Stephen's in the Daphne were the right hand of the proto-martyr and St. Matthew's gospel written by St. Barnabas. At St. Saviour's in the Chalce John Zimisces placed the hair of St. John the Baptist. The Oratory of St. Theodore, in the Chrysotriclinium, enshrined the rod of Moses. Our Lady of the Pharos was the richest sanctuary of all; here was the autograph letter from Our Lord to Abgar, the Lance of the Passion, with its fresh blood stain, a nail, still unrusted, from the Cross, the crown of thorns, still miraculously green, and the stone rolled away from the Holy Sepulchre. The Nea, or New Church, the splendid edifice of Basil I, housed part of the mantle and the girdle of the prophet Elijah.

In the long years of the empire, saints had gone in and out of fashion; emperors, not unnaturally, promoted the cult of their own favourite patrons. Thus Basil I had a particular devotion to the prophet Elijah, for example, and Constantine Porphyrogenitus to St. John Chrysostom. Theodosius the Great, at the end of the fourth century, brought a head of St. John the Baptist to Constantinople, wrapped in his own purple mantle, but it so rapidly lost popularity that an entirely new head was discovered in the following century.

The relics and treasure of the Great Palace were pillaged by the Latins in 1204; Robert of Clari, one only among many pious relic-thieves, brought to the monastery of Corbie small relics of the True Cross, the Crown of Thorns and the Sudarium, stolen thence. Much, however, remained hidden; the relics of Constantinople moved about from church to church, and later pilgrims still found much for their veneration, though now no longer in the palace.

[1] *The works of Liudprand of Cremona*, tr. F. A. Wright (London, 1930).

The palace particularly attracted the admiration of Robert of Clari;[1] he says it was 'very rich and was made in such a way as I shall tell you. Within this palace, which was held by the marquis (Baldwin), there were fully five hundred halls, all connected with one another, and all made of gold mosaic. And in it there were fully thirty chapels, great and small, and there was one of them which was called the Holy Chapel [i.e. Our Lady of the Pharos], which was so rich and noble that there was not a hinge nor a band nor any other part such as is usually made of iron that was not all of silver, and there was no column that was not of jasper or porphyry or some other precious stone'.

Of all this splendour nothing remains, except for those treasures that were carried away to the west, and have survived the French revolution and other vicissitudes; too often the crusading pirates were content to throw away the relic, and to melt down the reliquary.

The only fragment of the palace yet uncovered that has an artistic interest is the splendid mosaic pavement, once the floor of the colonnade on one side of an *atrium*; it is admirable fifth-century work. On a white ground, with a rich border, a series of detached scenes are depicted; there is no coherent design uniting the whole, but each scene is a small and satisfying work of art. There are the usual hunting scenes and country scenes of Greco-Roman mosaic, real and imaginary animals (a lion, for example, with an eagle's beak), a fine scene of two men hunting a tiger, and another of children playing in the hippodrome with little toy carts, as they still play today. The work is of great fineness, the colour vivid, the movement lively, and the figure-drawing, classical in its inspiration, greatly superior to that in later work in Constantinople. Work here is still in progress, as in Kariye, and, as there, the kindness and helpfulness of the archaeologists (if you can ever manage to get in) is a welcome contrast to the Turkish obstructiveness that seeks to bar the door.

Other monuments of Byzantine Constantinople, long vanished, may be mentioned here. There was the *Milion* or mile-post, north-west of St. Sophia, from which distances were reckoned. It was a double arch of triumph, with a cupola resting on the four arches. Above it St. Constantine and St. Helen held the Cross, turned towards the east. Along the central street, the Mese, that rose thence, where the silversmiths had their shops, there were marble lions. Near the *Forum Tauri* (now Aksaray) was

---

[1] *The Conquest of Constantinople*, by Robert of Clari, tr. Edgar Holmes McNeal (New York, 1936).

the *Anemodoulion* of Theodosius III; a figure of a woman stood for the weathercock, and the structure was decorated with charming bronzes. At various points in the city there were at least seven clocks. Haroum-ibn-Yaya, a prisoner in Constantinople about the year 900, thus describes the clock at St. Sophia: 'At the gate of the church is a building in which twenty-four little doors open, each of a square span; there is one for every hour of the night and day. When an hour finishes, a door opens by itself.'

The Water-works

From the first, Constantinople had an organized system of water-works to keep the city supplied both in peace and war. Private houses and public buildings had their own cisterns, and emperors constructed aqueducts to bring water from sources in the forest of Belgrade and elsewhere.

The greatest surviving work of this sort is the aqueduct of Valens, which bridges the valley between the third and fourth hills. He built it in 366; according to legend he used for its construction stone from the walls of Chalcedon, which he had destroyed as an act of vengeance.

Gyllius (who calls this 'the aqueduct of Valentinian') tells us: 'In the Reign of *Constantine*, the son of *Leo* the Emperor (who was a declared enemy to Images in Churches) and in the Year of Our Lord 759, there was so great a drought at *Constantinople*, that the Dew ceas'd to fall from Heaven, and all the Cisterns, *Bagnios*, and Fountains of the City were dry'd up; which the Emperor observing, he began to repair the *Aqueduct* of *Valentinian*, which [had] continued in good Order, till the Reign of *Heraclius*, when it was demolished by the *Avares*. Upon this he sent for workmen from many Places to rebuild it; from Asia and Pontus he had a thousand Builders, and two hundred Whitewashers; from *Greece* five hundred Brick-makers, and from *Thrace* a thousand Day-Labourers, over whom there presided a Nobleman, and some of the principal Men of the City, as Surveyors of the Works. When the *Aqueduct* was finished, the City was again supplied with Water, which was conveyed into the Town through a Passage between the ninth and tenth ward. There are many subterraneous *Aqueducts* which run through six of the Hills, but the *Aqueduct of Valentinian* has its Course above Ground, which the Historians who have wrote of the *Actions* of *Andronicus* tell you, passed through the Great *Forum*, that the Water of it was clear and pleasant, that it was repaired and enlarged by *Andronicus* himself, and that he encreased its Current by the River *Hydrales*. At the Spring-head ... he built a tower and a Palace, where he used to divert himself in the Summer. He also brought the Water from the same River into the *Blachernae*, which is a Part of the *Suburbs*.'

The great double arcade of round arches is a noble feature in the view from Galata. It is most familiarly known, where it spans the new Atatürk Boulevard just before the top of the hill, which it climbs from the Golden Horn. Sad and ruinous, it skirts the courtyard of the Shehzade Mosque, and the sad little church of Christ Akataleptos nestles against it. It is most charming when it bridges a side street, and the arches give the illusory impression of being gates in a city wall.

I leave unmentioned the more distant aqueducts or 'bends', Byzantine or Ottoman, which are to be sought out in the forest of Belgrade; nor can most of the surviving cisterns be mentioned.

The open cisterns, counting only those that still exist, have been computed to be capable of holding 900,000 cubic metres. Several survive, planted as kitchen gardens, and partially built over; each has been called *Çukur Bostan* (hollow garden) by the Turks. The cistern of Aetius is probably the depression near the Adrianople Gate; that of Aspar is probably that near the Mosque of Selim; the cistern of Mocius has been certainly identified with the enormous sunk area of Altimermer, on the seventh hill. The name *Çukur Bostan*, surviving without the depression itself, proves the site of the cistern of St. Benedict at Galata. We do not know how many more there may have been.

It has been suggested that the open cisterns were used to store water to fill the fosse, but it is more than doubtful that the fosse was ever filled, even in time of siege; already, before the Fall, they are said to have been turned into gardens. They are rather dismal, untidy places, though that near the Mosque of Selim is agreeably green.

More than eighty covered cisterns have been discovered in the city and the suburbs; people to this day inadvertently discover them, by falling into them. Not that every subterranean construction is a cistern; many such substructures have been built merely to correct the irregularity of a site.

The cistern most easily accessible is the Basilican Cistern, or the Yere-batan Saray (the underground palace); this is one of the loveliest and most exciting buildings in Constantinople. Hutton had to descend to it through a trap-door and some worn steps, 'lighted by a torch extemporized of sacking steeped in naphtha, and wrapped round a pole'. Now there is a little ticket-office erected on top of it; it is shown to the public on set days at set hours, and it is lighted by electricity. I did not (1953) see a boat at the foot of the stairs, but in 1938 my brother and I were rowed about in a dinghy, under the mysterious arches and between the columns of this enchanting Byzantine cavern.

This ancient cistern, enlarged by Justinian, has three hundred and thirty-six columns, arranged in twenty-eight symmetrical ranks. Here the Corinthian impost capital is used, a Byzantine invention; and, if it is not tried out here for the first time, it is at least an early instance of its extensive use. The depth, the gloom, the wonderful perspectives, the earthy and aqueous character of the Yerebatan Saray are frequently said to make it a subterranean counterpart to the height of the Great Church. I wish I could see in the Great Church sufficient elements of air and fire that would complete the contrast.

Gyllius recounts his discovery of it. 'Through the Carelessness and Contempt of everything that is curious in the Inhabitants, it was never discover'd but by me, who was a stranger among them, after a long and diligent search after it. The whole Ground was built upon, which made it less suspected there was a *Cistern* there. The People had not the least Suspicion of it, although they daily drew their Water out of the Wells which were sunk into it. I went by Chance into a House, where there was a descent into it, and went aboard a little skiff. The Master of the House, having lighted some Torches, rowing me here and there across, through the Pillars, which lay very deep in Water, I made a Discovery of it. He was very intent upon catching his Fish, with which the *Cistern* abounds, and spear'd some of them by the Light of the Torches. There is also a small Light which descends from the Mouth of the Well, and reflects upon the Water, where the Fish usually come for Air. This *cistern* is three hundred and thirty six Foot long, a hundred and eighty two Foot broad, and two hundred and twenty four Roman Paces in Compass. The Roof, and Arches, and Sides, are all Brickwork, and cover'd with Terrass, which is not the least impair'd by Time . . . Over the Abacus of every Pillar is placed a large Stone, which seems to be another Abacus, and supports four Arches. There are abundance of Wells which fall into the *Cistern*. I have seen, when it was filling in the Winter-time, a large Stream of Water falling from a great Pipe with a mighty Noise, till the Pillars, up to the Middle of the *Capitals*, have been cover'd with Water.'

The Walls

Three walls are to be distinguished. The outer fortification of the city was the Long Wall, reaching from the Marmara to the Black Sea; this wall never proved so useful a defence as it was hoped. Gyllius writes of it: 'The Suburbs and Fields adjoining were inclosed with Walls of such an immoderate Length, that they extended themselves from the City to the Distance of a two Days Journey. They were built by Anastasius the Emperor to prevent the Incursions of the *Scythians* and *Bulgarians*, reach'd from the *Black Sea* to the Propontis, were forty thousand Paces remote from the City, and twenty *Roman* Foot in Breadth. These Walls were often taken and batter'd by the barbarous Nations, but repair'd by Justinian . . .' Some vestiges of these walls remain at Kushkaya and at Horaçköy.

The wall of Constantine's original city is said to have been divinely planned; he walked, spear in hand, tracing the boundaries, and when asked how far he meant to go, he replied: 'Until He tarries, Who now goes before me.' The best authorities are unwilling to be dogmatic about the position of these walls; they appear to have remained standing to some extent so late as the ninth century, after which they are spoken of in the past tense.[1] In the Constitutions of Justinian larger pay is allowed to undertakers who attend a corpse outside the *new* walls, which implies the existence of burying-grounds between the (still-standing) walls of Constantine, and those of Theodosius II. The ancient Golden Gate, that of Constantine, is marked by the crumbling remains of a Byzantine church, turned into a mosque called Isa Kapu Cami (Mosque of the Gate of Jesus), and reduced to a dismal pile of rubble by the earthquake of 1894; it is one of the few points where we can be certain that the old wall passed. It can be seen (not that it is worth seeing) in a garden not far from the Mosque of Daoud Pasha.

Theodosius II gave Constantinople a new *enceinte*, while Honorius in Rome was contenting himself with a restoration of the wall of Aurelian. Extension was imperative. By the end of the fourth century there is

---

[1] R. Janin: *Constantinople Byzantine*.

ample evidence of overcrowding; the corn fleets of Alexandria, Asia, Syria and Phoenicia were not able to provide enough bread for the growing population, houses were oppressively full, and streets dangerous from the number of beasts. Piles had even been driven in, near the shore, to provide more building sites.

The sea walls, built in 439, were the least important part of the *enceinte*; the emperor's command of the sea made them of secondary importance. Moreover, the northern shore could be protected by a chain across the Golden Horn, and the other shores were protected by the dangerous currents of the Marmara. The only successful assault of Constantinople by sea was the gallant exploit of the Venetians in 1204.

The wall along the Golden Horn is some way inland; it is ruinous, and its course lies through depressing and evil-smelling slums, for the most part. Here there was a single wall, ten metres high, with a hundred and ten towers and fourteen gates; it comprised part of Constantine's wall, which seems to have ended in Unkapan, somewhere near the modern Atatürk bridge. The westernmost gate was the Koiliomeni (Rolling gate) at what is now called Ayvan Saray (the great palace): this was the gate for the imperial wharf, for the great palace of Blachernae, and for its church, which held the girdle of Our Lady, the palladium of the 'God-defended City'. The next gate, that of the Kynigos (the hunter) is probably to be identified with the Balatkapi (Porta Palatina), in the Jewish quarter now called Balat; some have supposed that the emperors set out thence from Blachernae on hunting expeditions, and others that a theatre of wild animals existed in this place. St. John the Baptist's gate is gone; we do not know where it was (unless it was another name for the Hunter's gate, for the Baptist is often given that appellation). The Fenerkapi, Porta Phanari, or Porta del Faro is in the quarter, once Greek, now only distinguished by the presence of the Patriarchate; there was a beacon here, and the name dates from before the conquest.

The Petrion was a citadel and a gate; it, also, is in the Phanar quarter, but not much remains of it. Petrius, master of the offices under Justinian, gave his name to the whole *enceinte*, which contained several famous churches. Ayakapi, or the gate of Dexiocrates, comes next, at the bottom of the fifth hill, near the church of St. Theodosia; afterwards came the Porta Platea or Unkapankapi, destroyed when the Atatürk Boulevard was made.

Thereafter the walls have been destroyed; in this quarter the sites of gates are known by the Turkish names which still commemorate them. There was the gate of Drongarion, where there was a timber-yard in Byzantine times; the Prison Gate, in the quarter granted to the Venetians; the Perama Gate, in the place that then, as now, was the fish-market. This name commemorated the ferry to Galata ('Transitus Sycarum') for the only ancient bridge was at the head of the Golden Horn; here was a Jewish colony, later moved to Hasköy, when a site was wanted for building the Yeni Cami.

Further on, nearer the point, was the Porta Hicanatissa (called after palace troops, the Hicanati); the Neorion, or Dockyard (later the Bahçe-kapi or Garden Gate under the Turks), and lastly the Porta Eugenii, where the brides-elect of Byzantine emperors were received, when they came by sea, and were invested with the imperial buskins. From the Porta Eugenii the harbour chains stretched across to Galata.

The walls of the Marmara are much nearer the shore; a breakwater of loose boulders was scattered along their base. These walls were five metres high, and had a hundred and eighty-eight towers, so Buondelmonti tells us; there were at least thirteen entrances. They follow an irregular line, turning with the shore, and always presenting as sharp a front as possible to the waves. They are best seen from the sea; on shore they are easier to follow from the inside. Nevertheless, a part of them can be followed along the narrow strip of shingle that lies between them and the sea. Melancholy, they are, and not very easy to follow. The railway line cuts through them, and parts of them are inside barracks.

Just south of the apex of Seraglio Point was Topkapu (Cannon Gate), called also the gate of St. Barbara from the church which once stood hard by; this gate existed till 1871, though in 1816 Sultan Mahmud II destroyed the two towers that flanked it, to construct his marble kiosque with their remains. The next gate, Degirmenkapi, is one of which the Greek name is unknown. Near it, on the curtain wall, was this inscription:

> Possessing Thee, O Christ, a wall unbreakable,
> Theophilus the King and pious emperor
> Has raised this wall upon a new foundation.
> O King of All Things, guard it under thy protection
> And show it till the end of time unshakeable
> And indestructible . . .

Facing, above: THE OLD WALLS ON THE LANDWARD SIDE.
below: SEA WALLS OF CONSTANTINOPLE, AT THE BOUCOLEON PORT.

left: THE PALACE OF CONSTANTINE PORPHYROGENITUS

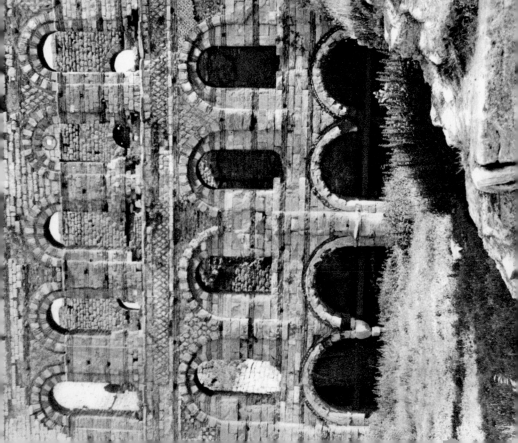

Through a small opening in this gate guilty harem women sewn in sacks were thrown into the sea. Behind it was the hollow of Kynegion, an amphitheatre for wild beasts.

At the Mangana, the Byzantine arsenal, there were also a church, a monastery and a palace; to the palace Alexius I, Comnenus (1081-1118), was taken for his health when he suffered from gout, and to the monastery John VI, Cantacuzene (1342-55), retired as a monk, till he sought the greater seclusion of Vatopedhi on Athos. Here was the tower which Manuel I, Comnenus (1143-80), attached with a chain to the tower of Damalis (now called that of Leander) at Scutari. Of these monuments the remains are mainly of archaeological or topographical interest. There are some remains of the façade of the church of St. Saviour Philanthropos, in the wall; near it is the elegant ruin of the Indjili kiosque of the Sultans (the Pearl Kiosque) built by Sinan Pasha, the Grand Vizir of Murad III in 1582. Here, as Thévenot and other travellers tell us, the Sultan liked to sit unseen in the windows on the feast of the Transfiguration (6 August), amusing himself with the sight of the Greek pilgrims to the holy fountain of St. Saviour, on its patronal festival; sometimes the sick were buried up to their necks in the sand as a cure.

There follows a series of gates, belonging to various convents, in particular to St. Mary Hodighietria and St. Lazarus. Hereabouts were found the topi, stone seats of one of the theatres constructed by Septimius Severus; near were the baths of Arcadius, and a church of St. Michael. 'Thus the whole area is an architectural palimpsest indeed!'[1]

Boucoleon, which follows, is the name given to two imperial villas near the sea; the lower was anciently called the house of Hormisdas and vestiges of a façade remain. The name was due to a marble group of statuary on the quay: a lion with its left foot on a bull's horn, in the act of twisting its victim's head to get at the throat. This group existed till the earthquake of 1532.

Beyond the church of SS. Sergius and Bacchus were two harbours, Port Sophian and Kontoscolion (the little harbour). There follows the Yenikapi (New Gate), near the ancient harbour of Eleutherius, now silted up and called Vlanga Bostan. Then came the gate of St. Emilianus (or of Daoud Pasha), and then that of Psamathia (Samatya) — where the whole quarter owes its name to the sand thrown up on the beach. The Narlikapi

---

[1] N. M. Penzer: *The Harem* (London, 1936).

G

(or Pomegranate Gate) gave access to the monastery of Studium; here the emperor was received in state by the abbot and the community, when he visited them on their feast (29 August). A lazy traveller, having toiled round the sea walls so far as the lighthouse, under the walls of the Serail, will probably be content to leave the rest of the five miles of the Marmara walls unvisited; they are sad beyond description, and the coast is beyond description filthy. They can be seen very well from inside in the tram to Yedikule; from a slight eminence, one looks down on the Samatya walls.

But the end of the sea walls must be seen, the Marble Tower; this is tiresome to find, gas works and railway lines are in the way. Tanneries also encroach upon it; it can be best seen from beside an evil-smelling rubbish-heap with scraps of hides, where one cannot stay long enough to admire its quiet, tragic dignity; one can hardly stay long enough to photograph it, without overpowering nausea. This lovely and venerable tower, and the intolerable squalor of its surroundings, seem to sum up all the enthusiastic traveller hopes for and fears and finds in Constantinople.

Some three miles outside the walls is the suburb of Makrikevi, now definitely identified with the Byzantine suburb of Hebdomon which Gyllius and Du Cange wrongly situated near Tekfur Saray. We know of the Hebdomon that it was seven miles from the city (presumably from the Milion, from which distance was reckoned), that it had a harbour on the sea of Marmara, and a plain of considerable extent on one side. This plain, in imitation of old Rome, was called the Campus Martius; it was a good camping ground, and for this reason many emperors were invested with the purple here, in front of the troops, to preserve another Roman tradition.

At the Hebdomon ceremony, the troops laid their standards on the earth, to show the desolation of the state without a ruler. Supplications went up to Heaven; at the accession of Leo the Wise they ran: 'Grant Leo life, let him reign. O God, Lover of mankind, the public voice demands Leo; the army demands him; the laws wait for him; the palace awaits him. The world expects Leo; the army waits for him. Let Leo, our common glory, come. Let Leo, our common good, reign.' The emperor-elect then went up to a tribune, where one officer placed a coronet on his head, and another an amulet on his right arm. The standards were raised again, and acclamations rang out: 'Leo, Augustus, thou hast conquered; thou art

Pius, August. God gave thee, God will guard thee. Ever conquer, worshipper of Christ. Long be thy reign. God will defend the Christian empire.'

Soldiers of the household troops (Candidati) held up a shield, behind which the emperor was invested with the imperial insignia; the shield was lowered, and the emperor appeared robed, crowned and armed, and received homage.

His first action was then to do homage to God, uncrowned, in the camp chapel; the next ceremony was the consecration of the crown at the church of St. John the Baptist, then followed the procession through the Golden Gate for the consecration of the emperor at St. Sophia.

Justinian had a palace here called *Jucundiae*, a pleasant country seat. There were many churches, including that of St. John the Evangelist (where Basil II was buried), the church built by Arcadius in 407 to receive the relics of the prophet Samuel, and that of the Holy Innocents, where emperors were welcomed on their return from the West.

Hebdomon was a convenient halting-place for people entering or leaving the city, and the large Campus Martius was a place of refuge in times of earthquake; it was also used as a place for public prayers for the cessation of earthquakes. Only insignificant remains now mark this spot, and indeed, had there been anything considerable left in the time of Gyllius, its identification would not have been so long delayed.

The land walls are great and tragic; the enormous length of them, sweeping uphill from the Marmara to Topkapu, down again into the Lycus valley, uphill to their highest point at the Adrianople Gate, and then down to the Golden Horn, must make them the most impressive fortification in Europe — one tower follows another from sea to sea. These walls, as noble as their history, are infinitely moving; they are best appreciated as a great expanse, for no small part of them can be picked out as especially good. Along all these miles are gaunt, red and grey towers, riven by earthquakes and battered by siege engines; green market-gardens are sometimes planted against them, maize is grown in part of the fosse, wooden houses sometimes hang in a rickety way from the crumbling wall. On the other side of the arterial road that follows them are green fields, or cemeteries dark with cypresses. It is the best walk near Constantinople.

These walls were built in 413 by Anthemius, early in the reign of

Theodosius II, and repaired and added to in 447, late in the same reign, by Constantine Cyrus; (from Tekfur Saray, *alias* the palace of Constantine Porphyrogenitus, a different wall, to be mentioned later, continues the *enceinte*). An earthquake in 447 had thrown down fifty-seven towers, and the restoration, made in less than three months, with Attila threatening, was a heroic effort.

Constantine Cyrus, the restorer, erected a second wall, with a broad and deep moat, in front of the wall of Anthemius. The fosse, the outermost protection of the city, is from fifteen to twenty metres broad, and from five to seven in depth; it has an escarpment and counter-escarpment, and is crossed here and there by low walls, that may have been aqueducts or dams; it is, however, doubtful if there were ever water in the fosse, even during sieges.

Between the fosse and the outer walls is a terrace, about sixty feet broad. The outer wall had ninety-two turrets, facing the curtain of the inner wall; fifty-six of these are still standing, of which thirty-four are square, eighteen are semi-circular and four are hexagonal. This wall sheltered the front line troops that defended the city from the inner terrace (περίβολος), a second embankment, varying from fifty to sixty-four feet in breadth.

The inner wall, of concrete, faced with limestone, was the main bulwark of the city. It was higher than the outer wall, with ramparts and ninety-six towers; of these seventy-four were square, and the remainder polygonal. The towers were distinct constructions, although connected with the wall; on the towers sentinels kept watch, day and night, shouting along the line to keep each other awake, as today one hears Egyptian soldiers crying 'Ha!' to each other in the night. The upper chambers of the towers also held engines for hurling stones or 'Greek fire' upon invaders; the lower chambers were guard-rooms. These towers are some one hundred and seventy-five to one hundred and eighty-one feet apart, and are fifty-seven to sixty feet high.

There were several gates and posterns in the walls. Some authorities like to class these as civil or as military gates; it is not certain that the distinction, based on no ancient text, is a valid one. The conjecture (pretty generally accepted) is that the military gates were those known as Deuteron, Triton and Pempton, and that they were only used to give access to the fortifications. The civil gates, connecting the city with the outside world and facing bridges over the fosse, that were cut in time of siege, are generally reckoned to have been the Golden Gate, the Gate of Xylokerkos, that of the Piyi, and those of Kalagros, Rhegion, St. Romanus and Charisius.

A great tower joins the land and sea walls, inscribed: 'Tower of Basil [II] and Constantine [VIII], Emperors believing in Christ, pious sovereigns of the Romans.' They had repaired it after the earthquake of 975. Another tower (now destroyed) bore an inscription of Romanus III; it had been repaired after the earthquakes of 1032 and the following year. Thus the Theodosian walls, in their thousand years of history, have seen a very great deal of rebuilding and repairing, though they remain, substantially, a monument of the fifth century.

The Golden Gate is said to have been built in 388-91 to commemorate the triumph of Theodosius the Great over Maximus, and to have been incorporated in his wall by Theodosius II. It is true that it would then, originally, have stood outside the walls of Constantine, but the Samatya quarter may have already existed. Perhaps it was a suburban arch, to welcome the emperor even before he entered his capital. Many emperors passed through it from the Hebdomon (Makrikevi) to their coronation, and others entered in triumph after conquests; the last was Michael VIII, the returning Greek Emperor, who walked hence on foot in 1261, as far as the church of the Studium.

The Propylaeon of the Golden Gate was famous for the statuary which adorned it; bas-reliefs of Prometheus's tortures, of the labours of Hercules, of Endymion and of Phaethon, were seen by travellers so late as 1778. Sir Thomas Roe, ambassador to the Porte, failed, in spite of all his diplomacy, to buy or steal them for the Earl of Arundel and the Duke of Buckingham.

'Promise to obteyne them I cannot,' he wrote in May 1625, 'because they stand upon the ancient gate, the most conspicuous of the cytte, though now mured up, beeing the entrance by the castell called the Seaven Towers, and never opened since the Greek emperors lost yt: to offer to steale them, no man dares to deface the cheefe seate of the grand signor: to procure them by favour is more impossible, such envy they bear unto us. There is only then one way left; by corruption of some churchman, to dislike them, as against their law; and under that pretence to take them downe to be brought into some privat place: from whence, after the matter is cold and unsuspected, they may be conveyed. I have practised for the four, and am offered to have it done for six hundred crounes.' A year later he corrupted the treasurer, who took his bribe, but then for superstitious reasons would not touch the reliefs.

The Golden Gate is stripped and bare, and walled up; Hutton, with a faint relish, records the tradition that a victorious Christian army will enter in one day and take the city. We, who live in an age when the Crescent and the Cross have learned to live peaceably side by side, and, with mutual respect, united by a fear of unbelievers of quite another stamp, do not very much like any idea of the city changing its masters again.

Behind is the Castle of the Seven Towers (Yedikule); this is not so much a castle as a fortified *enceinte*. Four of the towers are Byzantine; the other three were added by Mehmet II, when he took the city. For a long period it was a state prison, and ambassadors were apt to find themselves here when their countries were at war with Turkey; for the Ottoman Empire treated foreign envoys no better than Nicephorus Phocas had treated Liudprand of Cremona. The little gate, called the Yedikule Gate, may have existed in Byzantine times, also under the name of the Golden Gate; it was probably used for ordinary traffic, while the ceremonial gate was kept for special occasions.

The next gate (now destroyed) is that of Xylokerkos, or the Belgrade Gate; hereabouts the walls are in good condition as far as the gate of Piyi or of Silivri (Selybria). By this gate the general of Michael VIII entered in 1261; it was restored by Manuel Bryennios Leontaris in 1438, he who defended the gate of Charisius in the siege of 1453. The gate owed its name of Piyi to the sacred spring at Balukli, where was the sanctuary of Our Lady, Source of Life, regularly visited by the Byzantine court every Ascension Day; the emperor would come by boat to the last wharf of the city, and ride up from the Marmara.

Balukli is some half a mile outside the walls; there is no longer a Christian village here, as there was until recently; the modern monastery and the pleasant, insignificant chapel over the holy spring are occasionally visited by Greeks from Pera. Sitting in a shady Greek café, I listened to a widow arguing over the fee for a requiem; she wanted it to be 'despotic' (pontifical), which comes more expensive, of course. The fountain owes its name Balukli (fishy) to the fish in it; they are supposed to be parti-coloured for this reason. The priest was frying fish on the day of the Fall, when news was brought him that the Turks had entered the city. 'I would sooner believe that these fish should leap from the frying-pan into the spring,' he cried; and so they did, done on one side though they were. Their descendants live there to this day. In a Turkish cemetery near Balukli is buried the head of the famous Ali Pasha of Yanina.

In the next stretch of wall there is a C-shaped inflexion, called the sigma from its form. There follows the Rhegion Gate (for the road led hence to Rhegion on the Marmara), also called Polyandrion, or the gate of many men, for the walls built by the Blue and Green factions met here in 449, the Blues building from Blachernae, and the Greens from the Golden Gate. It is called Yenimevlevihanekapi by the Turks. The next section of the wall is called the Mesoteichion, for it is the central stretch; on one of the towers is an inscription in brick letters: 'Christ, God, preserve the city from trouble and war, and give victories to our kings.'

The gate of St. Romanus, where the last emperor is said to have fallen, is still called Topkapu (Cannon Gate), from the position of Mehmet II's great cannon during the siege. From here the wall descends into the Lycus valley; hereabouts it was called the Murus Bachatareus (perhaps after Bahadur, a Seljuk warrior in the service of Andronicus III). It was notoriously the weakest part of the wall, on account of the configuration of the soil; the besiegers, on the upper slopes of the Lycus valley, were above the heads of the defenders of the wall at the bottom of the channel.

Here the wall is at its most shattered; some of the cracked towers look as if they would go over with a breath, and the next earthquake will do havoc among them. Nevertheless, the sweep of walls down into the valley, and up again to the next gate, is an impressive sight. The sixth hill, just inside the gate, is dominated by the splendid mosque of Mihrimah, built on the site of a church dedicated to St. George, who often showed himself upon that spot. The Edirne Kapu, or Adrianople Gate, was in Byzantine times called after Charisius, the chief of the Blue faction, while the Theodosian walls were building; shortly before it is the Pempton, a 'military gate'.

After the Adrianople Gate, their greatest height, the walls begin to descend towards the Golden Horn. A small iron stair now leads to a splendid viewpoint on the ramparts; here can be seen one of those sublime panoramas which, at their best hour, that before dusk, are the chief consolations of Constantinople.

To the right are the ramparts, then the great lantern of the mosque of Mihrimah, the Propontis with its islands, the dome and minarets of the Conqueror's mosque, the University tower (too far off to be seen in its full hideousness), the Süleymaniye, Haydar Pasha and the sea, the Mosque of Selim I, Scutari, Galata and Pera, the Golden Horn (with the ugly tower of the Greek school in front), and then the walls again. Behind you, outside the city walls, can be seen the curl of the Golden Horn towards the Sweet Waters of Europe, the Turkish cemeteries, and Eyüp.

Following the wall, one soon reaches that ruined building now called Tekfur Saray, commonly called the Palace of Constantine Porphyrogenitus, though for no very good reason; it is more likely that it was a twelfth-century construction of the Comnene emperors, and a part of their additions to Blachernae, their favourite residence. It is an oblong, three-storeyed building; its northern façade has an open arcade on the ground floor. The windows are framed with marble, and there are graceful balconies on the east and south. The most remarkable feature is the polychrome decoration in brick and stone; this has been attributed to the Palaeologue emperors,[1] whose escutcheon is to be seen on the walls. It is a very pretty building, one of the few domestic buildings of Byzantium that survives intact enough to be worth a visit.

A sixteenth-century traveller says of it: 'A fragment, standing memory of the ould Emperiall pallas, with certayne galleries, waist romes, and pillors within itselfe, doth well shewe the great power of time the distroyer and overthrower of all, that a prince of the wourld his pallas is nowe become a lodge for olifants, panthars, and other beasts.'[2]

Here the Theodosian walls end. It is not certain how the walls originally descended to the sea; perhaps Blachernae was a fortified suburb, with pre-Theodosian walls; perhaps the Theodosian walls turned eastwards, and went down the easternmost of the three spurs of the sixth hill. The walls from henceforth are the work of several periods. From the palace of Constantine Porphyrogenitus the wall of Manuel I, Comnenus, begins; this is a single wall, with no fosse or external wall, but protected

[1] R. Janin: Constantinople Byzantine.
[2] John Sanderson: Travels in the Levant, 1584-1602 (Hakluyt Soc., 1931).

by the steepness of the slope. It is very strong, perhaps a reinforcement of the walls of the former fortified suburb, and its nine towers are more massive than those of Theodosius. There is one gate in it, Egrikapi, or the Porta Caligaria (where soldiers' boots were made); it owes its Turkish name, 'the Oblique Gate', to the tomb of Hasreti Hafiz which blocks a part of it. It is from a tower near this gate that Phrantzes and Constantine Dragases observed the Turkish host, a few hours before the fall of the city.

The next portion of the wall provides most puzzles for those who seek to identify points that we know well by name; it is also uncertain if it be the work of Manuel — smaller blocks of stone and slighter bricks are used, and the square towers are much inferior to the towers in Manuel's undoubted work.

Here was the tower of Isaac Angelus, built either to defend the palace of Blachernae, or as a residence.

Here also was the tower called the prison of Anemas, from Michael Anemas who was imprisoned here for conspiracy against Alexius I, Comnenus. Anna Comnena gives a moving account of how he was led out with his companions for blinding: the prisoners were attired in sacking, their beards were plucked out, their heads were shorn, and crowned with the intestines of oxen and sheep. They rode, mounted sideways on oxen. Anna herself was so horrified that she brought her mother the empress, who interceded for the prisoners' eyes. Alexius's messenger arrived just before they reached the bas-relief of two hands pierced by a spear, beyond which mark even imperial clemency was of no avail.

Andronicus I later occupied the same prison, from which he was led to the hippodrome for execution, dressed as a slave, blinded in one eye, and mounted on a mangy camel; his beard had already been plucked, his teeth knocked out, and his right hand struck off with an axe. The Ottoman Empire could hardly outdo the late Roman Empire in atrocities.

Beyond the towers new walls begin, two parallel walls down to the Golden Horn. The inner wall was erected by Heraclius in 627, to strengthen the suburb of Blachernae after the attack of the Avars; the outer wall, with its four small towers, was built by Leo III in 813, because of the preparations of the Bulgarians under Krum, who wished to avenge his attempted murder. At their extremity is the Xyloporta, called 'the Wooden Gate' from its material, where the walls along the Golden Horn begin.

Within the last stretch of wall, below the palace of Constantine Porphyrogenitus, which may have been a part of it, was the great palace of Blachernae. Its site included a partially artificial hill, whence there was a view praised by the crusader, Odon de Deuil: 'offering its inhabitants a threefold pleasure, it looks over sea, meadow and city'.

Today there are Turkish houses, gardens, building operations, a few lumps of masonry, but little more than misery and confusion where once the palace stood. The aghiasma of Blachernae should be visited; there is only a modern and ugly Greek church, but the ancient source is there (though now running rather nastily through taps), and an old black icon. It is one of the most sacred places in the 'God-defended City', the former home of Our Lady's robe, the City's main defence.

In the reign of Leo I two senators, Galbius and Candidus, were shown the robe of Our Lady at Capernaum, in the house of a Jewess, where they lodged. They went to Jerusalem and had a copy made of the box in which it was kept, and, returning to Capernaum, they stole the relic by substitution. They brought it to Constantinople, and placed it in the church of SS. Peter and Mark near the gate of Ayvan Saray; thence it is said to have been moved by Leo I to a new sanctuary at Blachernae. It was incorruptible, and exhaled a sweet smell. The icon of the Blachernitissa represented her as an *orante*, bearing the Holy Child in a medallion on her breast; the original, at Blachernae, was miraculous, and one could pray to her for favours secretly desired.

The ceremonies of Blachernae were based upon those of the Great Palace; in the time of Constantine Porphyrogenitus the court came here on the feast of the Purification; on the first Sunday in Lent (the feast of Orthodoxy, or the thanksgiving for the suppression of iconoclasm, for the church of Blachernae had been an iconodule stronghold); and on Good Friday.

The Comnene emperors more and more forsook the Sacred Palace for Blachernae, which they loved partly because of its convenience for hunting expeditions outside the city walls. In their time took place what Anna Comnena calls 'the regular miracle', a parting of the veil in front of the icon, which happened every Friday evening, as a matter of course, like the annual Easter miracle of the Holy Fire which still takes place at the Holy Sepulchre in Jerusalem. The revealed icon appeared, animated by the soul of Our Lady. When the Crusaders came, Blachernae was able to rival the Great Palace in beauty and splendour and, like the Great Palace, it suffered from their uncontrolled rapacity. In the later empire when John VI, Cantacuzene, and his consort were crowned here (St. Sophia being then under repair), imperial poverty was such that the royal banquet was served on pewter or earthenware, bits of coloured glass in the diadems had to stand for precious stones. Cavafy has celebrated this fact in a noble poem:

> Nothing
> That is mean or that is unseemly
> Do they have in my eyes, those little bits
> Of coloured glass. They seem on the contrary
> Like a sorrowful protestation
> Against the unjust misfortune of those being crowned.[1]

But the poem with which one inevitably connects the former home of the Blachernitissa is the greatest hymn of the Byzantine Church, the Acathistus hymn (so-called, Ἀκάθιστος because it is sung standing), said to have been composed by the Patriarch Sergius when the Avars were threatening the city in 626. This hymn is still sung (divided into four parts and called the *Chaeretismoi* or Salutations of Our Lady) on the first four Fridays of Lent; on the fifth Friday it is sung in its entirety. Twenty-four troparia (each beginning in turn with one of the letters of the alphabet) celebrate the events from the Annunciation to the flight into Egypt; these are dramatic, often in dialogue. Alternate troparia are followed by panegyrics of the Mother of God, put into the mouths of the Angel of the Annunciation, the Saints, the narrator and the crowd.[2] Four or more times the *kontakion* of the Saviour of the city is sung: 'To thee, our defending general, the songs of victory! Thanksgiving, as having been saved from perils, I render to thee, I thy City, Mother of God.'

This great *kontakion*, so familiar, and so often sung to its beautiful melody on public occasions of thanksgiving in the Greek world, is inscribed now over the holy spring, on the spot where (so near to the walls) the Mother of God was posted through the centuries as the guardian of the 'God-defended City'. It is a sad and appropriate place to end a visit to the land walls, before escaping from this miserable quarter at the wharf of Ayvan Saray.

---

[1] *The Poems of C. P. Cavafy*, tr. by John Mavrogordato (London, 1951).
[2] Egon Wellesz: *A History of Byzantine Music and Hymnography* (Oxford, 1949).

CHAPTER V

THE FALL

IN February, 1451, the Sultan Murad II died at Adrianople; three days later a courier reached his son Mehmet in Magnesia. The new Sultan was twenty-one years of age, a linguist, an art-lover, something of a scientist, and an admirable soldier, abstemious but sensual, proud and over-poweringly ambitious, cruel and utterly without mercy. Though outwardly conforming to the doctrines and practices of Islam, he is suspected of having been a free-thinker, and it is likely that desire for the earthly glory of conquest motivated his greatest exploit rather than zeal for the triumph of his faith. He hastened without a stop to seize his inheritance; this he further secured by having his baby half-brother strangled in his bath. He now turned all his mind to the conquest of Constantinople, which had been promised by the Prophet to Moslem arms, and was therefore expected by his people; a conquest that at one time had seemed likely to be achieved by his great-grandfather, Bayazit I.

Mehmet II prepared for this exploit by making peace all round in the Asiatic provinces; he also promised peace when the compliments of the Roman Emperor were brought to him upon his succession. At Byzantium perhaps too much credence was placed in his reassurances, perhaps the character of this ambitious young prince was still unguessed at, or perhaps it is true that 'God maddens those whom He wishes to destroy'. The Constantinopolitans precipitated trouble by clamouring unseasonably for the arrears due on the allowance paid to them for the custody of Prince Orkhan, and threatened to loose this possible pretender to the Ottoman throne if these arrears were not paid. Khalil the Grand Vizir, who was secretly their friend, remonstrated against this folly.

'Ye foolish and miserable Romans,' he said (in the words of Gibbon), 'we know your devices, and ye are ignorant of your own danger! The scrupulous Amurath is no more; his throne is occupied by a young conqueror, whom no laws can bind, and no obstacles can resist: and if you escape from his hands, give praise to the divine clemency, which yet delays the chastisement of your sins. Why do ye seek to affright us by vain and indirect menaces? Release the fugitive Orchan, crown him sultan of Romania; call the Hungarians from beyond the Danube; arm against us the nations of the West; and be assured, that you will only provoke and precipitate your ruin.'

In the winter of 1451 Mehmet chose a site at Asomaton, on the European banks of the Bosphorus, for a new fortress, now called Rumeli Hisar. There was panic at Constantinople. The Emperor Constantine XI sent a protest; it is said that he even wished to oppose the construction by force, and was only put off by the prayers of his horrified councillors. The Sultan answered the emperor's envoy, saying that he was merely carrying out a plan of his father's to make the crossing of the Bosphorus safe. 'Have you the right or the power to regulate what it is my pleasure to do on my territory?' he said. 'The two shores are mine: that of Asia because it is inhabited by the Ottomans, that of Europe, because you cannot defend it. Go and tell your master that the reigning Sultan is not at all like his predecessors, and that their aspirations were not so far-reaching as my power. I allow you to retire, but if anyone approaches me again with such messages, I will have him flayed.'

The church of St. Michael was destroyed to make room for the new castle. Material arrived in March, 1452, and six thousand workmen were employed: Rumeli Hisar was completed during the summer, and Constantinople was thus cut off from the Black Sea. Constantine petitioned for the safety of the harvest in Greek villages by the Bosphorus; Mehmet, on the contrary, ordered his men to graze their mules and horses on Greek lands. An 'incident' followed, as it inevitably must, at Epivatos, and in June Mehmet ordered his soldiers to massacre the harvesters there in revenge. This was the *casus belli*. The emperor closed the gates of the city, thus imprisoning some Turks inside, but three days later, still wishing to avoid hostilities, he loosed some young eunuchs from among them, and sent them to Mehmet with a pacific message. Mehmet now unequivocally declared war upon the city, without any pretext.

The winter was spent by each side in preparations. Constantine had for months been provisioning the city; he had the gates walled, and occupied himself with an attempt to get allies. The first step to conciliate the West was another effort to reunite the Churches. Cardinal Isidore, formerly the Metropolitan of Kieff, arrived as Papal Legate; in his presence, and that of the Patriarch Gregory, of the Basileus and of three hundred priests, the reunion of the Churches was proclaimed in St. Sophia on 12 December. This reunion did not go deep; even the emperor's sincerity in the matter is open to doubt. The general unpopularity of this measure very much impaired his personal authority and was to weaken his power of stimulating resistance against the Turks. Meanwhile fanatical zealots gathered round George Scholarius, who was thundering away against Rome at the Pantocrator, and there were street riots against the 'azymites' (those whose Host is of unleavened bread), in which the lower clergy took part. The Grand Admiral, Luke Notaras, said that he would rather see the Turkish turban than the Cardinal's hat in Constantinople; he may perhaps have felt differently the following year, when he died for refusing his young son to the Conqueror's bed. The common people, for all their traditional and well-earned hatred of the West, are said to have expressed a preference for people who at least believed in Christ and in Our Lady; but a nun went so far in anti-Roman enthusiasm that she disconcerted everyone by turning Turk, eating meat, and worshipping the Prophet.

Mehmet, having reconnoitred the fosse of Constantinople, went to Adrianople on 1 September. He sent an envoy to the despots of the Morea, to discourage them from sending aid to their brother, the emperor; he himself remained in Adrianople, absorbed in his preparations. 'To sound the disposition of his soldiers,' says Gibbon, 'he often wandered through the streets alone, and in disguise; and it was fatal to discover the Sultan, when he wished to escape from the vulgar eye. His hours were spent in delineating the plan of the hostile city, in debating with his generals and engineers on what spot he should erect his batteries; on which side he should assault the walls; to what place he should apply his scaling ladders; and the exercises of the day repeated and proved the lucubrations of the night.' To him there fled a Hungarian cannon-founder, Orban, who had been underpaid in Constantinople; he was charged with the construction of a huge cannon. A smaller cannon from his workshop was placed in Rumeli Hisar, and sank a Venetian ship in the Bosphorus; the great cannon, dragged by fifty yoke of oxen, was tried out in Adrianople, the townspeople having been previously warned; it gave equal satisfaction. In February the cannon left Adrianople, drawn again by fifty yoke of oxen; two hundred men marched on either side of it, to hold it balanced, and it took two months to make the two days' journey.

On 6 April, Friday after Easter, Mehmet arrived and pitched his tent behind the hill facing the Caligaria gate, by Blachernae. The cannon was placed there too, but the gate had lately been newly fortified, and it was thought it could do more damage opposite the gate of St. Romanus; it was therefore later moved to the second situation and that gate is still named Topkapu from its presence there during the siege. Smaller cannon were placed on either side of it, for more continuous artillery fire, for the great cannon took two hours to be charged. Shortly afterwards, the great cannon burst, and killed its founder; though it was patched up again, it never quite fulfilled Mehmet's hopes of it. There were also other siege engines, including movable towers for fighting from, against the defenders of the walls; and medieval apparatus for stone-slinging, as well as battering-rams, were used side by side with the most advanced artillery of the age.

On 7 April Mehmet's army took up positions along the land walls; in the centre was the Sultan with a hundred and fifty thousand Janissaries, on his right a hundred thousand infantry faced the walls down to the Golden Gate, and on his left wing were fifty thousand opposite the northern part of the walls down to Blachernae. The cavalry was drawn up in the rear. Including the navy, the Turks had a twenty to one majority over the defenders of the city: there were fewer than fifty thousand Byzantines under arms, and only two thousand foreigners on their side, including the five hundred men who had come in January, with the great soldier John Giustiniani. Nevertheless, on this day a thousand men, crews of allied ships, marched the whole length of the land walls as a demonstration.

On 12 April the batteries began, obliging those inside to a constant repair of the walls; by the 18th, part of the outer wall and two great towers of the inner wall were broken in the Lycus valley. On the latter day a double assault was repelled; an unsuccessful attempt was made by the land forces to fire the patched walls that the defenders had botched up with beams or anything they had handy, and to break into the city; an equally unsuccessful attempt was made by the Turkish fleet to force the harbour boom.

On 20 April the defenders were heartened by a further success. Three Genoese ships, possibly aid sent by the Pope, having been delayed by north winds off Chios, joined with an imperial corn ship from Sicily. They fought by the Turkish fleet at Seraglio Point, under the eyes of the defenders and of Mehmet himself; and at the last minute a favourable wind enabled them to crash through into safety – more help coming at this time might have saved the city. The furious Sultan ordered his admiral to be bastinadoed for this defeat, and gave him a hundred blows with his own hand.

It was after this set-back that the idea was conceived, perhaps by Mehmet himself, of transporting the Turkish fleet overland, from its harbourage at Beşiktaş into the port; there were many historical parallels for such an enterprise, the most recent instance was ten years before, when the Venetians dragged their fleet from Adige to Garda. The transport of the ships was intended to weaken the defence at the land walls, to control the activities of the neutral Genoese in Galata (who were sending help to the garrison) without going to war with Genoa, and to establish communication with the fortress Rumeli Hisar. A narrow canal was dug and fitted with rollers. This feat was carried out unperceived, and the last stage of the transport was accomplished by night; suddenly the Constantinopolitans found seventy Turkish vessels in their port, with drums beating, trumpets sounding and streamers waving. Giustiniani's plan of burning it was betrayed, perhaps by the Genoese of Galata, and his ship was sunk. Mehmet was now master of the port, and built a bridge across the Golden Horn at Blachernae.

It is at this point in the story, according to Ducas, that Constantine offered to pay a tribute, if Mehmet would raise the siege, and that Mehmet made a counter-offer to Constantine of safe departure, and a principate in the Morea if he would yield the city. The other historians are silent. If Mehmet indeed made the offer, it is natural that Constantine should have doubted its sincerity, and should have refused it.

Early in May, provisions were getting short. On 3 May a brigantine was sent out to look for the reinforcements which had been promised by the Venetians; the crew were disguised as Turks, and the Turkish flag was flown – thus the vessel sailed unnoticed through the Turkish fleet. No trace of Venetian ships was to be seen, and the crew were well entitled to seek their own safety and to abandon the city for which they had taken great risks, and which was now almost certainly doomed, but by a majority decision they chose a nobler course: 'Whether the city be taken or not, whether it is to life or to death, our duty is to return.' They returned on 23 May with their hopeless news, making their way back in the disguise in which they had sailed out.

Facing: RUMELI HISAR.

Meanwhile the Patriarch and senators had urged Constantine to escape before it was too late, and, once abroad, to gather an army for the relief of the city. A Slavonic MS.[1] records the scene that followed. 'The Emperor listened to all this quietly and patiently. At last, after having been for some time in deep thought, he began to speak: "I thank you all for the advice which you have given me. I know that my going out of the city might be of some benefit to me, inasmuch as all that you foresee might really happen. But it is impossible for me to go away: how could I leave the churches of Our Lord, and His servants the clergy, and the throne and my people in such a plight? What would the world say of me? I pray you, my friends, in future do not say to me anything else but, 'Nay, Sire, do not leave us.' Never, never, will I leave you. I am resolved to die here with you." And, saying this, the Emperor turned his head aside, because tears filled his eyes; and with him wept the Patriarch and all who were there.'

In the following days an ever widening breach was made in the walls by the Romanus Gate; the battery of the great cannon began to tell, though in all its four hundred and fifty times of firing it only scored one direct casualty — a famous beauty, who was hit by a stone dislodged from the wall. An assault was beaten back on 7 May, and a second on 12 May near the palace of Constantine Porphyrogenitus. The courage and ingenuity of the besieged secured two further triumphs; on 16 May the Austrian, John Grant, defeated an attempt to undermine the walls by destroying the Turkish mine, and on 18 May the defenders of the walls managed to blow up a wooden turret, one of Mehmet's siege-works, that had been brought up near the Romanus Gate.

On 23 May, the day the ship returned with its hopeless message, Constantine refused to see the Sultan's envoy, who came with another offer of conditions. In these days signs and wonders were seen. In a procession the image of Our Lady fell to the ground, and was as heavy as lead when they tried to raise it; a light seemed to settle upon the dome of St. Sophia, and scared besieged and besiegers alike. The prophecies were canvassed again, and on the whole they pointed towards the fall: the Constantino-politans remembered some uncomfortable sayings of the Erythraean Sibyl, and others of Leo the Wise, while the Turks had the Prophet's promise: 'Constantinople will be conquered; what joy for the army that

[1] Cit. W. H. Hutton: *The Story of Constantinople*.

H

Facing: THE BAGHDAD KIOSQUE, INTERIOR.

makes this conquest, and what glory for its leader' — words now inscribed at the entrance to the Conqueror's Mosque.

According to one story, the Patriarch told Constantine that the light on the dome of the great church meant that God had abandoned the hitherto God-guarded city, and urged him to leave with the empress. This story must in part be apocryphal, for there was no empress, and there never had been one: Constantine Dragases was a widower, and had been since 1442, before his accession. The rest of the story may be true, that the emperor fainted at the Patriarch's words, and said, on regaining consciousness: 'If it is the will of God, whither can we fly before His anger?'

The guns were still pounding in the Lycus valley, and frantic attempts were made to repair the shattered walls; stones fallen from the wall, baulks of timber, trees and branches, crates full of straw were all hastily crowded into the breaches, and cemented with earth and clay. The whole city shook every time the great cannon threw its twelve-hundred-pound ball against the walls.

On Thursday, 24 May, Mehmet ordered a general assault upon the city for the 29th, by land and sea. Astrology had indicated that this was a propitious day. A trumpet proclaimed a general illumination, and all the tents shone out in Galata, on the Bosphorus, and along the land walls; among the besiegers there was music and feasting, and despair among the besieged. On the 26th there was another illumination, the whole length of the wall, and prayers and fasting, as in the month of Ramazan.

Within the city, Constantine visited every post in person. Many, he found, had left places on the ramparts that were under fire, for no one thought the Turks would dare to mount the wall; the emperor reproached deserters and threatened them with punishment. He also had the difficult and delicate task of settling dissensions among the defenders: Greeks and Latins were straining apart; for example the admiral, Notaras, was refusing Giustiniani his essential co-operation, out of jealousy and mistrust. While, among the Latins themselves, there were dissensions between the Venetians and the Genoese: the Venetians within the walls had a simple choice before them, they must help the defenders or they must go; the Genoese, with their own walled city of Galata, could take a more independent line — their policy, on the whole, was a neutrality favourable to the empire, for which their countryman Giustiniani was fighting with the utmost valour, but individual Genoese seem to have succumbed to the temptation of profitable dealing with the Turks.

Outside the walls, there was still hesitation; many among the Turkish army could not believe that Europe would allow Constantinople to fall into their hands. There were rumours of a Hungarian army coming to the rescue of the city; rumours of a papally aided navy, of which the van was said to have reached Chios; above all, there was weariness with the seven weeks' siege. On the 26th or 27th a council was held; Christians outside shot letters into the city, and the besieged were able to follow all that was going on. Khalil Pasha, the pro-Christian grand vizir, advocated the raising of the siege; the city was invincible, he maintained, and Christendom was bound to interfere in its favour. Zagan Pasha, an Albanian, led the opposite party; Alexander, he said, had conquered the world with a smaller army than that of Mehmet. The younger members of the Council urged Mehmet to attack, and carried the day. Even at this moment, two days before the fall, signs of effective European intervention would probably have been enough to avert the last assault; and if help had arrived in time, the last assault, even if it were carried out, might well have been repelled.

On the 28th, Whitsun Monday, Mehmet addressed his troops: 'I give you today', he said (according to Critobulos), 'a grand and populous city, the capital of the ancient Romans, the very summit of splendour and of glory, which has become, so to say, the centre of the world. I give it over for you to pillage, to seize its incalculable treasures of men, women and boys, and everything that adorns it. You will henceforward live in great happiness and leave great wealth to your children.' He assured them that the city no longer was invincible, for the fosse was levelled, the walls were tattered, and the defenders were few and weak; moreover, its conquest had been foretold by the Prophet.

Within, the two walls were well manned, icons and relics were brought to the danger spots, and monks were posted to encourage the defenders. All who were not required on the walls took part in a procession, and Constantine made a last speech to his people. He told them that it was a man's duty, at need, to die for his faith, his country, his sovereign, or his family, and that all these duties now met in the defence of the city — the queen of cities, the pride and joy of all Greeks, which was now coveted as a prize by an enemy who would supplant there the worship of God by that of the Prophet. 'Brothers and fellow-soldiers,' he said, 'be ready for the morn. If God gives us grace and valour, and the Holy Trinity help us, in Whom alone we trust, we will do such deeds that the foe shall fall back with shame before our arms.'

The leaders embraced, and asked mutual forgiveness, and went with the emperor to St. Sophia. The great church had been almost deserted, as if it had suffered pollution, since the ceremony of the reunion of the churches on St. Spyridon's day, in December. Now the liturgy was celebrated there for the last time, and the emperor did penance and received holy communion. Later in the day, Constantine visited Blachernae; there he asked pardon all round of anyone he might have offended: 'if a man had been made of wood or stone,' wrote Phrantzes, his friend and chronicler, 'he must have wept over the scene'.

Nor was even Gibbon unmoved by its contemplation. 'The distress and fall of the last Constantine', he wrote, 'are more glorious than the long prosperity of the Byzantine Caesars.'

Outside there was a night of silence, even more ominous than the previous nights of feasting and music. Within, the defenders manned the walls, and locked the gates behind them, voluntarily cutting themselves off from retreat.

A Venetian writer makes a Homeric comment upon this moment: 'Each side having prayed to its God, we to ours and they to theirs, the Lord Almighty with His Mother in Heaven decided that They must be avenged in this battle of the morrow, for all the sins committed.' The scales were weighted in favour of Mehmet.

Round midnight the emperor and Phrantzes inspected stations together; from the tower now called the tower of Phrantzes, in the wall of Manuel Comnenus, they looked on at the nocturnal preparations of the Turks; at about one or two in the morning of Tuesday, 29 May, they separated for ever.

The assault appears to have begun in the small hours; accounts are confused. The first attack was made by the Bashibazouks – mixed foreign troops, who were the least valuable part of the army; the Janissaries were stationed behind to cut off their flight. This attack was repulsed after two hours of fighting. The Anatolian division next attacked, still in darkness; an hour before dawn the great cannon brought down part of the stockade that replaced the outer wall, and three hundred men poured in – they too were repulsed.

So far there had been no success recorded against the northern part of the wall. There was now an assault by the élite of Mehmet's army, in which he himself took part; twelve thousand Janissaries, fresh and untired, were brought up against the worn-out defenders.

This brigade, the terror of Christendom, was formed of the flower of the youth of conquered Christian nations, paid as tribute to the Sultan, rigidly educated in religion and in arms, in order to be a means of subjugating yet other Christians to his domination. They were unmarried, and had no father but the Sultan, these Yeni-Tscheri (new soldiers), and no hopes save in the plunder they could win in this world, and the promise of Paradise if they died in action.

Two misfortunes were the immediate cause of the city's capture. First, Giustiniani was wounded and had to retire, against the wish of Constantine, who knew the panic that his departure would provoke. Some authorities deny that his withdrawal was justified, and accuse him of pusillanimity, but the fact that he died of his wound a few days later, on the way to Chios, seems to exonerate him from blame, if exoneration is needed, in view of his notorious heroism. The second accident was the leaving open of a postern, the Kerkoporta, near the palace of Constantine Porphyrogenitus; this had been opened for a sortie on the night of 27 May. Fifty Janissaries entered, Turkish standards were displayed upon the walls, and a cry went up, 'Εάλω ἡ Πόλις, 'the city is taken'.

The city was not taken yet, but, in spite of the emperor's superb courage, the broken morale of his people was now beyond mending. Janissaries got in near the Charisius gate, opened it from inside, and now there was a rush into the city; Mehmet from without, seated on horseback, with his standard displayed above him, watched the entry. This, the fall of the city, took place between five and six in the morning.

The end of Constantine is unknown. In his fear of falling into enemy hands, he is said to have cried for some Christian to cut off his head. According to Critobulos, he cried: 'The city is taken, and I am still alive', and threw himself into the midst of the enemy, where he was at once cut down.

'Ducas kills him with two blows of Turkish soldiers,' so Gibbon summarizes; 'Chalcondyles wounds him in the shoulder, and then tramples him in the gate. The grief of Phranzes, carrying him among the enemy, escapes from the precise image of his death.'

Tradition places his death by the Romanus Gate. We do not know where his body found a grave, though there are several mythical accounts of his burial. Mehmet had his head (or what was believed to be his head) brought to him, and for a time this was exposed on a column in front of the Great Church.

Looting and slaughter continued until noon. In the Great Church, thousands were gathered, putting their trust in the legend that an angel would descend there at the last minute and check the advance of the Moslems. There was no angelic intervention.

'Had that angel appeared,' cried Ducas to his defeated fellow-countrymen, 'had he offered to exterminate your foes if you would consent to the union of the Church, even then, in that fatal moment, you would have rejected your safety, or have deceived your God.'

The victors burst in, tore down the ornaments of the church, slaughtered many of the suppliants waiting there, and indulged in orgies of eating and drinking and rape; not even the Crusaders had behaved so badly. The Byzantine casualties in the siege have been reckoned as four thousand dead and fifty thousand taken captive.

If the rank and file of the Turks behaved as ill as any Crusader two hundred and fifty years before, yet Mehmet's conduct was moderate and contrasts favourably with that of any Latin leader; he was, after all, a cultivated man and a lover of the arts, and he meant to make the city his home, not to pillage it in favour of Adrianople. He entered in the afternoon by the Romanus Gate, and rode down the main street to St. Sophia; there he dismounted, took earth from the ground, and poured it on his head, as a token that the grave is the end of all earthly conquests. In the Great Church he struck a soldier, who was breaking up the pavement with his axe; in granting the loot of the city to his troops, he had reserved the buildings for himself, and this man was destroying his property. He declared himself protector of the Christians, and bade priests and people go in peace — then he had the Koran read, and himself prayed, and henceforward the Great Church was a mosque.

Thus the city fell, and now Western Europe, which had not exerted itself to save this outpost of Christendom, grieved too late at its fall, and was to live in fear of the Great Turk for two hundred and fifty years more, until the victory of John Sobieski. 'If the city had not fallen once, if it had not fallen twice', no one can tell what would have happened; a Greco-

Roman renaissance might possibly have taken place in this Greek city, the capital of the Roman Empire. As it is, Byzantium had guarded Greek civilization, and had necessarily, in protecting itself, served for centuries as the bulwark of Europe. It had done its work, and earned the eternal gratitude of the world. Perhaps we should not grieve unduly over its fall, natural as it is to give our sympathy to Constantine Dragases, that noble defender of a lost cause.

And yet a regret for the beauty destroyed at the fall – and much that had survived the Crusaders' vandalism was then destroyed – must not make us disparage the Turks and their sixteenth century, one of the great ages of Constantinople. 'No art, no literature, no handicraft even, nothing that the world would gladly keep, has come since 1453 from the Queen City', writes a Byzantine enthusiast. 'Its capture, as far as human eyes can see, has been for the world a misfortune almost without any compensatory advantage.'[1] It is quite time that people stopped talking in such a way: Kariye is the only monument of the Roman Empire, after the Latin conquest, that is at all worthy to rank with those of the reigns of Süleyman the Magnificent, Selim II and Murad III.

The fall of 1204 may have been an unmitigated misfortune; that of 1453, which replaced a dying empire by a younger and more vital people, may be regarded with less unmixed feeling.

[1] Sir Edwin Pears.

CHAPTER VI

OTTOMAN CONSTANTINOPLE

On the fourth day after the fall, Mehmet II made his triumphal entry into Constantinople. His first act was to declare himself the protector of the Christians. He sent for George Scholarius, the bitter opponent of the reunion of the Churches, who was glad enough to collaborate with him. Scholarius was invested as the Patriarch Gennadius, with most of the traditional Byzantine rites, and was established on his throne in the church of the Holy Apostles, till that ruinous building was pulled down to make room for the conqueror's own mosque; the patriarchate was then transferred to the Pammacaristos. In return for his patronage of the Church, Mehmet hoped to get acceptance of Moslem rule from the Greeks remaining in the city, and from Greek settlers whom he wished to attract; he was not disappointed.

The walls of Galata were destroyed, and the Genoese were taught that Mehmet was master on both sides of the Golden Horn. The first stone of the Mosque of Eyüp was laid by Mehmet himself; the relics of this companion of the Prophet had been miraculously revealed during the siege. Workmen were imported to restore the shattered walls of the city. Then the conqueror returned to Adrianople, where he made a solemn entry.

During the remaining thirty years of his reign, Mehmet restored the city to populousness and prosperity, granting land free to rich families from other places, to induce them to settle there, and forcibly importing many Albanians and Greeks. Gradually he gave it an oriental, Moslem appearance; he turned eight churches into mosques, and built four new mosques, of which the greatest was that (now rebuilt) which bears his name, on the site of the Holy Apostles on the Fourth Hill. He founded eight colleges, an *imaret* (refectory), a hospital, khans for the free lodging of travellers, and a library, and schools at Ayasofya and at Eyüp. He built the castle of the Seven Towers and began the construction of the Serail, borrowing from Byzantium the notion of a remote and sacred palace for the sovereign, and the Byzantine institution of a body of attendant eunuchs; but in the exterior court he lodged his fiercest fighting-men, the Janissaries.

He provided for a peaceful succession, elevating his own action on his father's death into a law. 'Most legists have declared', he said, 'that those of my illustrious sons or grandsons who ascend the throne may have their brothers executed to assure the repose of the world.' The sons of his daughters were to die at birth.

Bayazit II, returning from a provincial governorate to claim his throne, was not quick enough to order the death of his brother Djem, who raised a rebel army, and escaped to Rhodes after defeat. He was the prisoner of the Knights of Rhodes, who later sent him to Europe; he died ten years later in Italy. Bayazit, called the 'Sofi' or the Philosopher, was a person of studious and simple tastes, pious and peaceful (though his reign was marked by great victories and the fleet owed its origin to him), and a great alms-giver. His monument is the 'Pigeons' Mosque', which stands on 'the navel of Constantinople'. He is also responsible for the restoration of the city 'in most beautifull manner'[1] after the great earthquake in 1509; 80,000 workmen were impressed for the task.

His reign again proved that the law of fratricide could not, as it stood, secure 'the peace of the world'; more than one prince was needed to maintain the succession, and these, coming to manhood in Bayazit's lifetime, troubled the last years of his reign with civil wars. Selim, who won over the Janissaries from his brother Ahmed, was the winner, and Bayazit abdicated in his favour. The ex-Sultan died shortly afterwards, on his way to his chosen place of retirement; he was believed to have been poisoned by his Jewish doctor.

Selim I, 'the Inflexible', was a cruel and pitiless soldier, called 'the Great' because of his conquests of Egypt and Jerusalem. He began his reign with a massacre of his brothers and nephews, and his favour was nearly as dangerous to a man as blood relationship: 'I wish you were Sultan Selim's vizir' was the worst curse you could pronounce upon an enemy. Selim cared little for the pleasures of the table or of the harem, but he loved fine clothes and Persian poetry, and brought Persian potters into the empire. He reorganized the corps of Janissaries, replacing their chief, who owed his position to seniority, by an *agha* of his own choosing, and also chose their second-in-command; he therefore got into his own

[1] Richard Knolles: *The General Historie of the Turks* (London, 1621).

hands the command of that force which could, if it wished, make and unmake Sultans – it had made him Sultan, and unmade his father.

Süleyman I, his son and successor, was the greatest of the Osmanli Sultans, with the possible exception of Mehmet II, the Conqueror. In Ottoman history he is known as 'the Legislator'; his titles 'the Great', or 'the Magnificent' are of Western provenance. Something of his prestige he owed to his fortunate name, and more to his birth in 1494, the year 900 of the Hegira. It was believed that a great man destined to dominate his age would be born at the beginning of each century, and the tenth century, that of Süleyman's birth, had a lucky number. He was the greatest ruler of the city since Justinian; to some lovers of Ottoman art his reign is the greatest age of Constantinople.

Süleyman came to the throne from the governorate of Magnesia; it was the custom to keep the reigning Sultan's sons outside Constantinople after they had reached manhood. With him he brought his favourite, Ibrahim, a Greek, born (says Knolles) 'at Parga, a base village in Acarnania, brought up in the court from his childhood with Solyman'. As a child, Ibrahim had been carried off by corsairs, and sold as a slave in Magnesia – sold, no doubt, at a high figure, for he was a good violinist. He had been given as a present to the young Süleyman while his grandfather Bayazit was still alive; he became the young prince's inseparable companion, and shared his bed even after he came to the throne. Süleyman at once showed his characteristic weakness in promoting favourites; he made Ibrahim chief of pages and first falconer, and later Grand Vizir: 'by which his great place, and the speciall favour he had with *Solyman*, he in magnificence, power and authority farre exceeded all the rest of the Bassaes, doing whatsoever pleased himselfe; and that with such sovereignty and the good liking of *Solyman*, that it was commonly said, hee was the commander of his thoughts'. Ibrahim was 'of countenance amiable, of feature comely, active of bodie, well spoken, pleasantly conceited, and sharpe of wit: so that he in shorter time than was thought possible, to the admiration of many, learned both to speake and write the Arabian tongue, and other languages used in the Turkes court, and could skilfully playe upon Sundrie kinds of instrument'. He was, perhaps, still European in outlook; he was friendly with Gritti, a bastard of the Doge's, and would 'manie times bring *Solyman* himselfe over the haven to Pera, to solace himselfe in *Grittus* his pleasant gardens and banqueting houses, which he had there most sumptuously made after the Italian manner'. Ibrahim's own house was palatial, containing 'a world of wealth and royall furniture'.

Nevertheless, as Knolles tells us, domestic architecture was of little account in Ottoman Constantinople: 'The Turks' private houses . . . are for the most part low and base, after the Turkish fashion, built some of wood, some of stone, and some of unburnt brick, laid with clay and dirt, which quickly decaieth againe: they are after their homely manner (by long custome received) never building anything sumptuously for their own private use, but contenting themselves with their simple cottages, how meane soever, commonly saying them to be good enough for the short time of their pilgrimage . . . Neverthelesse, there are yet in Constantinople some other houses built high and comely enough; but these be few, and very old, all inhabited by the Christians and Jewes, and not by the Turks.'

'The soule of *Solyman* lived in Abraham,' says Knolles, 'whereat many of the great men of the court secretly repined; but especially *Solyman's* mother, and *Roxelana* his faire concubine, whom of all women he held dearest.'

Ibrahim's favour increased; on 22 May, 1524, he was married to the Sultan's sister, with a great feast in the hippodrome. When he was sent as governor to Egypt, a post worthy of a member of the imperial family, Süleyman accompanied him as far as Prinkipo. But the harem was biding its time. When Süleyman returned from his Persian expedition, which had been by no means an unqualified success, he looked with some coldness at Ibrahim, who had inspired it, though the Grand Vizir was anxious to represent the return as a triumph, and had covered the shore of the Bosphorus, where Süleyman was to land, with Persian silk.

'Envie, the fatall and cruell companion of princes immoderate favours, had with her prying eies quickly discovered in court *Solyman's* changed countenance upon the great Bassa, and began now to shew her gastly face. They which before were most readie to do him all the honour possible, yea to have laid their hands under his feet, sought now by all secret means to work his disgrace and confusion.' Süleyman's mother was embittered at the ill-success of the Persian expedition, and Roxelana because he favoured Prince Mustafa, Süleyman's eldest son, rather than her own children. It is even said that Süleyman was induced to suspect Ibrahim of remaining at heart a Christian. Ibrahim's end was near: 'An eunuch cut his throat with a crooked knife', says Knolles; others say he was strangled. Süleyman, having promised never to kill him while he was 'alive', was, by the casuistry of the Imams, allowed to have him murdered while sleeping.

A later vizir, also a personal appointment of Süleyman's, was Rustem his son-in-law, husband of Roxelana's daughter Mihrimah, and the tool of his ambitious mother-in-law. Rustem, by some accounts a Croat, was, according to Knolles, 'a man basely borne in Epirus, altogether composed of dissimulation and flatterie, ever serving his own turne'. He was suspected of being a leper; Süleyman is even said to have introduced a boy into his harem in order to find out if this were so. Rustem was cleared by the evidence of a flea, for fleas were believed never to touch lepers. He was grasping and avaricious, and a great enemy of the poets of Constantinople; yet, though most that we know of him was evil, his name permanently lives in his lovely mosque.

Roxelana, meanwhile, was pursuing her ambition, which was to be Sultana Validé, or Queen Mother, after Süleyman's death, the most exalted position for a woman in Constantinople, and very much more exalted than that of wife, or chief concubine.

First, however, she attained the status of legal wife, a status given to no woman for many generations of the imperial family. This she cunningly achieved by deciding to build a mosque for the good of her soul. Such an act, the mufti told her, was no good to a bondwoman, whose good works could only acquire merit for her lord. She therefore asked for her freedom; once free, she refused to lie with Süleyman, for the mufti told her that what a bondwoman might do at her lord's command would be sinful compliance in one free. Süleyman was then induced by her Pamela-like tactics to make her his wife; it was further said that she had bewitched him 'by the meanes of *Trongilla* a Jew'. This was the beginning of the fatal influence of the harem, that was for so long to dominate Turkish court life.

Roxelana and Rustem planned the removal of Prince Mustafa, who stood between Roxelana's sons and the throne: his accession would have made her rival the Validé. Rustem brought Süleyman stories that Mustafa was allying himself with the Shah of Persia, to make himself Sultan, and that the Janissaries were murmuring for his abdication in favour of his son. Süleyman, on his Syrian campaign, ordered his son to appear before him.

On 21 September, 1553, Mustafa was brought to the Sultan's tent at Amasia. When he entered, expecting to see his father, he found only seven mutes and a bow-string awaiting him; his father, from behind a silk curtain, witnessed his murder. The witty hunchback, Prince Djihanghir, Süleyman's favourite son, and son of Roxelana, either stabbed himself or died of grief because of his half-brother's murder.

Roxelana died not long after, not surviving her husband, and therefore never occupying the position of Validé for which she committed her crime. The later years of the reign were darkened by civil war between her sons, Selim and Bayazit. Rustem, however, was succeeded by the excellent and upright Serbian Vizir, Mehmet Sokullu, who continued Süleyman's aims and influence under the reign of Selim II.

A brother-in-law of Süleyman, also raised to power through his imperial marriage, fell into disgrace because he failed to get on with his wife. 'Sister, I give thee this man for thy slave', was the formula addressed by the Sultan to an imperial bride, who was given a dagger with which to take the law into her own hands in case of necessity; this lady, however, appealed to Süleyman against the 'Lütfi' of Knolles's story. 'This great Bassa then in credit and authoritee next unto *Solyman* himself, fell at ods with his wife, *Solyman's* sister: for that he after the unnatural manner of those barbarous people kept in his house a most delicat youth, in whom he tooke more pleasure than in his wife; which she being a woman of great spirit not able to endure, and knowing her husband by marrying of her to have bin from base degree advanced unto the highest honours that the emperor her brother could heape upon him, in great rage reproved him with most bitter words saying, that she had married him to be of him beloved, and used as his wife, and not contemptuously abused by minions. Wherewith the Bassa moved, gave her a blow on the eare, and caused her as a foolish and unquiet woman to be shut up in her chamber.' She complained to Süleyman, and her husband was degraded. Knolles sums up:

> On daintie boies, thou filthie man, why dost thou fire thine eye
> Whilst princely dame of royall blood doth in thy chamber lie?
> From base estate to honour's height blind fortune did thee call,
> And set thee up with princes great, to worke thy greater fall.

Süleyman's faults as a ruler were not only the promotion of favourites, and the toleration of harem influence on public life, but also his tendency to retire from the Divan and to allow himself to be represented there by his viziers. However, his reign is memorable and splendid for his thirteen campaigns (here not discussed, where his reign is reviewed from its metropolitan aspect); for his strict observance of Islam, combined with toleration of other religions; for his order, economy and splendour, and for his encouragement of art and science.

The ten poets of his reign, Baki, Khiali, Djelili and others, were patronized by the Sultan. Sinan, the great architect, transformed Constantinople during the reigns of Süleyman, Selim II and Murad III, doing his greatest work under Süleyman, who was the paymaster for many of his mosques and other buildings. The festivals at the marriage or circumcision of members of the imperial family were of a splendour that recalls the great days of Byzantium; such, for example, was the three weeks' festival that celebrated the circumcision of five princes during the summer of 1530; the Doge was invited on this occasion, and sent a representative. There were processions, fireworks, learned disputes, tilting and horse-racing; a noble renaissance festival, perhaps part of Süleyman's propaganda, intended to represent Constantinople as a great, civilized capital.

There was another side to Süleyman's Constantinople, and it is forcibly put before us by Busbecq, the emperor's ambassador, who arrived at his post in January, 1554. He complains bitterly of the squalor in which he had to live; though he enjoyed a distant view of the Marmara, and of 'the Dolphins skipping and playing therein', yet if he hung up his hat in his house, he was likely to find it next 'surrounded with a snake, as with a terrible hatband'. Snakes, weasels, lizards, scorpions and toads, were inmates of his house; to them (in the horrible boredom which has in all times since 1453 afflicted foreign residents in the city) he voluntarily added apes, wolves, bears, stags and a hog: 'Seeing we were debarred of Human society, what better conversation could we have to drive Grief out of our Minds, than among the Wild Beasts?'

The cleanliness of the Turkish army, however, impressed and surprised Busbecq; the soldiers were careful (as European soldiers were not) to bury their excrement. He found no dicing or drinking in camp, but a wonderful sobriety: 'They showed me a Janizarie sitting by, who in an earthern dish had killed a turnep, an onion, a head of garluke, a parsneip and a cowcumber, al sauced with salt and vinegar, or more truly to say with hunger, whereon he fed as savorly as if they had been feasants or patridges:

his drinke was the common drinke of all living creatures, even faire water.'

Here is the austerity and sobriety of Islam; on the other hand, like most Christians who have lived in an Islamic country, he suffered at times from the fanatical superstition of the ignorant, and from the obstructiveness of officialdom. Straight off, on his way, he suffered from the Turkish reverence for paper; who knows (certainly not the illiterate) but that the name of God *may* be written on it? The Turks therefore, at this time at least, would pick up any bits of paper they found lying about, and would stuff them into chinks in walls. 'My *Turkish* Guides were once very angry with my Servants for making use of Paper to cleanse their *Posteriors*' — a horrible piece of infidel sacrilege, it must have seemed to them. While, at the highest level, the emperor's ambassador was refused permission by the Grand Vizir, Rustem Pasha, to leave Constantinople for Prinkipo, to flee from the plague; what was the sense when, if God meant him to get the plague, he would necessarily get it?

In spite of his enforced preference for animal society, Busbecq had, like many other visitors to Constantinople, an interest in *mœurs*. He tells a pleasant story about an elderly woman who fell in love with a girl at the baths, but was given no encouragement. Such was her passion that she dressed as a man, hired a house near that of the girl's father, proposed to him for his daughter, and was accepted. The marriage was performed, 'and this doughty Bridegroom went unto the Bridechamber to his Spouse; after some Discourse, and plucking off her Head-gear, She was found to be a woman'.[1] The girl escaped, and the woman was brought before the Governor of the city. 'He chid her soundly for her beastly Love; what, says he, are you not ashamed, an old Beldam as you are, to attempt so notorious a Bestiality, and so filthy a fact? "Away, Sir," says she, "you do not know the Force of Love, and God grant you never may." At this absurd Reply, the Governour could scarce forbear Laughter, but commanded her presently to be pack'd away and drown'd in the Deep; such was the unfortunate Issue of her Wild Amours.'

Selim II, 'The Sot', had few of the abilities of his parents, Süleyman and Roxelana, and little of the latter's beauty; he was short and stout, his face flushed with Cyprus wine. This was his undoing; he used a new

[1] *The Four Epistles of A. G. Busbequius concerning his Embassy into Turkey* (done into English, London, 1694).

bath, of which the walls were still damp, and drank a bottle of Cyprus wine at a draught to counteract this. In consequence he slipped on the marble floor, fell, and took a fever of which he died. He was the first of the Constantinopolitan Sultans to live a life of indolence in the Seraglio, with eunuchs and women for his associates. His reign is principally significant for an important concession to the Janissaries, made when a revolt had to be checked; their children might now be enrolled in the ranks, which were no longer to consist entirely of captive or tribute children from non-Moslem families. This strengthened the power of the body, and of its officers, against the Sultan, on whom it had previously depended as on a unique source of benefits.

Knolles records a reception of the emperor's ambassadors by Selim II. 'The embassadours entred the first gate of the Grand Turk's pallace . . . so passing through the base Court . . . they came to the second gate, where al such as come in riding, must of necessitie alight . . . Entring in at this second gate, in one part of the Court, which seemed rather like some large street, they saw the whole company of the *Solaches* set in goodly ranke, which are archers keeping alwaies neare unto the person of the Grand Turke, and serving as his footmen when he rideth: they use high plumes of feathers, which are set bolt upright on their foreheads. In another place there stood the *Capitzi* in like array, with black staves of Indian canes in their hands: they are the porters and warders at the gates of the pallace . . . And among the rest, the Mutfarachas, men of all nations and all religions (for their valour the onely freemen which live at their owne libertie in the Turkish Empire) stood there apparalled in damaske, velvet, and cloth of gold, and garments of silke of sundrie kinds and colours: their pompe was great, and the greater for the turbans that they wore upon their heads, being as white as whitenesse itself, made a most brave and goodly shew well worth the beholding.'

The ambassadors ate with the pashas, but their followers were fed on the ground, on cloths spread on carpets. They were offered 'two and fortie great platters of earth, full of rice pottage of three or foure kinds, differing one from another; some of them seasoned with hony, and of the colour of hony, some with soure milk, and white of colour; and some with sugar: they had fritters also which were made of like batter, and mutten beside, or rather a daintie and toothsome morsell of an old sodden ewe'.

After the meal, the ambassadors went forward with their train to the third gate and were then led into the audience room silently, one by one: 'on both sides of which roome, when all things else were whist and in a deep silence, certaine little birds onely were heard to warble out their sweet notes, and to flicker up and downe the green trees of the gardens (which all along cast a pleasant shadow from them) as if they alone had obtained licence to make a noise'. Selim, almost invisible, saw them from an inner chamber, and received their homage.

During this reign occurred the naval victory of Don John of Austria at Lepanto; in revenge, the Sultan ordered the massacre of all the Christians in the capital, and they owed their survival to the wisdom of the Grand Vizir, Mehmet Sokullu, who delayed the execution of the order until it was cancelled.

Fiery crosses were seen in the air above Constantinople at the time of Lepanto. Earlier in the century there had also been superstitious fears of a Moslem downfall. There was the traditional prophecy of the Red Apple, differently interpreted: 'After twelve years from the time that he (the Sultan) hath captured the Red Apple, the sword of the Infidel shall come forth and put the Turk to flight.' Rhodes fell to the Turks in 1522; some derived the name 'Ρόδος from ροΐδι (pomegranate), and in 1534, it is said that the lion of Boucoleon turned its head away from Europe and towards Asia. Later in the century the millennium of the Hejira (1592-93) also excited fears, like the fears of Christians at the end of the tenth century, and there were further outbreaks of fanaticism against the Christians of Constantinople.

Murad III began his reign with a merciful attempt to save his brothers' lives: for hours he argued with his ministers, delaying his own proclamation, but finally, in tears, he was forced to send nine handkerchiefs to strangle the nine princes in the Seraglio. Unlike his father, he was abstemious – perhaps a choice forced upon him by his sufferings from the stone – and he had been addicted to intellectual pursuits and had served as a soldier. But, after his accession, he spent his mornings with fools and, when afternoon prayers were done, he retired to the harem. He had no fewer than forty Khassekis, that is, favourite concubines, who were mothers of his sons. His sexual excesses brought on epileptic attacks.

During his reign the harem was wonderfully adorned with those superb tiled rooms that bear his name, and preserve it for ever from

I

contempt. Beneath his bed, in one of those wonderful rooms, was a marble well into which he threw the gold to which he was insanely devoted, and which he amassed by the sale of ancient works of art and of public offices. Ambassadors describe how he would receive them with a stupid stare, then he 'went back to his garden, where in deep sequestered spots his women played before him, danced and sang, or his dwarfs made sport for him, or his mutes, awkward and mounted on as awkward horses, engaged with him in ludicrous combats, in which he struck now at the rider now at the horse, or where certain Jews performed lascivious comedies before him'. The Ottoman Empire was indeed a New Rome, and a new Tacitus and Suetonius would, had they flourished there, have found infinite material for Annals, or lives of the Caesars.

Sokullu maintained government until 1579, when he was murdered in the Divan by a man dressed as a Dervish — either a man with a grievance, or one set on by others. After his death Murad yielded more and more to female influence, that of his mother, the Validé, till her death in 1583, of his Khassekis and of Djanfeda Kadoun, the *grande gouvernante*; he also had an ambitious aunt, a daughter, three sisters, and five spiritual directors. Nevertheless he liked to see things for himself, on nocturnal rambles in the city, like those of Haroun-al-Raschid in Baghdad: on one such expedition, hearing a cook, Ferhat, complain of one of his ministers, he deposed the minister and raised the cook to his place, from which he rose to be Grand Vizir.

It was a reign of great external splendour, and still perfect taste. Beautiful must have been the festival at which the circumcision of Prince Mehmet was celebrated. Kiosques were set up in the hippodrome. The young prince was in scarlet, gold-embroidered satin, wore a turban with two black heron's plumes, and a ruby in his right ear and an emerald on his right hand. He was armed with a sword with a jewelled hilt, and a steel mace with a crystal head. The confectionery offered on this occasion included nine sugar elephants, seventeen lions, nineteen leopards, twenty-two horses, twenty-one camels, four giraffes, nine sirens, twenty-five falcons and eleven storks.

During the feast, prisoners from Hungary and Bosnia hacked each other in gladiatorial combats, and their blood flowed in streams. More than a hundred Greeks demanded the surrender of their Christianity; it was enough to bare your head and raise your finger — you were taken to the

Serail and circumcised. The Christian slaves of Esmakhan Sultan, the small, ugly daughter of Selim II, and widow of Sokullu Mehmet, performed a masque of St. George and the Dragon; the Admiral, Kiliç Ali Pasha, exhibited a masque of elephants and castles, and a Greek priest produced an artificial forest of cypresses. On 7 July the prince was circumcised by the Grand Vizir, Djerrah Mehmet Pasha; the foreskin was sent in a golden cup to the Khasseki, his mother, and the Validé, his grandmother, received the blood-stained knife.

Murad died in January, 1595. Sitting in a kiosque, he made his musicians play him sad airs; suddenly a salvo from two Egyptian galleys broke the glass. 'Once,' said Murad, 'the salvoes of the whole fleet would not have broken these windows, and now they fall at the sound of these cannons. I see it is the end of the kiosque of my existence.' Tears wet his cheeks and beard; he died the following night. Murad was better than many sultans; though feeble and superstitious, he was not cruel. His dislike of fratricide was not insincere, and he did not execute dismissed vizirs.

Mehmet III was the last prince to return to rule from the governorate of a province; most of his successors came out of the Serail, a less propitious school for empire. The Validé concealed Murad's death, and sent the *bostandji-baschi*, the head-gardener and executioner, to summon Mehmet. On his arrival, he ordered his nineteen brothers to be strangled; at the same time seven slaves, pregnant by Murad III, were thrown into the sea – Amurath indeed succeeded to Amurath, as Shakespeare was to write two or three years later; perhaps he was thinking of this horrible massacre. The nineteen coffins, crowned with state turbans, were laid by those of Murad III, Mehmet being chief mourner. Later the plague made an almost equal havoc of Mehmet's sisters, carrying off seventeen of them.

Mehmet sent the Sultan Khasseki, his mother, and the *grande gouvernante* to the Old Palace, and he and the Serail were ruled by the Validé Safiye, his mother; her eunuch ministers provoked a rebellion, and they were given up and strangled. In spite of his submission to harem influence, Mehmet headed a successful army; and he showed himself to his people, making public Friday prayers in Constantinople, whereas Murad had not made a public appearance during the last two years of his life.

A pleasant incident in the reign of Mehmet III was the visit of Thomas Dallam the organ-builder, maker of the organ at King's College, Cambridge, which was destroyed in the Civil Wars. He brought with him a splendid organ of his own making, a present to the Grand Signior from Queen Elizabeth, who wished for a Turkish alliance against her Catholic enemies. She had previously appealed to Murad III for help 'against that idolator the King of Spain, who relying on the Pope and all idolatrous princes, designs to crush the Queen of England, and then to turn his whole power to the destruction of the Sultan, and make himself universal monarch'. In the nineteenth century the Germans were to make similar attempts to represent Protestantism as being much the same thing as Islam.

Dallam had to start at short notice, with barely time to buy a suit of sackcloth to wear at sea, and another of kersey. On his arrival, the organ was first set up in the house of the English ambassador, Sir Henry Lello, in Pera. There was much to be done: 'the extremeties of the heete in the hould of the shipe, with the workinge of the sea and the hootnes of the cuntrie, was the cause that all glewinge fayled.' The repaired organ was then conveyed across the Golden Horn. The ship fired a salutation to the Sultan which Dallam records as a wasted civility to an infidel, for it cost two Christian lives: the ship's carpenter died at the report of the first great piece, and a sailor blew himself to bits when the last gun fired. A room (apparently) in the second court of the Seraglio was chosen for further setting up of the organ 'bulte for no other use but for the stranglinge of everie Emperor's bretherin'.

The ambassador's speech had been discouraging. 'You are come hether wythe a present from our gratious Quene, not to an ordinarie prince or Kinge, but to a myghtie monarke of the worlde, but better had it bene for yow yf it had bene sente to any Christian prince, for then should yow have bene sure to have receaved for your paines a great rewarde; but you muste consider what he is unto whom yow have broughte this ritche presente, a monarke but an infidell, and the grande enymye to all Christians. What we or other Christians can bring unto him he dothe thinke that we dow it in dutie or in feare of him, or in hoppe of some greate favoure we expeckte at his handes. It was never knowne that upon the receaving of any presente he gave any rewarde unto any Christian, and tharfore you must loake for nothing at his handes.' The organ, the ambassador added, must be a success at first sight; if the Grand Turk tired of it next day, it did not matter, but if it disappointed on a first view he might trample on it and smash it, and all their pains would go for nothing.

Dallam first fixed up the organ for a mechanical performance: a clock struck twenty-two, a chime of sixteen bells played a song of four parts, two figures on the organ raised silver trumpets and sounded them, and then the organ played a song of five parts twice. 'In the tope of the orgon, being sixteen foute hie, did stand a holly bushe full of blacke birds and thrushis, which at the end of the musick did singe and shake theire wynges.' It was now the turn of the west to delight Constantinople with a splendid mechanical toy.

Dallam, contrary to Lello's expectation, was asked to appear before the Sultan and to play, and was rewarded with gold. He was also offered two wives if he would remain in the Sultan's service, either two imperial concubines or two virgins of his choice.

When Mehmet died, on 22 December, 1603, the decadence of the empire was well begun. The Divan met, when the throne was vacant, and puzzled over a message from the new Sultan. A throne had been placed, no one knew how or why, in the second court: suddenly the Door of Felicity opened, and a fourteen-year-old boy in a black turban came out and sat in it. The new Sultan absolutely refused to sanction the usual fratricide; his able elder brother had been liquidated during his father's reign, and his surviving younger brother, Mustafa, was half-witted. On 4 January the Sultan was girt with the sword of Eyüp, and on the 23rd he was circumcised. He began with good intentions, but soon abandoned himself to religious and feminine guidance.

Of the Janissary revolt in 1601, Knolles tells us: 'Which their so great insolencie *Mahomet* imputing unto their excessive drinking of wine, contrarie to the law of their great Prophet; by the persuasion of the Mufti, commanded all such as had wine in their houses in Constantinople or Pera, upon paine of death to bring it out and to stave it, except the embassadours of the Queene of England, the French king, and of the state of Venice: So that (as some report) wine for a space ran down the channels of the streets in Constantinople, as if it had water after a great shower of raine.'

In this reign Constantinople was severely attacked by the plague:

'The greatness of this mortalitie', wrote Knolles, of the plague victims, 'is not to bee imputed so much to the corruption of the aire, as to the wilful negligence of the Turkes, who would not vouchsafe to turne away from a bodie dead of this disease, when it goes to buriall, nor to forbeare to visite their friends being infected. The obstinate beliefs they have of predestination makes them brutishly contemne all sorts of dangers: for, say they, as soone as man goes out of his mother's wombe to enioy the light of the world, God writes in his forehead all the good or evill shall happen unto him, and particularly of what death hee shall die, the necessitie whereof no humane power can avoid. All is governed (say they) by destinie, and therefore they regard not any infection, but contrariwise when anyone is dead, another takes his clothes and weares them: which is the cause that Constantinople, and the grand Caire are seldom free; and when as the aire is anything disposed to contagion, there dies such a multitude of people, as they do not number them but by hundreds of thousands.'

One is reminded of Busbecq's refusal of permission to leave the city by Rustem Pasha. The only legitimate precaution was prayer, and public prayers against the pest were not made until it had numbered a thousand victims a day. In the plague of 1626, Sir Thomas Roe speaks of such prayers, said 'at a little moschy on the edge of the plain of Ackmadan over on Pera's side'.

Sandys describes Ahmed (in 1610) as 'of a just stature, yet greatly inclined to be fat: in so much as sometimes he is ready to choke as he feeds, and some do purposely attend to free him from that danger. His face is full and duly proportioned: only his eyes are extraordinarily great, by them esteemed (as is said before) an excellency in beauty. Fleame hath the predominancy in his complexion. He hath a little haire on his upper lip, but lesse on his chin, of a darksome colour. His aspect is as hauty as his empire is large. His occupation (for they are all tied to have one) is the making of ivory rings, which they weare on their thumb when they shoote, whereupon he works daily.' Sandys witnessed Ahmed's procession to St. Sophia on the first day of the feast of Bayram. 'Upon his returne we saw a sort of Christians, some of them half earth already, crooked with age, and trembling with palsies; who by the throwing away of their bonnets and lifting up of their forefingers, did proffer themselves to become *Mahometans*. A sight full of horror and trouble, to see these desperate wretches that had professed Christ all their life, and had suffred, no doubt, for his sake much contumely and oppression, now almost dying to forsake their Redeemer, even then when they were to receive the reward of their patience. To these the Tyrant a little retired his body: who before not so much as cast his eye aside, but sate like the adored statue of an Idol.'

A plague of acridians, also in Ahmed's reign, was checked by a Greek religious procession from the Adrianople Gate. It is interesting to observe such an example of religious toleration, and gratifying that it was rewarded.

Knolles describes the splendid wedding procession of Ahmed's daughter: 'Eleven caroches full of young maidens, slaves to serve the bride: these caroches were covered and shut, and either of them attended by two eunuches Moores: after these followed twenty-eight virgins slaves, attired in cloth of gold, and accompanied by twenty-eight blacke eunuches all on horseback, and richly clad. After which were seene two hundred and forty mules, loaden with tents of tapistry, cloth of gold, satin, velvet with the ground of gold, with many cushions, which are the chaires the ladies of Turkie use, with many other rich and sumptuous moveables. Such was the Trusse which this yong princesse brought to her spouse's house.' A show as splendid as those of Byzantium, and a palace as disturbed and violent as the Sacred Palace or Boucoleon; next day Ahmed beat the Khasseki, and stabbed her through the cheek, and trod her under his feet, because she had had one of his favourite female slaves strangled.

Sandys, though he did justice to the advantages of the site and the harbour of Constantinople, was very sensible to its drawbacks. 'For I know not by what fate or misfortune, subject it hath bin to sundry horrible combustions . . . The fall of houses heretofore by terrible and long-lasting earthquakes; now by negligence, tempests, and the matter that they consist of, is here also most frequent, many (as it hath beene said) being built of sun-dried bricks. And although it enjoyes a delicate aire, and serene skies, even during the winter, when the East, the West, or South wind bloweth: yet the boysterous *Tramontana*, that from the blacke Sea doth sweepe his blacke substance, here most violently rages; bringing often with it such stormes of snowe, that in September I have seen the then flourishing trees so overcharged therewith, that their branches have broken: accompanied with bitter frost; which dissolving, resolve therewith the infirme matter that sustaines them. Lastly the plague (either hapning through the vice of the Clime, or of those mis-beleevers, or hither brought by the many frequenting Nations) for the most part miserably infesteth this City . . . To these adde the Scepter of a Tyrant, with the insolencie of slaves: and then, ô New Rome, how are thy balanced profits and delights to be valued?'

Ahmed, by his own directions, was succeeded by the feeble-witted brother, Mustafa I, whose life he had spared. Mustafa extravagantly appointed his favourite pages to the highest positions, and further showed his imbecility by passing his time in throwing gold coins into the sea. He was deposed, and sent back to the Serail, while Osman II, Ahmed's young son, was placed on the throne.

Osman, like Murad III, imitated Haroun-al-Raschid: 'his dayly haunting the streets on foot, sometimes disguised, with a page or two, prying into houses and taverns like a petty officer, encreased his contempt even in the City', said Sir Thomas Roe.

A Janissary revolt dragged Mustafa from his prison in the Serail and replaced the poor, terrified creature on the throne. The crowd was whipped up against Osman who, after a struggle, was carried off to the Castle of the Seven Towers and murdered there. The wretched Mustafa ran about the Serail, frantically knocking on doors, and looking for Osman; he even tried to ride into a boat, to escape, by his craziness acquiring no mean a reputation for sanctity.

Mustafa was again deposed, and an eleven-year-old brother of Osman, Murad IV, was set upon the throne. He was a monster of unparalleled brutality. A Janissary revolt, which demanded and obtained the 'seventeen heads' of the Sultan's chief counsellors and favourites, embittered him; the leaders of this revolt were subsequently assassinated, one by one. He became a terrible tyrant, with a fine system of espionage, and the number of executions that took place was fantastic and horrible; there were more than fifty thousand during the last seven years of his life. Moreover, he dealt out death summarily to people who annoyed him; a servant was impaled on the suspicion of theft, women whose dancing disturbed the Sultan were drowned, and a boat full of women was sunk, because it sailed too near the Serail. But this brutal and drunken monster was the last Sultan to return in triumph to Constantinople from a victorious campaign in which he himself had been the leader, 'with a leopard's skin thrown over his shoulders, after the manner of a brave huffing Champion', and he celebrated his conquest of Baghdad by the erection of the Baghdad Kiosque in the Serail, surely one of the loveliest and most harmonious rooms in the world.

Murad was another Sultan who imitated Haroun-al-Raschid. 'It was the common custom of the Grand Signior to walk the streets in disguise,' says Ricaut, 'when meeting with any drunken person, he would imprison him, and almost drub him to death. It was his fortune to meet a deaf man one day in the streets, who not hearing the noise of the people, nor the rumor of his approach did not so readily shift out of the way, as was consistent with the fear and dread of so awful an Emperor, from which default he was strangled immediately, and his body thrown into the streets. All people feared and trembled at these practices, and were as careful to look out abroad for the Grand Signior, lest they should be surprised with the bluster of his presence, as Mariners are of being taken unprovided by some hidden Gust or hurricane; for there was scarce a day, that one innocent or other was not sacrificed to his fury and tyrannical fancy.'

The Turkish traveller, Evliya Chelebi, gives an account of the Alay, or procession of the trades, in Constantinople in 1638, which illustrates much of the life of the time. In it walked the Chief Executioner, 'a model hangman', who was, 'girt with a fiery sword, his belt bulging with all the instruments of his craft such as nails, gimlets, matches, razors for scorching, steel plates, different kinds of powder for blinding people, clubs for breaking the hands and feet, hatchets and spoons'. He was followed by his suite, carrying the remainder of the seventy-seven instruments of torture.

The night-watchmen also inspired wholesome fear: 'they carry lanthorns, wax-lights and torches, all alight though it be midday, and iron-capped staves . . . As they pass along they strike their staves on the ground and cry out, as if they were after a thief: "Hie! Catch him! Don't let him get away! There he goes!" and by way of a joke, they lay hold of the nearest spectators. . . .'[1]

The coffee-house story-tellers, eighty in number, were carried past in litters, with their prompt-books stuck in their girdles, reciting as they passed.

[1] Alexander Pallis: *In the Days of the Janissaries* (London, 1951).

Keepers from the asylums led chained lunatics, from two to three hundred in number, who filed past, some weeping, others laughing and swearing. They physicked their patients, or beat them to keep them quiet.

Divers (mostly Greeks from the island of Symi) went by stark naked, crying out: 'O thou, All-diving, Thou All-bestowing!'

Bear-leaders called out to their bears: 'Vassil, show thy skill . . . As the water-wheel turns round irrigating the garden, even so do thou turn and dance.'

The tripe-cooks had a distinguished place in the procession, for the Prophet had said: 'Tripe is the prince of dishes.' They were all Greeks, as were the fish-cooks, fishermen and fishmongers, and also the sweet-sellers, who came from Chios. These last also were honoured, for the Prophet had a very sweet tooth and is believed to have said: 'The love of sweetmeats comes from the Faith.'

There were many other trades represented: furriers, nightingale-dealers, arrow-makers, soothsayers, tumblers, tavern-keepers, and even professional tipplers.

Evliya is also interesting as a gastronomic guide to the city of his time: he speaks of the oysters and white wine of Tersane Park, the rose jam of Kasim Pasha, the sweet-shops of Galata with their Chios preserves and helva, and of Greek taverns there with muscat from Ancona or Tenedos, of grilled swordfish wrapped in vineleaves at Beykos, and trout from above Broussa. Coffee-houses, as possible homes of sedition, were forbidden in the metropolitan area under Murad IV, but Ibrahim rescinded the order.

The English traveller Sandys had already commented on the coffee-houses, when coffee was still unknown in the west. 'Although they be destitute of Taverns, yet have they their Coffa-houses, which something resemble them. There they sit chatting most of the Day, and sip of a drink called Coffa (of the Berry that is made of) in little *China* Dishes, as hot as they can suffer it: black as soot, and tasting not much unlike it (why not that black broth which was in use among the Lacedemonians?). Which helpeth, as they say, digestion, and procureth alacrity: many of the Coffa-man keeping beautiful Boys, who serve as stales to procure them Customers.' In the taverns, in the early nineteenth century, Pertusier similarly observed Greek boys, dressed as women, with flowers in their hair.

Ibrahim, Murad's successor, was his only brother, and the last of the race of Osman; for this reason great care had been taken by the Greek Validé, Koesem, to prevent Murad from killing him. Almost as imbecile and more degenerate than Mustafa I, he was equally terrified at his accession; he was sure that it was a trick, and that it would be fatal to him, until the Validé showed him his brother's body, then he screamed with delight: 'The empire is at last delivered from its butcher.'

As Ibrahim was the last of the race of Osman, it was necessary that he should breed successors; this he was fortunately willing and able to do. Every Friday the Validé and the vizirs brought him new concubines; and at one time, we are told, his powers were such that twenty-four slaves could visit his bed within twenty-four hours. His physician, consulted about his nerves, advised greater moderation, and was banished to the islands for his pains. Ibrahim had seven Khassekis, each with her own court. Once he sent for the largest possible woman, thinking the pleasure would thereby be extended; an Armenian giantess was brought to the Serail, and Ibrahim rewarded her with the government of Damascus, which she exercised by deputy, but the jealous Validé invited her to a banquet and had her strangled.

Ibrahim would drink amber, dissolved in boiling coffee, for his nerves. One night they were out of amber, and a court official mentioned a huge pyramidal lump of it, the property of an English merchant at Galata. The merchant, in fear, was brought to the Serail before dawn, where he found himself able to strike a wonderful bargain. Women, scent and furs were Ibrahim's passion: lynx and ermine and other exotic skins. Instead of heron plumes, he would weave flowers in his hair and behind his ears, which was considered very effeminate. English cloth, French silk and Venetian velvet and cloth of gold abounded in the Serail. Shops were made to light up, and to remain open all night, so that they could be pillaged for Ibrahim's favourites, and English boats were robbed on their way to the port. Charles I's ambassador appeared before the Sultan with a lighted lamp on his head (which signifies sighs rising to heaven for vengeance), and he lit up thirteen vessels in the port, and placed them round the Serail as a sign of pleading. We hear of a boat enriched with precious stones, and of a kiosque hung with fur for a favourite Khasseki: the Validé was banished from the Serail for her protests against Ibrahim's senseless luxury.

The governor of the harem was an elderly eunuch, Sunbullu (rich in hyacinths) — names of flowers (e.g. narcissus) and scents were commonly bestowed upon eunuchs. To keep up his position, Sunbullu had a perfectly useless harem of his own. When the Kizlar Agha (governor of the harem) and the Validé are friends, there is peace in the Serail; but in Ibrahim's time they were bitter rivals. Sunbullu, thinking it advisable to absent himself on a pilgrimage to Mecca, could not restrain his impatience for the proper equipment of his vessel, and fell a victim to pirates off Carpathos. With him was taken Mohammed Effendi, the child of a favourite slave, who later joined the Dominican order, was known under the picturesque appellation of Padre Ottomano, and was believed to be the true heir to the throne of the Sultans.

Ibrahim, forcibly deposed by a Janissary rising for his follies and iniquities, was sent back to the princes' prison in the Serail, where a few days later his life was ended by a bowstring.

On 8 August, 1648, Mehmet IV, aged seven years, was enthroned outside the Gate of Felicity. At once there was a contest between the old Validé, Koesem, Mehmet's grandmother, and his Russian mother, the young Validé, Turhan. Koesem and his Grand Vizir wished to place another young prince on the throne, and were opposed by Tarkham and the agha of the Janissaries. Civil war was narrowly evaded.

'The Visier', says Paul Ricaut,[1] 'had given order to all the Pashaws and Beglerbegs, and other his Friends, that without delay they should repair to the Seraglio with all the force they could make, bringing with them three days Provision, obliging them under pain of Death to this Duty. In a short space so great was this concourse, that all the Gardens of the Seraglio, the outward Courts and all the adjoining Streets were filled with armed Men: from Galata and Tophana came boats and barges loaden with Powder and Ammunition and other necessaries, so that in the morning by break of day appeared such an Army of Horse and Foot in the Streets, and Ships and Gallies on the Sea, as administered no small terrour to the Janissaries; of which being advised, and seeing the concourse of the people run to the assistance of the King, they thought it high time to bestir themselves; and therefore armed a great company of Albaneses, Greeks and other Christians to whom they offered Money and the Title and Priviledges of Janizaries, promising to free them from the Harach, and

---

[1] *The History of the Present State of the Ottoman Empire.*

Impositions paid by the Christians, which Arguments were so prevalent, that most taking Arms, you might see the Court and City divided, and ready to enter into a most dread confusion of a Civil War.' The side of Mehmet's supporters triumphed: the murder of the Validé is related in the chapter on the Serail; the Vizir and agha of the Janissaries also fell victims.

The Validé Tarkham wisely educated Mehmet, and during her regency the admirable Grand Vizir Köprülü Mehmet was appointed, founder of a line of prudent and honourable vizirs, who directed the fortunes of the empire for nearly fifty years.

Mehmet, principally remembered as a great huntsman, was distinguished by his love of the chase, and his hatred of his capital. He lived principally in Adrianople: 'His aversion to *Constantinople* so much increased, that he could not endure so much as the name of the place: and if accidentally in his Hunting (as is reported) he chanced to fall into the road which led thither, and remembering himself thereof, would immediately turn thence, as one that corrects himself of some desperate error, or avoids a path which tends to an evitable destruction.'

There, in 1675, he celebrated the circumcision of Prince Mustafa, his son by his favourite Cretan Khasseki, Rebia Gülmisch ('she who has drunk the roses of spring') with a splendour that recalled the reign of Murad IV. His reign was further distinguished by the vast luxury and the epicurism of the ruling class; no longer, in this trough period of Turkish architecture, did they spend their wealth in the adornment of the City.

Süleyman II, Mehmet's younger brother, was set upon the throne by a revolution which followed a military defeat. This Sultan ruled in accordance with the principles of the Koran, and was tolerant to the Christians, whom he allowed to restore their churches. His Grand Vizir was Köprülü Mustafa, 'the virtuous', and his too-short reign brought internal peace to the City; this peace was marred, however, by the earthquake of 1690, which destroyed several of the domes of the Conqueror's mosques.

The same virtuous Grand Vizir ruled through the reigns of the next two Sultans, who were lacking both in vices and in vitality. Ahmed II was devout and melancholy, and a lover of music and poetry; he died of the dropsy that had carried off his two brothers and predecessors. Mustafa II, son of Mehmet IV, was also humane and cultured, and a fine calligrapher. From now on there was very much less savagery both in public and in private life.

Ahmed III, whom a revolution placed on the throne of his brother, Mustafa II, though he did not care to rule personally, had the good sense to depute his power to a wise Grand Vizir, Damad Ibrahim Pasha, and not to indiscriminately favoured eunuchs or women. His reign was externally glorious for the success of Turkish arms and diplomacy, and at home there was a sumptuousness that recalled Ahmed I or Murad III. In this reign both religious and secular buildings were erected in large numbers; the ceramic workers, successors of those brought to Nicaea by Selim I, were set up in a factory at Tekfur Seray, and reinforced by others brought from Tabriz by Damad Ibrahim; their work, though lacking the fineness of that of earlier days, has still quality and charm, and the Turkish rococo of Ahmed is among the last architecture or decoration in the long history of Constantinople that can be looked at with pleasure. It was under Ahmed that the first printing press was set up in the city, by one Ibrahim, a Hungarian renegade; an Arabic dictionary and a number of historical works were published.

Ahmed's public life consisted in visits to the Grand Vizir, and to the Treasury, to gaze upon the sums that the latter had collected. His private life was taken up with fêtes in the harem — elsewhere his tulip feasts are described — and with his wives and his fifty children. He had the satisfaction of begetting sons not destined to the bowstring: it is strange, and pathetic, as well as horrible, to think of the love many previous Sultans displayed for their ill-fated younger sons, and the splendid feasts they gave at their circumcisions. But philoprogenitiveness is an oriental quality, and Lady Mary Wortley Montagu found it displayed equally, about this time, among the lower classes, who had indeed not the bow-string to fear for their young, but rather starvation. When she asked how they could hope to provide for the numerous progeny which they brought into the world, she was told resignedly that the plague was sure to carry off half of them.

Ahmed and Damad Ibrahim were mild men, executions were few and iust, and in this reign the vast majority of public men who died, died natural deaths: almost in inverse ratio to the deaths of the eminent under Mehmet IV.

Ahmed delighted in the strange dances of Egyptian opium-eaters, and in the performances of tame animals. The zoological garden had been a feature of Constantinople palaces since Byzantine times; the Crusaders, wantonly breaking into Blachernae, had killed a lion. The Conqueror kept up the tradition, and in 1533 Barbarossa had brought Süleyman 'wild beasts of Libya, as lyons, leopards, and such like'. Sanderson (1592–97) visited the zoological garden: 'The admirablest and fairest beaste that I ever sawe was a jarraff, as tame as a domesticale deere *and of a reddish deere colour, white brested and cloven* footed: He was of a very great hieth; his foreleggs longer than the hinder; a very longe necke; and headed like a camel, except two stumps of horne one his head. This fairest anymale was sent out of Ethiopia to this great Turkes father for a present. To Turks the keeper of him would make him kneele, but not before any Christian for any money.' And we have seen Busbecq with his private collection of animals, to cheer the miseries of his embassy.

A charming feast recorded in Ahmed's reign was that of the first lesson of three young princes. The Sultan sat on the throne, and, left and right, on rich carpets, sat the princes, the Grand Vizir, the mufti, the sheikh of Ayasofya and other notables; the rest were upright. After the sheikh of Ayasofya had opened the proceedings with a prayer, the Grand Vizir took the eldest prince in his arms and put him on the carpet opposite the mufti; a desk covered with scarlet cloth was brought, and the mufti taught the little prince the first five letters of the alphabet. After the letters had been correctly repeated, Ahmed tried to kiss the mufti's hand, but he refused, and kissed the Sultan's shoulder. The same ceremony was then repeated for the other two princes. The young pages stood behind on tip-toe, straining to watch the goings on, and it is charming and characteristic of Ahmed that he invited them nearer, where they could see.

Lady Mary Wortley Montagu, whose husband was ambassador to the Porte during the 'tulip reign', was unusually Turcophil, and reports the prosperity of Constantinople under Ahmed III.

'The exchanges are all noble buildings, full of fine alleys, the greatest part supported with pillars and kept wonderfully neat. Every trade has its distinct alley, where the merchandise is disposed in the same order as in the New Exchange at London. The *besisten*, or jewellers' quarter, shows so much riches, such a vast quantity of diamonds, and all kinds of precious stones, that they dazzle the sight. The embroiderers' also is very glittering, and people walk here as much for diversion as business. The markets are most of them handsome squares, and admirably well provided, perhaps better than in any other part of the world.'

One imagines Lady Mary as almost defiantly Turcophil, and going very far in her defence of Constantinople in the attempt to counteract western prejudice; had the *New Statesman* existed in her day, one can imagine the severity with which her letters would have been treated.

Slaves, she said boldly, were 'never ill treated', and Turkish women were almost as spoiled as American women today. She found them: 'The only women in the world that lead a life of uninterrupted pleasure exempt from cares; the whole time being spent in visiting, bathing, or in the agreeable amusement of spending money, and inventing new fashions. A husband would be thought mad that exacted any degree of economy from his wife, whose expenses are in no way limited but by her own fancy. It is his business to get money, and hers to spend it.'

Miss Emmeline Lott,[1] more than a hundred years later, who knew harem life as a governess to the Khedivial family of Egypt, criticizes Lady Mary for superficiality. 'The interior of these Harems were to her Ladyship a *terra incognita*, and even although she passed through those gaudy halls like a beautiful meteor, all was *couleur de rose*, and not the slightest opportunity was permitted her to study the daily life of the odalisques. True, she had witnessed the

"Strange fascination of Eastern gorgeousness, reverie and passion"

but yet, as she had not been allowed to penetrate beyond the reception halls, nor to pollute the floors of those "Castles of Indolence" with her defiling footsteps, the social manners, habits and customs of the *Crème de la Crème* of both Turkish and Egyptian noblesse, and the Star Chamber of Ottoman intrigue, were to her all unexplored regions.'

A Turkish woman,[2] writing a little later than Miss Lott, chiefly complains of the monotony of the harem, of the lack of family life: after his morning levée, the Pasha only comes in for a quarter of an hour at five o'clock, to change his clothes, and is out until he retires for the night at eleven-thirty, attended by a eunuch; the chief relief to boredom is in the charm of the eunuchs' society.

Nevertheless, Lady Mary was under no illusions about Turkish government. 'Here is, indeed, a much greater appearance of subjection than amongst us; a minister of state is not spoke to, but upon the knee; should a

[1] *Harem life in Egypt and Constantinople* (London, 1866).
[2] Mme Kibrizli Mehmet Pasha: *Thirty Years in the Harem* (London, 1872).

reflection on his conduct be dropt in a coffee-house (for they have spies everywhere) the house would be raz'd to the ground, and perhaps the whole company put to torture ... None of our harmless calling names! but when a minister here displeases the people, in three hours time he is dragged even from his master's arms. They cut off his hands, head, and feet, and throw them before the palace gate, with all the respect in the world; while the Sultan (to whom they all profess an unlimited adoration) sits trembling in his apartment, and dares neither defend nor revenge his favourite. This is the blessed condition of the most absolute monarch upon earth, who owns no law but his will.'

A Janissary revolt deposed Ahmed III in 1730, and set Mahmud I, son of Mustafa II, upon the throne. The destruction of Ahmed's pleasure-houses by the Sweet Waters was demanded by the insurgents; Mahmud, showing a sensitiveness to Western opinion that was now developing in Turkey, refused to allow them to be burnt, for fear of provoking Christian mockery, but he allowed them to be otherwise demolished. As a reaction from Ahmed's extravagance, sumptuary laws were passed; women were forbidden the huge, voluminous burnous, also embroidered slippers and transparent veils. Some women were drowned, as an example; of one a Turkish historian says with satisfaction that her 'naked body now had only the blue tissue of the waves of the sea for clothing'. The forty embroiderers, established near the mosque of Bayazit, were driven out of the city, lest they should be a temptation for 'weak heads'.

Nevertheless, Mahmud much resembled Ahmed in temperament, and was also a great builder, though few of his constructions were useful or permanent. He also built pleasure-houses, mostly by the Bosphorus: the Garden of Joy, the House of Happiness, the House of the Emperor, the House of Gaiety, the House of Security, the House of Khosroes, the House of Spring. To these his mother, the Validé, added the House of Desire.

Ahmed's tulip feasts and other gaieties were abolished, but the birthday of the Prophet was celebrated in this reign with much pomp. Three panegyrics on the Prophet were pronounced by the sheikhs of three of the imperial mosques. Aloes and essence of roses were offered to the Sultan to whom, after the solemn singing of a nativity ode, a letter was handed from the Sherif of Mecca. There was a great distribution of elaborate sweets.

A pleasant procession recorded during this reign was that of the trades,

K

in 1736; ten thousand people took part in it, and it lasted six hours. In front went a cart, drawn by oxen, followed by a sower, scattering grain (and one can imagine that the myriad pigeons of the City must have fluttered about him, taking their part in the ceremony). A young man on horseback followed, with the Koran on a desk in front of him. Bakers followed, with portable ovens, escorted by the verifier of weights and measures whose duty it was to cut off their ears, or the tips of their noses, if they gave false weight. Millers carried handmills, shepherds led sheep on golden reins, butchers followed with the implements of their trade. Sixty-four corporations, mostly of Greeks and Armenians, were represented; masters and apprentices followed, crowned with flowers; and triumphal cars, symbolizing every trade. After the musicians, the rear was brought up by furriers, displaying rare skins on poles, and by gardeners carrying fruit trees or baskets of fruit.

Shortly before Mahmud's death, a terrible fire burnt 6667 houses. This reign was distinguished by the gentleness of the administration at home, by the peace of Belgrade, and by the foundation of four great libraries. The Sultan died suddenly on 13 December, 1754, on his return from Friday prayers.

Osman III, his successor, was a neckless hunchback, serious and obstinate, but not cruel. He had spent half a century in the Serail, and revenged himself upon the feminine world of his prison by forbidding women the streets on Sundays, Thursdays and Fridays, the days when he himself wished to go out. His acts as a ruler were restricted to the passing of sumptuary laws, and the frequent changing of his viziers; he also was addicted to wanderings in the manner of Haroun-al-Raschid. Some pretty building was done in the Serail during his reign, and the great mosque begun by Mahmud, the work of a Greek architect, was completed. Its name Nuruosmaniye, 'the light of Osman', celebrates the memory not only of Osman III, but also that of Osman the third Caliph who, having married two daughters of the Prophet, was called 'possessor of two lights'; the lightness of the many-windowed mosque is also referred to, and the inscription inside the dome is: 'It is from God that the light of heaven and earth emanates.'

Mustafa III bore a name generally ominous in Ottoman history, and his reign was marked by many public disasters. Like Osman III, he had spent years in the Serail, but he was more intelligent. Every prince learned a craft, in imitation of the great kings, David and Solomon; but while Osman had chosen to make slippers, Mustafa was a bookbinder. He also was fond of visiting all parts of the city, in a great variety of disguises. He had a passion for astrology; he asked his ambassador in Berlin to send him an astrologer from Germany, and tried to hire another from Morocco. The same ambassador in Berlin had reported that the people of that city 'did not deny the prophetic character of Mohammed's mission, and were not ashamed to agree that they would willingly become Moslems', but he himself was a renegade, and perhaps had a convert's zeal for proselytism.

The eighteenth century was the period of greatest prosperity for the Greek aristocracy of the Phanar, established near the Patriarchate in old, often medieval houses. Few vestiges of this once distinguished quarter now remain, an occasional house-front with an arched door or corbelled windows. Until 1922 many such houses survived, often with the escutcheons of Wallachia and Moldavia over the door, testifying that one of the owners had been 'Hospodar' of one of the Danubian principalities. Since 1634, when the last Catholic church in Stamboul was turned into a mosque, the Venetians and Ragusans had crossed to Pera, leaving this quarter to the Greeks. Two or three Phanariot families had Byzantine origins, others rose in the world after the conquest, and there were affiliated to them families of other origin, such as the Albanian Ghikas, the Italian Mavroyennis, and others from Dalmatia, but the newcomers became Orthodox and Hellenized; some eighteen families in all were reckoned as the Phanariot nobility. As early as the seventeenth century some of them had been given diplomatic appointments; the Turks thought it beneath them to learn European languages and had need of Greek secretaries and interpreters. The two great posts at home filled by Greeks were those of the Dragoman of the Porte, and the Dragoman of the Fleet. In the eighteenth century Phanariots administered Dalmatia and Wallachia, offices were sold to Greeks, who hoped to recoup the price on the rich provinces, though the charges of extortionate conduct that have been made against them have often been greatly exaggerated. While loyally serving the Turks, the Phanariots helped their fellow-countrymen, and their involvement in the War of Independence broke them up as a community. The survivors settled in Athens, disliked there at first for their cosmopolitan view of life, and inclined to be snobbish. The Phanar, apart from the Patriarchate, is now no more than a Turkish slum.

The earthquake of April, 1766, wrecked the Conqueror's Mosque, and severely damaged many others. This reign was also marked by the religious fanaticism and massacres which attended the unfurling of the sacred standard in 1769 for the Russian war; and the burning of the Turkish fleet in the Bosphorus by the Russians was the worst naval defeat endured by the Turks after Lepanto. Despite Mustafa's passion for astrology, that war was begun under the most unpropitious stars.

In this reign the lovely Tulip Mosque, the last good Ottoman religious building in Constantinople, was erected near the Tulip fountain. The Conqueror's Mosque was rebuilt, and Mustafa honoured his mother by the erection of the Validé Mosque at Scutari.

The Turkish army was reformed, with European assistance, at the instance of the French ambassador Saint Priest; the Baron de Tott formed a training school, and introduced the bayonet.

Mustafa was succeeded by his brother, Abdul Hamid I, who had been forty-four years in the Serail before his accession, and came to the throne stultified, and with a very complete ignorance of the world.

During his reign Russian advances were believed to have made the Ottoman Empire little more than a kind of province; nevertheless, internal splendour was still kept up. Elizabeth, Lady Craven, visiting Constantinople at this time, saw 'the Sultan sitting on a silver sofa, while his boats, and many of the people who were to accompany him, were lining the banks of the garden'. Like Lady Mary Wortley Montagu before her, she thought well of harem life: 'I think I never saw a country where women may enjoy so much liberty, and free from all reproach, as in Turkey.' She was impressed by the rule that slippers put at the harem door always kept the husband from entering, in case a strange woman might be visiting his wives.

Selim III, who succeeded in 1789, had been allowed unusual liberty in his youth, for an Ottoman prince: he had had an Italian doctor for his friend, and had corresponded with the French King. When he came to the throne he attempted to reform the government, to check the powers of the pashas in the provinces, and to promote education. Instead of closing the Greek school and suppressing the Greek press for their revolutionary tendencies, he tried to counteract these by getting Greek clergy to write in defence of the Turkish government. He tried to introduce European military methods, learned of a prisoner taken in the Russian wars, but the conservative Janissaries obstinately refused, and their revolt was, as usual, successful. A further revolution in 1807 deposed him, because his reforms were causing alarm among the more privileged class, and he was murdered in 1808 when the reform party tried to replace him on the throne.

Mustafa Bairacter Pasha of Rustchuk, who was under great obligations to Selim, came with the sacred standard of the Prophet, and demanded to enter the Serail. He was told that the gates were only opened at the bidding of Mustafa IV, the new Sultan. 'Do not talk to me of Sultan Mustafa,' he replied, 'let us see Sultan Selim, our Padischah and yours.' The eunuchs threw out the strangled corpse, crying: 'Behold the Selim you seek!' Mustafa IV had also ordered the death of his own brother, Mahmud; he would then be left the sole representative of the house of Osman, and secure against violence; but a slave had hidden Mahmud in the furnace of a bath. Mustafa was deposed, and Mahmud II was made Sultan. Mustafa, banished to the princes' prison, was shortly afterwards put to death, otherwise the Janissaries would certainly have replaced him on the throne, after their revolt.

Mahmud was an intelligent prince, a great man who might have saved the tottering empire had Russia left him in peace. His mother was possibly a French woman, Aimée Dubuc de Rivery of Martinique, the home of the Empress Josephine; she had been captured by Algerian pirates on a journey from France, purchased by the Dey of Algiers, and by him presented to his suzerain, Abdul Hamid I. From her, Mahmud may have learned his liberal ideas; it is said that he spoke good French and read French books.

He was, however, forced to swear to uphold old abuses and to repudiate all European innovations by the mutiny of the Janissaries in the first year of his reign. The English traveller, MacFarlane, has left a graphic account of the bloodshed and destruction, and of the fire which raged unchecked in the city. 'Soon the most populous quarter of Constantinople was covered with a sheet of fire. The cries, the groans of women, and old men and children, attracted no attention and excited no pity. In vain they raised their suppliant hands, in vain they begged for beams or planks to save themselves from their burning houses by their roofs: their supplications were vain: they were seen with indifference to fall and to disappear among the flames. The desire of destruction was the only feeling that then prevailed. Sultan Mahmood beheld the awful spectacle from one of the lofty towers of the Seraglio, but not like "another Nero", as some have unjustly asserted — the flames were not of his lighting, and he was anxious that they should cease. He ordered Cadi-Pasha to stop his carriage, and to retire with his troops within the walls of the Seraglio, and despatched a hatti-sheriff to the Janissary-agha, commanding him, as he valued his head, to exert himself to stay the conflagration. As Mahmood was Sultan, and, from the pledge he had in his hands, was likely to continue so, even when the revolt should end, the Janissary-agha trembled at the imperial mandate and obeyed; but the fire was too intense and active to be subdued or arrested, even by throwing to the ground whole stacks of houses; it vaulted over the chasm thus made, and only found "sufficient obstacles in the public squares and in the mosques, whose vast cupolas and massy stone walls have frequently preserved Constantinople from entire destruction".'

It is no wonder that Mahmud was profoundly impressed when he learned how, in the same year, Murat had used cannon to clear the streets of Madrid, but he bided his time; he was determined to overthrow the power of the Janissaries for ever. Some of their supporters were detached by gifts, others were arrested on one charge or another, and executed. In June, 1826, having carefully prepared his way, he decreed that, for the sake of the triumph of Islam, the infidels must be faced with a disciplined army, therefore European training must be imposed on the Janissaries. A few days later the Janissaries revolted, overturned their kettles (the traditional sign that they would eat the Sultan's bread no longer), marched on the Serail, and demanded the heads of Mahmud's ministers. Mahmud unfurled the sacred standard of the Prophet and called all believers to rally to the side of their Caliph. The Janissaries were repelled and fell back on their barracks in the Atmeidan (the old hippodrome); to these the Sultan set fire, and those who tried to escape were slaughtered. Probably some four thousand Janissaries were killed on that occasion in the capital, and many afterwards were hunted down throughout the provinces; the name of the corps was proscribed, and their monuments were destroyed. A solitary stele of a Janissary, somehow overlooked in the general destruction, stands in the graveyard of the Ayiasma Mosque at Scutari.

Mahmud's liberal tendencies and western outlook made him an object of suspicion and hatred to the Orthodox Moslems. The Ulemas taught people to pray for deliverance from the 'Giaour Sultan', and his reforms were met with the obstinate passive resistance that, in the East, can break any reformer's heart. A pleasant story is that of the dervish who seized Mahmud's bridle one day as he rode over the Galata bridge and cried that he was ruining Islam. The attendant officers exclaimed that he was a madman. 'Not mad,' he answered. 'Allah speaks through me, and has promised me the crown of martyrdom if I speak truly.' 'Very well,' rejoined Mahmud. 'Give the good man his crown of glory. Hang him!'

Against the rock of Moslem obscurantism, Mahmud beat in vain: it was an age when many of the highest notables could not bring themselves to believe that the earth was round. But when we remember the excesses of so many Christians, the fundamentalism of America, the unthinking, blind puritanism of some English nonconformists and of some Irish Catholics, perhaps we shall feel more tolerant of Moslem fanaticism, and shall find ourselves able to respect the pure monotheism and the high, austere morality of Islam, though in all centuries some of its adherents have shown their faith in a very unattractive fashion, by hostile screams of xenophobia.

Lord Stratford de Redcliffe thus sums up his reign. 'His reign of more than thirty years was marked by disastrous wars and compulsory cessions. Greece, Egypt, and Algiers escaped successively from his rule. He had to lament the destruction of his fleet at Navarino. On the other hand he gathered up the reins of sovereign power, which had fallen from the hands of his immediate predecessors; he repressed rebellion in more than one of the provinces, and his just resentment crushed the mutinous Janissaries once and for ever. Checked no longer by them, he introduced a system of reforms which has tended greatly to renovate the Ottoman Empire, and to bring it into friendly communion with the Powers of Christendom. To him, moreover, is due the formation of a regular and disciplined army in place of a factitious fanatical militia, more dangerous to the country than to its foes.'

Lord Stratford de Redcliffe, then Stratford Canning, came first to Constantinople in 1808; he was later to be Kinglake's 'great Elchi', altogether going beyond his later functions as ambassador to the Porte, and acting as Turkey's guide, philosopher and friend, the protector of her fortunes and promoter of her civilization. At first his services in Turkey were not altogether a labour of love: in 1810, when he learned he had been made minister-plenipotentiary in Constantinople, he locked his door, and burst into tears; one can understand his reaction.

On one occasion he wrote of his boredom: 'In the dearth of diplomatic business, a fire, an earthquake, a storm, a revolt, and almost a visitation of the plague was welcome, if not for its own sake, at least as a relief from the dull nightmare of monotony. A disinterested love of events is the natural consequence of that pressure, and the mind, rather than prey upon itself, is ready to accept calamity as a cordial not to be rejected.' Constantinople, fortunately for him, was fertile in events.

English visitors to Constantinople at this time included Byron, who did not greatly care for it. He was given the opportunity to wait upon the Sultan in the train of the British ambassador, and at first sulkily refused because no precedence could be allowed him, as a peer, on this occasion. Later, curiosity got the better of him, and he repented, saying that he was content to follow the Ambassador as his 'ox or ass, or anything that was his'. Lady Hester Stanhope, accompanied by her doctor, was also in Constantinople, and somewhat of a thorn in the side of Stratford Canning.

She particularly annoyed him by hobnobbing with the French ambassador, though an enemy, because of her insatiable curiosity to see Napoleon. In answer to his rebuke, she sent him the draft of a letter which she pretended she was going to send to the Foreign Office, in which she mocked him as 'a religious and political methodist', and suggested that: 'The best reward for his services would be to appoint him Commander-in-chief at home and ambassador extraordinary abroad to the various societies for the suppression of vice and cultivation of patriotism. The latter consists in putting one's self into greater convulsions than the dervishes at the mention of Buonaparte's name.'

Abdul Mejid, the son and successor of Mahmud II, was a well-meaning prince, trained for rulership by the father whom he lost when he was only sixteen. He had some prudent ministers, and had the great advantage of Canning's presence in his capital from 1842 to 1852, and again from 1852 to 1858. The great triumph of Canning was the Hatti-Humayun (Illustrious Rescript) of 1856 which abolished all restrictions against non-Moslems, and especially the death-penalty for those who forsook Islam for Christianity.

He was largely moved to action by the horrible martyrdom of a young Armenian, which he records in 1843. 'In spite of threats, promises and blows, he maintained his resolution, refused to save his life by a fresh disavowal of Christianity, and was finally decapitated in one of the most frequented parts of the city with circumstances of great barbarity. The first intelligence received in Pera of this occurrence was the appearance in the streets of the unfortunate lad's mother, tearing her grey hair and rushing distractedly from the scene of bloodshed. The poor old woman, when assured of her boy's fate, returned and sat in grief by the corpse, from which she was afterwards removed. A petition of the Armenians for the corpse was rejected, and it was after three days exposure cast into the sea.' When an appeal for the abolition of such atrocities was made to the Grand Vizir, he replied that he, personally, had not the heart to kill a fowl, but that the Koran was inexorable about the death-penalty for apostasy from Islam. Canning then 'searched the scriptures', and found nothing explicit upon the subject in the Koran; the law about apostasy rested upon the traditions (*Sunna*) which, though of great authority, could with less difficulty be set on one side.

The Hatti-Humayun was hailed as a Turkish Magna Carta, but from the first it was defied; Canning himself had to intervene to save a proselyte from Islam from death. Although he wrote of this hardly won reform that 'it was the first dagger thrust into the side of the false prophet and his creed', nevertheless he ended almost in despair of real reform in Turkey. 'There is no such thing as system in Turkey', he wrote. 'Every man according to his means and opportunities gets what he can, commands when he dares, and submits when he must.'

The Crimean War is a story that has been lately and well told; in another chapter I shall speak of its chief monument in Constantinople, the cemetery at Haydar Pasha, and of Florence Nightingale's hospital at Scutari.

Of Abdul Mejid it is related that he married a slave, Besmé, and entrusted to her the care of one of his sons, whom she bit in the arm. A harem slave, in Hamlet fashion, revealed the true state of affairs to the Sultan in a *Kara Gheuz* shadow play, in which the Sultan married a slave who prostituted herself to her servants, and ill-treated the heir. Abdul Mejid was mild enough to punish her by banishment, instead of having her thrown into the Bosphorus in a sack.

When Abdul Mejid had drunk himself to death, he was succeeded by his brother, Abdul Aziz. This prince had visited Europe, but had brought back few recollections save those of broad streets and squares decorated in his honour. He was mastered by his Circassian mistress, Mihri Hanum, and he was principally distinguished by an insensate extravagance, and a passion for building; unfortunate in his epoch, he has left no monument that greatly adorns the city or the Bosphorus. He was deposed by a mutiny and shortly afterwards was found dead. He may or may not have taken his own life by severing his arteries with a pair of scissors; it is very certain that the accusation brought years later against Midhat, the chief of the reforming party, of complicity in his murder, was no more than a trumped-up charge.

Murad V, the eldest son of Abdul Mejid, was placed on the throne. In England, the public learned of this from the press before the cabinet knew of it. An enterprising newspaperman, with a prearranged code, was able to send a seemingly private telegram with the message: 'The doctors have found it necessary to bleed poor Jane [Abdul Aziz]. Grandmamma [the Validé] is with her. Cousin John [Murad] has taken charge of the business.' Murad himself was shortly afterwards deposed for mental incapacity.

Abdul Hamid II, Murad's younger brother, was now girt with the sword. He dissolved the chamber within a year of his accession, and dismissed the reforming Grand Vizir, Midhat. From henceforth, till 1908, there was no longer any pretence of constitutional government.

Abdul 'the damned', 'the Great Assassin', lived ensconced in his palace on the hill of Yildiz, the 'starry'. To increase its grounds he ruthlessly appropriated houses, also two Christian cemeteries. There were many kiosques in his park, and he rarely slept twice in the same building, until, after the earthquake of 1894, he built an unshakeable kiosque upon a rock. Great security precautions were taken at Yildiz; a second encircling wall was added to the park, and the barracks of the imperial guard were set against it. Inside the walls were a farm, a lake, stables, workshops, a menagerie and an aviary; 5000 people lived in the enclosure.

Abdul Hamid's hobbies were carpentry, fretwork and pistol shooting; a guard threw oranges into the air for him, and he rarely missed them. He also dabbled in chemistry, and sailed on a clockwork boat upon the lake. Sometimes he gave excessively boring dinner parties, or had plays performed by theatrical troupes; he insisted on the women's parts being taken by men. He was no sensualist; his harem was small, and his meals light, for he suffered from chronic dyspepsia. His chief occupation was in reading *djournals* (the daily reports of his spies) and plotting. Out of this tedious seclusion he hardly ever emerged; he attended Friday prayers in a mosque in the grounds, and only visited Stamboul once a year on the 15th of Ramazan, for the annual veneration of the Prophet's relics. On this occasion, such was his fear of assassination, that he never let it be known until the last moment which of the three possible routes he would take; all were strictly guarded in advance. Such was his fear that all works describing the violent deaths of princes were banned by his order, including, naturally, a number of plays of Shakespeare; and his terror of darkness caused the kiosques and park of Yildiz to be brilliantly lit with electric light, which he would not allow elsewhere in Constantinople. He was never without a revolver, and those to whom he granted an audience were likely to be threatened with it, if by any gesture they aroused his fear.

This horrible and unhappy man, the last absolute ruler in Constantinople, was a more complete despot than any Sultan or Byzantine emperor before him. He was jealous of any able minister, and nearly always placed by him an assistant minister who was his own creature; he had the very greatest dislike for his Christian subjects, and further increased the inefficiency of the administration by replacing the more intelligent and better-educated Christian employees of the government by Moslems as often as he could; he was the instigator of the 'Bulgarian atrocities', and the fomenter of Armenian massacres in Constantinople. His reign was a long period of recrudescence, of espionage, and of censorship. Of the last, many ridiculous stories are told, and it is probable that they are, for the most part, true . . . the hymn book that was prohibited because 'Shall we gather at the river?' must have a military significance, and the school book in which the formula H_2O aroused suspicion — H_2 must mean Hamid II, and the O must signify that he was good for nothing.[1] At the same time the army was ill paid, and the ships were rusting.

Meanwhile the 'Committee of Union and Progress', i.e. the union of all nations and creeds in the Ottoman Empire, was forming outside Turkey, and the 'Young Turks', as they were otherwise called, managed to force a constitution on Abdul Hamid in 1908. In the following year he was deposed, after an attempt on his part to regain his former status. The only pleasant story about this terrible old man, with his fez too large, and his clothes hanging loosely, like Macbeth's, is that he was devoted to

[1] Recently an Egyptian censor objected to Pascal's *Traité de la Passion*, as probably an obscene work.

his favourite cat, and obtained permission to take the creature with him
into exile.

Mehmet V succeeded him. His reign is chiefly notable for the entry of
Turkey into the war on the side of the Central European Powers. The
German interest in Turkey began with the Baghdad railway: in 1870
Bismarck said that he did not give himself the trouble to open the mailbag
from Constantinople, but in 1889 William II visited Abdul Hamid, and in
1898 declared that the 300,000,000 Moslems who reverenced the Sultan
as their Caliph, could count on the German Emperor as their friend. The
Turks were encouraged to believe that Lutherans differed little in their
tenets from Moslems, an idea which had also occurred to the Turkish
ambassador to Frederick II. British incomprehension, and lack of
sympathy with the 'Young Turks', contributed to the same result, and,
like all neighbours of Russia (always the worst of neighbours), Turkey
was inclined to take the opposite side from her. 'The ideal of our nation
and people leads us towards the destruction of our Muscovite Enemies,'
the 'Young Turks' declared, 'in order to obtain thereby a natural frontier
to our Empire, which should include and unite all branches of our race.'

This declaration of Pan-Turanianism, instead of the rather indefinite
Pan-Ottomanism with which the 'Young Turks' started, marks a further
stage in the development of Turkey from an international empire into a
nationalist state, a development which was to leave Constantinople as only
the second city of the new republic.

Mehmet VI reigned until the victory of the nationalists under Mustafa
Kemal put him to flight. The Sultanate was then abolished, but Abdul
Mejid was allowed to reign as Caliph in his stead until 1924, as a concession
to Islam. The Caliphate was then abolished, from a fear that it might be
used as a step to the restoration of the Sultanate, and all members of the
imperial house were banished from Turkey. The Byzantine Empire was
now finally ended, and replaced by the new republic of Ankara – a return
of the Turks to Asia from the denationalizing temptations of Constantinople. In 1928 it was proclaimed that the republic had no national religion.

The last flicker of Byzantinism had now gone out: the priest-kingship
of the Basileus, half extinguished with the Sultanate, was finally put out
with the Caliphate; it was the end of the Byzantine and Ottoman court,
whose pomp and ceremony were so similar from before Justinian until
after Abdul Hamid, for the Ottomans had modelled themselves on

Byzantium, and both owed much to Persia. Indeed, had Mehmet II been a Christian, he might have been regarded as another of the many Asiatics who ruled in East Rome, a successor to the Isaurian, Amorian and Paphlagonian emperors. Both empires ended as little more than tax-gathering organizations, making large demands on the provinces, and doing nothing for them. Any writer on Constantinople, and most European observers, must naturally be largely concerned with the Christians of Constantinople and their plight under the Turks; but they, and most Constantinopolitans above the line of severe poverty, were privileged in comparison with the tax-ridden, Moslem farmers of Anatolia, who were bled white by the capital city.

The Sultans had followed the emperors' example by granting large capitulations to foreigners, to the diminution of their own sovereignty; they also had split the population of their empire into nearly autonomous compartments; they also ruled over a mixed people, employed foreign mercenaries, and were supported, or held in check, by an official nobility and a ruling race.

The new Turkey had become more homogeneous; provinces inhabited by non-Turanians had been lost, one after another, from the time of Mahmud II onwards, the final step being the compulsory exchange of population between Turkey and Greece.

Modern Turkey has its capital at Ankara, in the bracing highlands of Anatolia, and has turned its back on the Bosphorus, where the lush, over-grown gardens of deserted embassies add to the melancholy of the scene. Constantinople is a dying city, the second capital only of a secular state, which has no religious capital any more; and, for all the vitality of the new republic, its sadness cannot but be felt. *Fuit* . . . the past has been so great, that it obtrudes at every minute, and crushes the present. Byzantium survives in the Greek patriarchate in the Phanar, but this is no Vatican. Islam is still there, and the muezzin still calls to prayer from the countless mosques, but some of the heart seems to have gone out of it. 'What love is to the world at large, that is Islam to the Eastern,' wrote a nineteenth-century author, 'it renders him architect, poet, metaphysician, carver, decorator, soldier, anything.' This love has grown cold in Constantinople. St. Sophia is now neither mosque nor church, but a museum; as such it symbolizes the fate of the city.

I saw a sight one day, in the Grande Rue de Péra, which for me more than anything typifies Byzantium and Istanbul. An old man was staggering up the narrow pavement of the steep street, bent beneath the weight of two coffins, tied together on his back; I have since seen this phenomenon several times, and I have not been able to discover why coffins should be delivered in braces. He seemed a perfect symbol of the city, old and decrepit, that has buried two empires.

CHAPTER VII

THE MOSQUES

IT is to the mosques that the city owes the development and perfection of its sky-line. The Byzantines saw the seven hills as if marked upon a map, grouped their buildings upon them in such a way as to preserve their distinction, but did not attempt to enhance their profile. The cistern of Mocius on the seventh hill was a big depression, and the small domes of the Holy Apostles on the fourth hill could not have been impressive from a distance. The Turks crowned the hills with their mosques, and magically transformed the silhouette of the city. Before the conquest, from the Tower of Galata, only the dome of St. Sophia rose appreciably above the ridge. Now it is lightened by its four minarets which, though no valuable addition to its confused exterior, unquestionably improve it as an element in a general view; and to the west rise the domes and minarets of Ahmed, Nuruosmaniye, Bayazit and Süleymaniye and, after the gap spanned by the aqueduct of Valens, the domes and minarets of Fatih, Selim and Mihrimah. The Golden Horn has a new beauty as the reflector of this lovely outline, and the lovely pyramid of the Yeni Cami, an ornament to the waterside and not to the skyline, shines reflected in its bright water in the evening, as you sail in from Asia.

No buildings are so important to the general appearance of the city as its mosques, not even the great land walls; and to no Islamic city do the mosques make such a contribution of beauty, not even to Cairo or Damascus.

No traveller can fail to admire the mosques as landscape, unless he is one of those many who wholly dislike Constantinople. It has, generally, been too much the fashion to decry their architectural merit.

John Galt, for example, no friend to the city, wrote of 'the moschs':[1] 'Though stately structures, it is impossible to look at them long without being disposed to think of old-fashioned cupboards, where punch-bowls, turned upside-down, are surrounded with inverted tea-cups, pepper-

[1] *Voyages and Travels* (London, 1812).

boxes, and candlesticks.' 'Their uniformity', he summed up, 'was, to me, exceedingly tiresome.'

And this passage by W. H. Hutton will stand for many other such. 'The inspiration felt so overpoweringly in the Church of the Divine Wisdom still abides in the buildings erected by the Emperors of past days. More open and evident still is the fact that architects of the mosques, built for Mohammedan worship since the Turks have ruled in the city of the Caesars, have done little more than copy the people whom they have conquered. In most of the great mosques of Stambul, St. Sophia is simply and directly imitated. In others the leading idea is developed with a variation or two. Of genuine originality the Turkish architects have shown not a trace.'[1]

Such ignorance and such extreme anti-Moslem prejudice must nowadays be uncommon, but there are admirers of Byzantium who will not gladly look at a building erected after 1453, and for whom it is the proof of a tourist's vulgarity if he prefers the mosque of Sultan Ahmed to St. Sophia. Such a one compares the museum of the Holy Wisdom to the mosques as a fresh pea to peas out of a tin; he finds a 'cold, almost death-like air' in the mosques, and a 'warmth of feeling'[2] in St. Sophia.

It will be seen that there are mosques of far greater architectural refinement than Sultan Ahmed's, whose size, convenient position, and blue interior all predestine it to be the tourist's paradise; it is the 'Blue Mosque' of all the conducted tours. However, it should be remembered that the achievement of Ottoman architects was extremely distinguished before ever they saw Constantinople; a visit should be made to Broussa. One can comfortably fly there and back from Constantinople, and visit the monuments in the inside of a day.

Broussa, the old Ottoman capital, is situated on the slopes of the Bithynian Olympus; great trees shade its broad, peaceful, main street, and the air is fresh and dry. The town has the quiet cheerfulness of a spa. The wooden houses are painted dark red, blue or ochre, a gay contrast to the dingy unpainted houses of Constantinople. Such is the welcoming charm of Broussa, that one finds it hard to sympathize with the Turkish desire of expansion towards the West. It is a treasure-house of early Ottoman architecture.

[1] *The Story of Constantinople* (London, 1900).
[2] Cecil Stewart: *Byzantine Legacy* (London, 1947).

Facing, above: SULTAN AHMED MOSQUE.
below: THE BAGHDAD KIOSQUE.

The late-fourteenth-century mosque of Ulu, in spite of hideous internal decoration, is a remarkable building: it consists of five aisles, each of five bays, and each bay is vaulted by a dome. Under the central dome of open iron-work (now glazed in) a fountain flows. Two Constantinopolitan mosques, Zindjirlikuyu (c. 1500) and Piyale Pasha (1573), each vaulted in six equal domes, derive their plan from that of the Ulu Cami; so do the lateral wings of the mosques of Bayazit II and Selim I.

The Yeşil Cami (Green Mosque) of 1419 is a much lovelier building; indeed it must be among the most beautiful of eastern buildings, in its stillness, fixity and repose, and in the superb control which has given it the effect both of austerity and of extreme richness. The exterior is simple, vaulted in two great domes, with a small flanking dome on either side at the west end. Inside it is T-shaped; two great domes surmount the sanctuary and the prayer-hall, and in the latter a grey stone fountain flows. To north and south of the prayer hall great transepts open. The sanctuary wall is lined, to about a third of its height, with splendid dark blue hexagonal tiles, edged in white, and the huge *mihrab*, with its stalactite-vaulted prayer niche, is all tiled. The transept walls are similarly decorated with hexagonal green and blue triangular tiles; a faint, gold arabesque, nearly rubbed off, can still be seen on the green tiles. At the west end are small tiled rooms below, and balconies above; the latter, set in the high, bare wall, are of infinite colour and richness.

A course of stalactites breaks the transition between the domes and the walls of the rooms beneath, heavy stalactites that seem to hang from the domes, which overhang the mosque instead of seeming to rise from it. A recent author has well said that no building in the world is so unlike Gothic, where everything aspires upwards; she also says that the Green Mosque, in its quietude, is like a room that has not been built, but has been hollowed out of a rock.[1]

The Yeşil Turbéh (Green Tomb) of Celebi Mehmet (1422), with its huge, external, blue-green, tiled panels that shine afar, is a companion building; and in both the tiles are the work of Persian potters from Tabriz. At the other end of Broussa there is a pretty group of domed tombs round the mosque of Murad (c. 1425): this is another mosque of two, big, domed bays, with small lateral domes; it has a fine peristyle, in which there is polychromatic brick- and stone-work.

[1] Ulya Vogt-Göknil: *Türkische Moscheen* (Zürich, 1953).

L

Facing: BAYAZIT MOSQUE.

In Broussa we can see, in the Yeşil Cami, a building of such beauty that no Ottoman work after the conquest ever eclipsed it; and in this mosque, the Ulu Cami, the Muradiye and other mosques, we can see the prototypes of the earliest mosques erected after the conquest in Constantinople. The model of St. Sophia was not copied until the mosque of Bayazit was erected in 1501.

Mehmet II, the conqueror, turned eight churches into mosques, including the great church of St. Sophia, the Pantepoptes, and the Pantócrator. He built four new mosques, of which the greatest was on the fourth hill; for this he destroyed the ruinous church of the Holy Apostles, once the imperial mausoleum, some of whose materials were used in his mosque. The architect is variously named Christodoulos and Atik Sinan, and these may both be names for the same person, if he were a Christian Greek induced later by the Sultan's favour to embrace Islam. Sixteenth-century travellers have described this mosque as a great domed room, with a half-dome on the east, over the *mihrab*, and small lateral domes on either side; it seems to have owed nothing to St. Sophia, except the eastern half-dome, unlike the big, undistinguished eighteenth-century mosque which now replaces it. Damaged in the earthquakes of 1677 and 1690, the original mosque of Fatih (the conqueror) is said to have been razed to the earth after the 1766 earthquake, to make place for the present building.

The mosques that survive from the reign of the conqueror are, as his own mosque appears to have been, modelled on the Ottoman mosques of Asia Minor, and the same is true of the first years of the following reign. The mosque of Murad Pasha, a renegade Palaeologue who died as a Turkish general, is an exact copy of the Broussa mosques: two bays vaulted by unequal domes. The small mosque of Rumi Mehmet Pasha, another renegade, in Scutari (1471), and of Atik Ali Pasha, the eunuch vizir of Bayazit II (1497), have a more interesting plan: a central dome flanked by lateral domes, with a half-dome in the east – the plan (as we are told) of the original mosque of Fatih, though this was surely very much larger.

In short, for nearly fifty years after the conquest no mosque was built in Constantinople so good as those in Broussa or Adrianople. If acquaintance with St. Sophia made any immediate effect upon Ottoman architects, the effect was one of discouragement and paralysis. The mosque of Bayazit II, built by Hayreddin between 1501 and 1506 was the first building directly inspired by St. Sophia.

Built on the third hill, which it shares with the mosque of Süleyman, the mosque of Bayazit stands at one of the great traffic centres of modern Constantinople; on another side of the square of Bayazit are the hideous buildings of the University of Istanbul, and it backs on to the covered bazaars. Nearby, shaded by trees, there is a pleasant outdoor restaurant and café. On the pavement outside the mosque, hundreds of pigeons strut and flutter and coo, descendants of a pair of pigeons given to Bayazit II by a poor widow for his mosque; they may not be killed and are as philoprogenitive as all their kind. The pigeon is a mosque fowl, unlucky in houses. It is an act of piety to feed them, and also a favourite pastime with tourists, and boys are at hand peddling corn or seeds for the purpose. Pigeons perch on the many domes of the court, on the window-sills and edge of the roof, and give the name of the 'Pigeons' Mosque' to the mosque of Bayazit. If you feed the pigeons outside this mosque with grain, you may expect to hear news of absent friends.

The exterior of this mosque is a little confused and fussy. The great rectangle made up of the square mosque and its square courtyard has sent out two small lateral wings at the west end of the mosque, each roofed with five small cupolas, a reminiscence of the Ulu Cami at Broussa, grafted on to a plan derived from St. Sophia. But the courtyard, the first of its kind and the model of so many that were to be built later, is distinguished both from outside and from within; Hayreddin's catholic tastes have here been an advantage, for he has given it three noble doorways in which he has gone back to Seljuk art for inspiration, high stalactite portals into whose geometric design no curves enter. The great court is surrounded by a cloister; ancient columns, of granite or of verd-antique, with stalactite capitals support the pointed arches, whose archivolts are of alternating red and white marble; each of the twenty-four bays is vaulted by a dome. This court, busy with book-stalls and with sellers of chaplets, has more life than any other mosque courtyard and preserves more of the atmosphere of old Turkey, though it lacks the repose of the great, tranquil courts of Fatih, of Selim or of Süleyman.

Before entering this, the earliest of the great imperial mosques, it is the moment to say something about the mosque as a religious and architectural conception. Its origin is the courtyard of the Prophet's house at Medina: a crier from the wall-top summoned his companions to join him for public worship, a well was nearby for ablution, and in the courtyard was a fallen tree-trunk on which the Prophet stood to preach. A stone indicated the direction of Jerusalem, the holy city. It was a place for prayer and preaching, like a meeting-house of the Society of Friends, where no spot is especially sacred or mysterious. Later ages encircled the courtyard with a cloister for cover, added a further covered building on the side towards which prayer was directed, built a fountain (*chadrivan*), erected a prayer-niche (*mihrab*) in place of the stone, a pulpit for preaching, and a minaret for the crier (*muezzin*).

'The Mosque,' says Mr. E. M. Forster,[1] 'sets itself against a profound tendency of human nature – the tendency to think one place holier than another... It does not fulfil what is to most of us the function of a religious building: the outward expression of an inward ecstasy. It embodies no crisis, leads up through no gradation of nave and choir, and employs no hierarchy of priests. Equality before God – so doubtfully proclaimed by Christianity – lies at the very root of Islam; and the mosque is essentially a courtyard for the Faithful to worship in, either in solitude or under due supervision.'

The mosque is a holy place, but not uncomfortably holy; it is often used as a school, and no one minds it being used as a place for quiet conversation. Though it is sanctified by prayer, and claims respect, yet it is not the special dwelling-place of an omnipresent Deity. It is therefore a kind and welcoming place to the stranger, whatever his religion may be; all that is asked of him is that he should be reverent and nice-mannered, and that he should not dirty the carpets on which prayer is to be made – for this reason he must take off his shoes, or (at the big, touristic mosques) cover them with slippers hired at the door. There are pigeon-holes for shoes at the door, or they may be carried in (with their soles together) and placed in one of the little wooden troughs provided in the mosque. It is pleasant to walk shoeless over the soft carpets after wearying one's feet on the seven hills of Constantinople, or to sit quietly on the floor listening to the hum of children, rocking themselves to and fro, learning the Koran by heart.

The reverent atmosphere of the mosques, and the attentiveness at prayers, were well described by Aaron Hill:[2] 'They Pray with Fervour and a fix'd Attention, never turning like too many Inconsiderate *Christians*

---

[1] *Abinger Harvest*: 'The Mosque'.
[2] *The Present State of the Ottoman Empire* (London, 1709).

in our Noisy Churches, to behold people pass behind them; all is *still*, and *softly* Sacred; no Man mutters Prayers of Course, and Gapes the while to see about him how his Neighbours Cloaths are Fashion'd; no loud Indecent Whispers Interrupt Devotion, to inform some busie *Irreligious* Asker, who Addresses such a Lady, and how much such a Woman brought her Husband; no *opening* Pews and *Shutting* them again, disturb the Congregation with their needless Clamour; no *Holy-Talking*, and *Conceited* Hypocrite outruns the *Parson* with her zealous Lips, while her lew'd *Eyes*, behind a Fan, are laughing heartily at some poor Jest her Ears have listen'd to; no turn'd up Eyelids seem to speak her Thoughts on Heaven, while a *Wry-mouth* or scornful turn of her affected Nostrils, declare her Observation running o'er the Faults or Ill *Contrivances* of her Neighbour's Pettycoat. A *Turkish Mosque* is free from Noise, and all within it so *sedately* bent on What they do, that 'tis a matter of Sufficient Wonder, to behold so many met together in so deep a stillness. And indeed, so very sacred do the Turks esteem the Act of Prayer, that if the casual sting of some small *Gnat*, the scratching of their Heads, or any other common Accident but chance to interrupt them, they begin again though almost *ended*, thinking such prevented *Prayers* of no *Effect*, or *Virtue* whatsoever but neglected as unworthy the Great Ear of Heaven.'

In Cairo the first mosques are huge courtyards, large enough to contain immense crowds for the Caliph's Friday prayers; such are the mosques of Ibn Tulun, of El Hakim and El Azhar. Later smaller mosques of the courtyard type were built, such as El Mardany, and small cruciform schools (*madrassas*). The colder climate of Turkey made the courtyard inadequate as a shelter for the Faithful, and in the Ulu Cami twenty-five domes covered them; after the mosque of Bayazit II we find great mosques based on the ground plan of the Great Church — the courtyard survives, but it is only a courtyard, though the side nearest the mosque is often covered with matting and ready for prayer should the mosque be shut, or overcrowded, and there are small balconies for the muezzins.

The imperial mosques of Constantinople, of which that of Bayazit II is the earliest, the foundations of Sultans, are the largest mosques in the city; each has two minarets (like the mosque of Bayazit) or more, an imperial tribune for the Sultan's use, and always a *mimber* (pulpit) for Friday prayers. Some of the lesser mosques, where the Friday prayers are not made, have only a reading-desk (*koursi*); they have not always a minaret.

The mosque of Bayazit II, like so many others, has been uglified by white-wash, and by hideous coloured stencil which does what it can to obscure the architectural features; it cannot do much, for a characteristic of Hayreddin's mosque, which sharply differentiates it from the Great Church that was its model, is the distinctness of the parts. While the dome of St. Sophia floats ethereally over the centre, the dome of Bayazit is clearly demarcated by a jutting row of stalactites supporting a kind of whispering gallery; it might have been screwed on like a lid. All the other component parts of the mosque stand out as clearly marked. The mystery of St. Sophia is not there, but it would not be appropriate to the spirit of Islam, any more than the dark narrow aisles of the Great Church would serve the purposes of a form of public worship which does not entail processions; the wide and lofty aisles of Bayazit, unencumbered by galleries, are integral parts of the great meeting-house.

The next imperial mosque to be erected was the mosque of Sultan Selim I, erected in 1522 on the fifth hill, by his son Süleyman the Magnificent. There is no good reason for supposing this to be an early work of the great architect Sinan, though the attribution is sometimes made. The main part of the mosque is a great, simple, square room whose dome rests on four unelaborate, stalactite pendentives; this mosque is only 'two-storeyed' and therefore the vast and beautifully proportioned dome hangs low and seems to form half of the room rather than to roof it. The plain walls are decorated only with faience lunettes over the lower doors and windows, and the *mihrab* and *mimber* are of quiet elegance. Such a building would be a far better model for a church of any Christian denomination that does not want provision for ritual than any Byzantine original; it is a great space, with admirable acoustics for public prayer and for preaching.

The exterior of the dome is less pleasing; it rises awkwardly from the square substructure, and the two lateral wings, vaulted with multiple domes in the Ulu fashion, like the wings of Bayazit, join awkwardly to the great prayer hall. The rectangular courtyard, with its noble doors, like those of Bayazit, and with splendid lunettes of early faience from Iznik over the windows of the cloister, is one of the most beautiful in Constantinople. The mosque stands in a conspicuous position, and is one of the landmarks seen from Pera or from the Golden Horn, and its terrace commands a splendid view towards the north.

The work of the great architect Sinan is first seen in the mosque of the

Shehzade. He was born of Christian parents in Caesarea, and first came to Constantinople as a janissary at the age of twenty. He served as a military engineer in Persia and Egypt, and thus had the opportunity of studying the architecture of other Islamic peoples. He was already over fifty when this, his first work, was completed in 1548; he was to live till over eighty, and some three hundred works are ascribed to him.

This mosque lies on the great central street that runs from St. Sophia to the Adrianople Gate, and its outer courtyard backs on to the aqueduct of Valens. Its name means 'the mosque of the prince', and it was erected by Süleyman, after a change of heart, to commemorate his eldest son, Prince Mustafa, whom he had had strangled.

In the mosque of Bayazit II, Hayreddin followed the model of St. Sophia in placing half-domes to east and west of his central dome, and filling his north and south arches with a window-pierced tympanum; Sinan in the Shehzade has thrown two additional half-cupolas to north and south, producing a great symmetrical cruciform space in the centre of his square mosque. Although particularly odious stencil obscures the lines of this monument, on repeated visits this strikes the eye less, and the real merit and grandeur of the design make themselves felt. The architect of the mosque of Ahmed I owed very much to this first work of Sinan, and outdoes its one fault of squareness and monotony; he also copies the fluting by which, on the upper part of the four great central piers, Sinan has sought to prolong the falling effect of his stalactites.

The great mosque of Süleyman the Magnificent on the third hill is Sinan's greatest work in Constantinople; it was erected between 1550 and 1557. In this work, reverting to a ground plan very like that of St. Sophia, Sinan raised upon it a building that is really a mosque and not a church. It at once impresses as no mere reproduction, but as a work of living art, and as an essentially religious work, though not the work of the Christian religion. The unity and majesty of this monument, which has not had to suffer the loss of surface beauty that befell St. Sophia, are so great that there are moments when one is tempted to think that Süleyman has nearly outdone Justinian.

Like the Shehzade, the Süleymaniye is a vast auditorium; it has not the mysterious exedras or the dark aisles of the Great Church, its open aisles are only extensions of the huge, central space. The central dome, smaller and higher in proportion than that of St. Sophia, seems to be a point to which the whole mosque rises, rather than an ethereal, floating covering, hanging down from Heaven by a golden chain; it rests on four gigantic piers, into which are inlet tall stalactite niches of exquisite beauty. The stalactite pendentives of the aisle domes are also of extreme elegance. The rich east end, not in itself holy or mysterious, draws the eyes in the direction in which they should be drawn for prayer; there are fine stained-glass windows, the work of Ibrahim the drunkard, and beautiful panels of faience round the elegantly carved *mihrab*. The arches of the aisles, beneath the great, window-pierced tympana (modelled on those of St. Sophia and of Bayazit) are supported by four huge, porphyry columns. One of these was the Column of Virginity, which once stood near the church of the Holy Apostles on the fourth hill; it has been shortened to serve its present purpose. A second column once stood in the Great Palace, perhaps as pedestal to an imperial statue; the other two were brought from Alexandretta.

The Süleymaniye is a pleasant and comforting place in which to linger; sitting restfully without one's shoes, leaning against a pier, one can watch the light pouring in through the transeptal windows, or from the west one can gaze into the solemn, blue sanctuary, with its white calligraphic ornamentation, and its jewelled windows. At dusk, when the great circle of little lights is lit, the effect is enchanting. One must admire the interior of St. Sophia more, but it is never such an agreeable place to be in . . . a cold museum, and not a place of life and prayer.

The exterior of the mosque of Süleyman is of a planned and ordered beauty that puts the muddled exterior of the Great Church into the shade; the great dome, the half-domes, and the lesser domes of the aisles are skilfully grouped, and are further set off by the little domes of the courtyard, and by the four minarets which rise one from each corner of it, a higher pair of minarets on the east, and a lower pair on the west. The eastern minarets are surrounded each by three, the western minarets by two, balconies: the four minarets signify that Süleyman was the fourth Sultan since the capture of Constantinople, the ten balconies that he was the tenth of the Osmanli line. The fountain in the court is rectangular, small and graceful, happily without one of those great extinguisher roofs which disfigure the fountains in so many mosques.

The huge mosque built by the architect Daoud for Ahmed I was built between 1609 and 1616 on the side of the hippodrome, and occupies part of the site of the Great Palace. The seventeenth-century traveller Grelot says this of its foundation: ' 'Tis true, that in regard it requires a vast expence to erect a Mosquee . . . the Grand Signors are expressly forbid to undertake so difficult an enterprise until they shall have won from the Infidels Cities, Provinces or Kingdoms sufficient to defray the excessive charges of such magnificent Piles. However Sultan Achmet, though he had not by any conquest extended the bounds of the Empire, resolv'd to Build a Mosquee, to the end he might eternize his name . . . and when he had finish'd the Pile, because he had slighted his Chaplains' exhortations, [they] call'd it . . . the Temple of the Incredulous.'[1]

Ahmed was also reproached for impiety by the Sherif of Mecca, because, in his anxiety for the glory of his mosque, he gave it six minarets, a number previously reserved for the mosque of the Qaaba; rather than pull one down, he gave a seventh minaret to Mecca, to preserve its superiority. His mosque is unique in Constantinople in having two minarets at the east end, as well as a minaret at each corner of the courtyard.

In this mosque Daoud returns to the cross-plan invented by Sinan in the Shehzade Mosque; he has produced the greatest and grandest central room, upheld only by four huge fluted piers, and this monument commands admiration. Unhappily the spaciousness due to this ground-plan only emphasizes the squareness and monotony which the rectangular plan of the Süleymaniye avoided. As Fergusson has written: 'If the plan were divided into quarters, each of the four quarters would be found to be identical, and the effect is consequently painfully mechanical and prosaic. The design of each wall is also nearly the same; they have the same number of windows spaced in the same manner, and the side of the Kibleh (*Mihrab*) is scarcely more richly decorated than the others.'

The mosque of Sultan Ahmed owes its title of 'Blue Mosque' to the magnificent Nicaean tiles, which begin above the lower windows and extend as a lining all round the gallery; the rest of the 'blueness' is bogus, produced by heavy blue stencil on the fluted piers and round the dome and on the archivolts of the four great arches: this very much detracts from the effect of the beautiful tiles and even gives a certain vulgarity to the great mosque, but unquestionably adds to its spurious attraction. The mosque, as a result of its open site, and the absence of stained glass (except for some modern windows at the east end), is flooded with a crude light

[1] Grelot: *A Late Voyage to Constantinople* (made English by J. Philips), (London, 1683).

which makes the genuine blue decoration hard to distinguish from the false, especially as there is none at eye-level.

Nevertheless, it is a noble and impressive interior, and the *mihrab*, the *mimber*, and the imperial gallery with its handsome gilt screen are all very fine work. No courtyard is more stately, and, like that of the Süleymaniye, it is fortunate in its fountain. And as for the exterior of the mosque, rising superbly, at the side of the hippodrome, it forms a contrast with the muddled dumpiness of St. Sophia, which tempts one to abandon any last regrets for the fall of Byzantium.

The last imperial mosque built in the great period of Ottoman architecture is the Yeni Cami (New Mosque), or more properly the mosque Yeni-Validé (new mosque of the queen-mother), on the square near the Galata bridge, marking the entrance to Stamboul. It was begun by the widow of Murad III, the mother of Mehmet III, 'who being one of the most aspiring and accomplish'd Lady's that ever entered the *Seraglio*, would most certainly spare for no cost, when she had once design'd to eternize her memory by a curiosity in architecture. To which intent she could not have chosen a situation more advantageous'.[1] Work on this mosque was interrupted at the death of Mehmet III in 1603, and it was only completed in 1663 by the mother of Mehmet IV.

This mosque is built on the cruciform plan of the Shehzade and Ahmed, but while the Shehzade has no galleries on the north and south, and those of Ahmed are pushed back far towards the wall and count for little in the general effect, the galleries of the Yeni Cami form broad enough aisles to obviate the squareness of the plan; they also help to differentiate the east wall. The great cruciform piers, covered with faience, that support the dome, are less fussy than the fluted piers of the Shehzade or of Ahmed. The interior of this mosque has great dignity and repose; light filters in through good stained-glass windows at the east, and the south side of the mosque is too much shaded to admit the crude burst of light that comes into the mosque of Ahmed. Good, though late, Nicaean tiles cover the walls and piers up to the sill of the upper windows – they can be studied at eye-level as those of Ahmed cannot; and the stencil decoration further up is light and inoffensive. The *koursi* is of very fine polygonal marquetry, with mother of pearl and ivory inlay; the fine grey stone *mihrab* with gilded stalactites is matched by the *mimber* on its south, and on a correspond-

[1] Grelot, loc. cit.

ing place on the north part of the east wall is a superb panel of inlaid marbles.

Lady Mary Wortley Montagu went far, perhaps, in describing this mosque as 'the most prodigious, and, I think, the most imposing structure I ever saw', but, after the Süleymaniye, it has a more satisfying and harmonious interior than any other of the greater mosques. The court, loftier in proportion, and smaller than that of Ahmed, has a beautiful fountain; its east wall is adapted for prayer, should the mosque be closed or overcrowded. On either side of the great door is one tall stalactite *mihrab*, panelled below in faience with a charming design of three sanctuary lamps, and there are pretty balconies for muezzins.

It may be well to leave the imperial mosques with this tribute from a Byzantinologist, one who has devoted a loving study to even the meanest monuments of Byzantium, to such ill-smelling ruins as the Gastria, that little reward it.[1] 'Strangely enough, the ideal of Byzantine architects is realized better in the imperial mosques that crown the summits of Stamboul, and rise above the hills on which they stand, as naturally and proudly as a peak lifts its head into the sky. How puny are the domes of the Pantocrator or those of the Pantepoptes compared with the dome of the Mosque of the Conqueror, or the dome over the Mosque of Süleyman the Magnificent, or the dome of the Mosque Shehzade, or even the dome of the Mosque of Sultan Selim! Nor is it only in their external aspect that the great mosques fulfil the Byzantine ideal. They do so likewise within. The long pillared lines of the basilica have vanished. In the Mosque of Süleyman the Magnificent only four piers and four columns, the latter from Byzantine building, break the interior view. In the Mosque of Sultan Ahmed only four piers uphold the roof. And at the same time, what spaciousness! What loftiness and grandeur!'

In the mosques, indeed, Anthemius's desire for a great, domed hall is fulfilled, and the purely Islamic elements are as important as the heritage of Byzantium: the stalactite design, whether in the pendentives of domes, in *mihrabs* or other wall-niches, or in the capitals of columns; the geometric, rectilinear Seljuk portals; and the faience, as characteristic a form of wall-decoration as the mosaics of Byzantine churches and palaces.

Faience provides a cool, bright covering to the walls; it does not shine

[1] Alexander van Millingen, *Constantinople* (London, 1906).

with a mysterious, inner luminosity like that of mosaic; it is a surface, and nothing more. Yet as a surface it is bright and luminous, not dulled by the grime of centuries like the marble revetment of several Byzantine churches, where all colours have turned to a uniform grey.

The earliest ceramic work in Constantinople is to be seen in the Çinili Kiosque (porcelain kiosque), that charming building erected by Mehmet II, which stands opposite the modern Museum of Antiquities. Here is preserved a magnificent Seljuk work, a *mihrab* from Karaman; the faience stalactites are great, plain, dark blue lumps. The walls of the Çinili Kiosque are decorated with monochrome tiles, blue or black, arranged in patterns on the same principle as mosaic, where no tessara is patterned or particoloured. Some of the tiles show traces of a rubbed-off gold arabesque, like that in the Green Mosque of Broussa.

The further history of Ottoman faience through all its stages, until the eighteenth century, may be studied in a small but well-chosen museum, arranged in one of the rooms of the Serail. A great date in its development is 1514, when Selim I entered Tabriz and directed seven hundred families of potters westwards; some were installed at Nicaea (Iznik).

The earlier Nicene tiles may be seen in Constantinople, as well as in the museum, in the mosque and tomb of Selim I, also in the mosques of Ibrahim Pasha (*c.* 1551) near the Silivri gate, and of Ahmed Pasha (*c.* 1554) near Topkapu. The colours employed in the first period are yellow, pistachio green, dark and light blue, aubergine, black and white. There are calligraphic inscriptions from the Koran, geometrical designs (notably in the peristyle of the tomb of Selim I, where the panels have a polygonal border that reminds one of the marquetry on a wooden *koursi*), and floral ornament. The tiles of this period are used to decorate a panel or a lunette, never to cover the walls of a building.

In the second half of the sixteenth century technical perfection was attained; pistachio green and yellow now disappear, and are replaced by leaf-green, and by a tomato-red made of liquefied coral which always stands up in low relief. The background is a matt white, on it are floral designs made up of imaginary flowers, but also of tulips, carnations, roses, long wild hyacinths, and almond blossom. This period could be studied in the tomb of Roxelana (if one were ever allowed into it); hardly more accessible are the rooms of Murad III in the harem of the Serail (1578). It can be seen with ease in the peristyle of the mosque of Rustem Pasha

(1560): here a flat *mihrab* looks like a brilliant Persian prayer rug hung against the wall; the niche is framed in a basket-design outline of tomato-red, within which is a lovely free pattern of flowering trees with aubergine trunks, of tulips, carnations and lilies. Equally splendid is the east wall of the lovely mosque of Sokullu Mehmet (1571), where the *mimber* has a faience spire; or the fine floral panels in the mosque of Atik Validé at Scutari (1583), where tomato-red vases hold sprays of blue fruit blossom; or the lovely red-currant panels in the little Tekiedj Ibrahim Agha (1591), an extra mural mosque built by Ibrahim Agha, a manufacturer of felt hats, not far outside Topkapu; or the panels with marvellous tomato-red borders, like those in the rooms of Murad III, in the small mosque of Ramazan effendi (1586), in Samatya; or the faience *mihrab*, the only *mihrab* in a Constantinople mosque in which the stalactites also are made of tiles, in the mosque of Piyale Pasha (1573), north of the Golden Horn.

In the early seventeenth century Nicaean ceramic, though still splendid, is in decline; red is rare, and becomes paler, and most tiles are only blue and white. This period can be studied in the mosques of Rustem Pasha, of Sultan Ahmed, in the Yeni Validé mosque, and in the Çinili Cami (1640) in Scutari; in the last the *mimber*, like that of Sokullu Mehmet, has a pointed spire of faience. The lovely blue and white Baghdad Kiosque in the Serail also belongs to this group.

By the beginning of the eighteenth century Iznik had almost ceased production. Under Ahmed III a number of potters established themselves in the Tekfur Saray, the palace of Constantine Porphyrogenitus. Their work was much less refined than that of Iznik, there are often large, empty spaces of greenish-white background, with a coarse, bold, blue design. Nevertheless, the Tekfur Saray tiles outside the tomb of Eyüp, or in the mosque of Hekimoğlu Ali Pasha (1734) are not ineffective.

The story of Ottoman ceramic ends sadly, in the later eighteenth century, with mass-produced stuff influenced by bad Italian models; some of this is to be seen in the harem of the Serail.

The smaller mosques of Sinan now claim attention. The Büyük Cami at Scutari, prominent on its raised platform opposite the wharf of the ferry-boats, from which it is also called Iskele Cami (or the mosque of the wharf) is an ingenious design; it was built in 1548. Here he has adapted, on a much smaller scale, the cruciform plans of the Shehzade, amputating the western half-dome and its frame, and creating a rectangular mosque with an entirely original plan. It was built for the Princess Mihrimah, daughter of Süleyman the Magnificent, and wife of Rustem Pasha.

In 1558 Sinan built another mosque for the same princess, on the sixth hill, near the Adrianople gate – the highest position of any mosque in the city. In this mosque, where he had again a smaller room to provide, he has reversed the plan of the Shehzade. There he adapted the plan of St. Sophia, opening out half-cupolas to north and south, where the Great Church had arches closed by window-pierced lunettes; here he has closed the east and west arches, and the dome rises on four lunettes. Inside, the effect is that of a grand lantern, into which light pours, silvered and diluted, for there is good glass throughout the mosque. Outside, the dome rises clear, unimpeded by half-domes; the three domes of the north and south aisles are too low and small to detract from its single effect. This grand mosque is well fitted for its site, and forms a striking feature in many views of the land walls, which run so near it. The interior, unfortunately, has been most cruelly stencilled, and there is almost as much pain as pleasure in looking at it; otherwise the restoration, that followed the 1894 earthquake, has been well carried out.

Five years later, Sinan built the lovely mosque of Mihrimah's husband, Rustem Pasha, near the Golden Horn. Here again there are low aisles, but the central room is an octagon; the dome rests on four closed arches, alternating with half-cupolas, and these are borne by the east and west walls, and by four octagonal piers, sheathed in faience. The walls of this mosque are entirely covered with faience up to the height of the capitals of these piers, and above there is more faience in the spandrels of the dome. In this mosque, as in the Yeni Cami and the mosque of Sultan Ahmed, the faience seems to be an integral part of the design of the mosque, and not an added decoration: Rustem Pasha is the finest tiled mosque in Constantinople, and it is right that it should be much visited by tourists, as it is.

The mosque of Sokullu Mehmet Pasha, a more estimable successor of Rustem in the dignity of Grand Vizir, was erected by his wife, the Princess Esmakhan, daughter of Selim II, in 1571, with Sinan as architect. It stands to the south-west of the hippodrome, on the site of the church of St. Anastasia; that martyr's relics had been translated here from Nicomedia, and her church was the rallying point of the Catholic party, under St. Gregory of Nazianzen, during the council of 381.

This lovely mosque has a hexagonal central space: the dome rests on the east and west walls, and on four half-cupolas, of which either pair is supported by a beautiful octagonal pier, gently fluted in its upper part. The north and south galleries, light and elegant, are supported on small, brass-bound, marble columns, with capitals of two orders of stalactites. There are plaques of faience with floral designs over the lower windows, and with Koranic inscriptions over the windows of the gallery; this, and the great faience east wall of the hexagon, with its floral panels, and Koranic labels and roundels, are all beyond praise. It is a mosque decorated with, not covered with, faience, unlike that of Rustem Pasha; perhaps it has the loveliest and most harmonious interior of any mosque in the city; the lighting is soft and peaceful, the recent restoration has been discreet, and there is very little modern decoration to regret. The beautiful mosque of Ahmed Pasha, an earlier experiment of Sinan with a hexagonal plan, was his prentice work for the masterpiece of Sokullu Mehmet.

The courtyard of Sokullu Mehmet has a low cloister with ogival arches, with a heavy-shaded fountain, and with a picturesque gatehouse on the west. The west end of the mosque has a seven-bay peristyle, with a high dome over the door.

In 1577 Sinan built a mosque at the orders of Sokullu Mehmet Pasha himself, on the north side of the Golden Horn, in Galata. This mosque, now generally known as the mosque of Azap Kapu, or of Mehmet Pasha, stands raised from street level on a lower construction, near the head of the Atatürk bridge; in its situation it is reminiscent of some London city churches.

The central space is octagonal, like that of Rustem Pasha: the polygonal piers, delicately fluted in the upper part, are as successful as those in the Sokullu Mehmet mosque; this form of pier decoration, so lovely in these small mosques, is awkward when applied to the massive piers of a great building like Ahmed or the Shehzade. The chancel-like east end is an innovation. The mosque is two-storeyed, like that of Selim I, and the dome, hanging low, seems with that of Selim to be the loveliest Ottoman dome in Constantinople.

In 1573, in the mosque of the admiral, Piyale Pasha, Sinan made a return to the Ulu type of ground plan, and erected a mosque vaulted in six domes, resting on two columns. A recent writer[1] sees this reversion to an old

[1] Ulya Vogt-Göknil, loc. cit.

plan as a way in which Sinan took a rest, after his triumphal creation, the Selimiye in Adrianople, to avoid the temptation of repeating himself. There was no successor to the Piyale Mosque, built by Sinan or his disciples; it is an isolated throw-back.

This is a beautiful and peaceful mosque, situated in a country village inland from the wharf of Kasim Pasha, on the north side of the Golden Horn: the surrounding cemetery and the ancient trees have the atmosphere of a country churchyard. It deserves a visit, not only for the beauty of its faience, but also for the prettiness of its exterior; there are cloisters on the north and south, and there is a lovely open colonnade in lieu of a peristyle on the west. The minaret rises, as a church tower might, in the middle of the façade.

Another experimental mosque is that of another admiral, Kiliç Ali Pasha, the colonizer of Samos, erected by Sinan in Tophane in 1580. This, like the two Mehmet Pasha mosques, has lately been very well restored. There is no mosque more like a church in design; the ground plan of St. Sophia has been followed in miniature, there is a projecting east end, and the galleries, instead of being recessed, cover the whole width of the aisles. It is as much a throw-back to St. Sophia, as the Piyale Mosque is to the mosques of Broussa. There is very good faience decoration at the east end and over the lower windows.

The seventeenth century, apart from the mosque of Ahmed I, and the completion of the Yeni Cami was no great period of building; to the eighteenth-century artistic revival, which began in the reign of Ahmed III, we owe some interesting work.

The Yeni Validé Mosque at Scutari was erected by Ahmed in memory of his mother, and finished in 1710; unlike later mosques, it is unaffected by Western influence – a pretty if decadent Ottoman building with an octagonal central space. The late greenish faience round the *mihrab* is not to be despised, but its chief attraction is the open-work *turbeh* (tomb), a stone frame whose sides and roof are metal grilles; inside are trees, and tiger-lilies and a tombstone. This pretty tomb (there is another such near the Burnt Column), together with a fountain of similar design, greatly ornaments the exterior of this mosque.

The Hekimoglu Ali Pasha Mosque (1734), on the south side of the seventh hill, also pure Ottoman work, is another charming example of eighteenth-century elegance. One entrance to the enclosure is through a

Facing, above: FATIH MOSQUE.
        below: UNIVERSITY QUARTER BUILT IN THE SIXTEENTH CENTURY
        BY SINAN. THE SÜLEYMAN MOSQUE IS IN THE DISTANCE.

beautiful gate-building with an open loggia, the other entrance is adorned by a *sebil* (drinking-fountain) with a pretty grille. It is a hexagonal mosque with aisles, on the model of Sokullu Mehmet Pasha, and the *mihrab* is set in an apse that is almost a chancel. The minor arts of the period make here a distinguished showing in the handsome stone and gilt *mihrab*, in the fine imperial tribune, and the tiles of bold, if coarse, design.

The mosque of Laleli (1763), the 'Tulip Mosque', owes its name to general admiration of its flower-like beauty, for it was not erected until long after the reign of the 'Tulip Prince', Ahmed III.

Unlike the Yeni Validé of Scutari, or the Hekimoğlu Ali Pasha Mosque, this mosque shows strong signs of Western influence. The plan is that of an octagon inscribed in a rectangle but, because of the arrangement of the columns, the interior effect is almost that of a cruciform, transeptal church, and the east end is a square-ended chancel. It is an elegant interior, full of light, with good marble panelling on the walls and the *mimber*; it has been fortunate in escaping lightly from the Italian white-wash-and-stencil vandals, who have so badly disfigured so many mosques in Constantinople. There is a certain amount of rococo detail which is highly offensive to purist admirers of Ottoman art; the almost purely Italian outside galleries do perhaps look strange on a building whose main conception is Turkish and Islamic, but it would be difficult to resent the charming, renaissance flying buttresses at the east end.

But the Nuruosmaniye Mosque, begun in 1748 by Mahmud I and finished by Osman III in 1755, marks the climax in eighteenth-century sacred architecture. This is, like the mosque of Selim I, a single, vast, aisle-less, domed room and, as in the mosque of Mihrimah, the dome rests on four great blocked arches, pierced by windows; the multitude and size of these windows make it a great lantern, to which it owes its name — 'Light of Osman'. There are no piers, but galleries in the thickness of the wall; a fine, heavy cornice with a gold inscription projects above the second course of windows, and the *mihrab* is in an apse large enough to hold an altar. The square fluted columns, and the trefoil arches in the gallery are wholly western, and this mosque, with a little adaptation, would make an admirable model for a Protestant place of worship. The horse-shoe-shaped court, in which there is no fountain, is a feature that is not found elsewhere.

M

Facing, left: SULTAN AHMED MOSQUE, INTERIOR.
    right: RUSTEM PASHA MOSQUE, INTERIOR.

The mosque of Fatih (the Conqueror), restored in 1771 after repeated earthquake damage, is a big, bright, dignified, but uninteresting mosque, built on the plan of the mosques of the Shehzade and of Sultan Ahmed. Within, it is disfigured by great black swags of stencilled arabesque, but the courtyard is stately, and the exterior is a splendid ornament to the fourth hill.

The mosques of Constantinople are, on the whole, the most beautiful class of buildings in the city, surpassing what now remains of the churches, and very much surpassing the secular buildings of either empire. They are the most welcoming buildings to the stranger. The greater mosques are open all day, and the lesser always open at the hours of prayer, nor is there any fanaticism or hostility on the part of the Faithful; a Christian may remain in the mosques even during the public prayers, and feels no discomfort in doing so.

The beauty of these buildings, protected as they are by Moslem iconoclasm from objects of piety, is often very much impaired by vile, coloured, stencil designs added early in this century or at the end of the last. And yet traces of older and better decoration survive and could serve as models for restoration: the dome of the Çinili Mosque in Scutari is painted with a faint, old, red and green diaper of Arabian design; in the Sokullu Mehmet there is a little patch of good pavement, and in the same mosque (under the western gallery) some good, original, panelled and painted roof; similar roof panels are to be seen in the Ahmed Pasha Mosque (under the galleries), in the Tekiedj Ibrahim Agha, and probably elsewhere.

The stained glass is of two kinds. In the Süleymaniye, and in many other places, it is the bright, jewelled window of the Arabian mosques of Cairo — floral or geometric designs in richly coloured glass, with an absence of white or light glass. These windows are set in an elaborate plaster tracery, which interferes with the effect if they are seen from too near. Often there is an outside window for protection, of plain glass in circular or hexagonal panes; this plain outer tracery may further complicate the effect of the delicate plaster frame within. Another kind of stained glass, to be seen in the Shehzade and elsewhere, is perhaps more suitable to pale Thracian skies than the glass designed to soften the blazing sun of Egypt — a pale, almost white background is set with jewelled lumps of bright translucent colour, arranged in a simple design, perhaps as an inner border.

After the Laleli Mosque, and the reconstruction of Fatih, there has been no mosque-building of consequence. The mosque of Ortaköy (1853) rises pleasantly enough beside the Bosphorus, and the Dolmabahçe Mosque, built in the same year, rises as a graceful silhouette against the Bosphorus and the shores of Scutari, when looked down upon from the hill behind, a pretty evening view. But the Validé Mosque (1871) at Aksaray is a disgusting building, hideously over-ornamented: a perverse butcher might have modelled it in lard. It is one of the many reproaches that may be made against Constantinople that there is no modern architecture in the City that is above contempt.

Of the tombs which stand in the outer enclosure of nearly all the greater mosques, and which flank many lesser mosques, very few can be seen; in Cairo such tombs may remain open, when the mosque is open, or some obliging attendant will be found to have the key. In Constantinople they remain sealed: the glum officialdom in charge of the monuments may wish to preserve them for posterity, but will not let the eyes of the present generation look at them; the main function of custodians seems to be to keep people out. Grudgingly, a few tombs are opened on Wednesday afternoons; it will surprise no one who has passed a few days in the city that the morose guardian of the tomb of Süleyman should not be able or willing to show also the beautiful tomb of Roxelana which stands in the same enclosure.

On Roxelana's separate tomb, Grelot remarks: 'As the *Turks* never admit their wives to pray with 'em when they are alive, so they never suffer them to lye with 'em in the same Tomb, when they are dead. Believing their old wives shall never be admitted to accompany them into Paradise, where they hope to find far younger and handsomer, leaving their cast terrestrial Wives to make much of the *Giaours*, whose lot they pretend it will be to stand without doors.'

The two tombs would not be too great responsibility for one man, who could close one and open the other for visitors, if jealous authority would not suffer them to visit unattended places from which there is nothing easy to steal.

At the Selimiye the tomb of Selim I may be seen, though other tombs in the enclosure are kept shut, and the main duty of the guardian seems to be to prevent people from photographing so much as the exterior. The portico with the fine panels of early Nicaean faience is of great beauty and interest, but the interior of the tomb is dull. The great octagonal tomb of Süleyman the Magnificent is a masterpiece of Sinan's, and one of the most beautiful interiors in Constantinople. The dome is supported by an arcade of eight blind arches, of which the archivolts are formed of alternate chevrons of dark red and white marble; this arcade rests on eight porphyry columns with stalactite capitals. There is faience up to a thick, calligraphic dado, that runs above the lower windows, and above this a red and white marble revetment; in the spandrels of the arches there is more faience. In the upper windows light enters through small, circular panes of bottle-glass, framed in a stained-glass border; all the faience and stained glass in this beautiful room is of a high quality. The dark red dome is decorated with a wonderful diaper, in which there are roses of rock crystal with emerald centres. Ivory and walnut rails protect the cenotaph of Süleyman, and the tombs of Süleyman II and Ahmed II. In this tomb, as in the Green Mosque of Broussa, or as in the Baghdad Kiosque of the next century in the Serail, we are really in the gorgeous East; each of these lovely build-ings is wholly Islamic in inspiration, and combines extreme richness with the control imposed by a most refined and fastidious good taste: it is hard to believe that the vanished beauties of Byzantium included anything much more satisfying.

From this lovely tomb, and from descriptions published in the past by privileged people, one can imagine some of the beauty that is shut away in many jealously closed monuments: the early yellow tiles of the tomb of the Shehzade, the exquisite work of the best Nicaean period in the tomb of Roxelana, and in those of St. Sophia. It is difficult to lament, with a Turkish writer,[1] that so much Ottoman faience has been carried away into countries where it is more generously exhibited. Berlin obtained panels from the Shehzade and the St. Sophia tombs, as well as some from mosques: these were due to the enterprise of a Constantinople dentist who was employed to repair the tiles in many monuments; he extracted them, and inserted painted plaster in their place. A second dentist imitated him a quarter of a century later. It would seem that the best protection for monuments would be for them to be open and well known; in the long years of official closure, it is probable that there have been further depre-dations, and it would not be possible to call them undeserved.

The fountains of Constantinople, so numerous and so beautiful, being

[1] Halil Edhem: *Nos Mosquées de Stamboul* (Stamboul, 1934).

for the most part the result of acts of piety, should no doubt be classed with the Ottoman religious monuments. Apart from the fountain of ablutions (*chadrivan*) in front of every mosque, there are many other fountains erected by benefactors for the good of their own souls, or for the souls of others. Fountains are of two sorts: there is the *çeşme* from which water is fetched, or the *sebil*, a drinking-fountain; often the two are combined.

The loveliest fountains date from the early eighteenth century and are in the charming Turkish rococo style introduced in the reign of Ahmed III by Yirmisekis Mehmed Efendi, his ambassador in Paris. The finest and best preserved of these is the fountain erected by Ahmed III himself in 1728 on the site of the ancient Byzantine fountain Yeranion, east of St. Sophia, and near the outer gate of the Serail. This is a square structure with a basin (*çeşme*) on each face, and a *sebil*, a semi-circular projection at each corner, protected by a grille, through which cups of water were taken when it was in use. Each face is superbly decorated with coloured marble inlay, with carving and inscriptions. The top-heavy, pagoda-like roof, with its five little domes, is a piece of the Far East that has come to Turkey by way of Paris.

Ahmed III also erected a fountain at Scutari, near the wharf of the ferry-boats; this has been sunk by the raising of the road level, only the side facing the sea retains its decoration – though that is most beautiful – and the *sebils* have lost their grilles.

The Tophane fountain, near the mosque of Kiliç Ali Pasha, was erected by Mahmud I in 1732; this is in the same rococo style, and an old engraving shows that it had a flat projecting roof, and a dome in the middle of it. Unfortunately the roof is gone, and a dull balustrade surrounds the top of the fountain, quite destroying its character. The two fountains of Mahmud I's mother have been even less fortunate. The Bereketzade fountain near the Dominican church, just below the Tower of Galata, is said to have been restored by Saliha, the widow of Mustafa II, but is almost certainly a new structure erected by her on the site of an early fountain; it has suffered much from moving, and there is not a great deal of her building left. The Azapkapu fountain, which she built in 1732, has now only one decorated face to show; this also is to be found in Galata, not far from the Azap-kapu mosque.

Pretty fountains abound, both in the city and in its outskirts, beyond the possibility of enumeration; they were built throughout the eighteenth century. A late fountain, built by Mihrishah Sultan under the reign of Selim III, is worth mentioning because of its idyllic situation. It stands on the shore of the Bosphorus (in front of a charming meadow), near the Small Sweet Waters of Asia.

CHAPTER VIII

THE SERAGLIO

THE palace of the Sultans, generally called Topkapu Saray, or Palace of the Cannon Gate, on account of the fortified sea-gate at Seraglio Point, has long captured the imagination of the West. As 'the Grand Turk's Seraglio' it was believed to be the scene of extraordinary orgies, and it was more difficult of access than almost anywhere else in Europe. Even today, when large parts of it are regularly shown to the public, it requires more than ordinary persistence to see rooms that are not generally shown; not a large personnel is employed, and it is hard to find anyone who has the leisure, the inclination and the power to unlock locked rooms. Moreover, some shame is felt about the disrepair of many parts of the Seraglio, where the floor is up and the walls crumbling; there may even be passages that are, in their present state, impassable. Two writers,[1] in the inter-war period, made a profound study of it, though in their plans of this labyrinth, and in a few other details, they are not always in agreement; they saw very much more than any visitor of today is likely to see.

European usage of the word *seraglio*, has made us think first of the harem and of the sultan's pleasures; in fact, the harem only came to Seraglio Point some time after the conquest, and the vast palace with its multitudinous buildings fulfilled many and diverse official and practical needs. Within its enclosure were the Divan, the mint, the treasury, a school, two bakeries, a flour mill, three store-rooms, two hospitals, a pharmacy, two athletic fields, seven bathing establishments, thirteen mosques, the privy stable of the Sultan, and a great stable for two to three thousand horses. At one time the inhabitants numbered from four to five thousand, and nearly as many more ate there on the four days a week when the Divan was held. It was a world of its own, and a world that some of its inhabitants never left.

After the conquest, Mehmet II at first lived on the fourth hill, either

---

[1] Dr. Barnette Miller: *Beyond the Sublime Porte* (New Haven, U.S.A., 1931) and N. M. Penzer: *The Harem* (London, 1936).

renovating the monastery of the Pantocrator, or building a new palace. The Byzantine palaces were too far decayed to be restored for his use; for a long time the Great Palace had been suffered to fall in ruins, and Blachernae had been badly damaged in the siege.

Only some years after the conquest did he begin work on the Yeni Saray, the new palace on the site of the ancient acropolis of Byzantium; here he moved his staff, but he left his harem of three hundred women with seventy eunuchs at the Pantocrator, which now became the Eski Saray, the old palace. Later, when the harem was moved to the new palace, the old palace at the Pantocrator became 'the palace of tears', i.e. a dower house for the harems of deceased sultans, etc.; previously 'the palace of tears' was at Adrianople.

During the whole Byzantine period the point was wooded, and was regarded as extra mural. Mehmet turned it into a pleasure-park, put in rare and exotic trees, and erected several kiosques or pavilions; every kiosque, we are told, was 'like a rose, every window like a vase of flowers, and every fountain like the fountain of eternal life'. The Çinili (or tile) Kiosque, opposite the modern building of the Archaeological Museum, is the only part of the Seraglio that can unquestionably be assigned to Mehmet II's reign; it was built between 1465-66 and 1472-73.

The principal entry to the Seraglio is by the *Bab-i-Humayun*, or the imperial gate; mistranslated as the 'Sublime Porte', it gave Europe its name for the Turkish Government. Within this is the vast, tree-grown expanse of the first court, which contains the church of St. Irene, once the imperial arsenal. This court, often known as the court of the Janissaries, was always open to all. 'Anybody may enter the first Court of the Seraglio,' says Tournefort (*c.* 1700), '... but everything is so still, the Motion of a Fly might be heard in a manner: and if any one should presume to raise his voice ever so little, or shew the least want of Respect to the Mansion-place of their Emperor he would instantly have the Bastinado by the Officers that go the rounds; nay, the very Horses seem to know where they are, and no doubt they are taught to tread softer than in the streets.' The silence deepened as one penetrated further.

All the buildings are now gone from this court, except for the mint and the church of St. Irene, though once there was a bakery here, built in 1616 by Ahmed I; we are told of the extreme whiteness of the bread made for the imperial family. There was also an infirmary in this court, under the jurisdiction of the Chief White Eunuch, for the use of the pages of the Palace School, who much enjoyed being there. Tavernier (1677) tells us: 'They continue there for the space of ten or twelve daies, and are diverted, according to their mode, with a wretched kind of vocal and instrumental Musick, which begins betimes in the morning, and holds on till night. The permission they have there to drink wine, which they never have elsewhere, is a greater inducement for their coming in thither, than the Musick.'

Near the gate to the second court, the Ortakapi, is the fountain of execution, where the executioner (who was also the head gardener) cleansed his hands after his work. The method was usually decapitation, though, as the blood of the ruling house might not be shed, the silken cord was employed on princely victims. The corpses might be handed over to relatives for burial; sometimes they were thrown into the sea through the gate of the Fish Market. Heads were exhibited, as an example, over the imperial gate; when there were too many of them, ears and noses alone were displayed, as gamekeepers sometimes nail up a beak or a wing.

Public execution is still the rule in Turkey, but as it takes place, usually, unannounced and in the small hours of the morning, its publicity is not particularly shocking. Visitors to St. Sophia, at an early hour of the day, have however sometimes been distressed to find a gallows still standing just outside, and a murderer still swinging from it.

The Ortakapi is very likely the work of Mehmet II; it is here that tickets are now sold, and cameras taken into custody. It was formerly the centre of Turkish court life, the place where processions formed on the days when the Divan met. Here were exhibited the heads of the executioner's victims when they were of high rank; those under the rank of Pasha adorned the *Bab-i-Humayun*.

Of the second court, that of the Divan, a traveller records that it was 'a little smaller than the first but much more beautiful, owing to its variety of elegant fountains, avenues flanked by very tall cypresses, and the presence of certain stretches of lawn where the growing grass provides pasture for a number of gazelles which breed and are regarded with pleasure'.

The fountains and the gazelles are gone, and the fussy diagonal paths and haphazard planting destroy the dignity of this court, which must rely for its effect on the wide open space, for the surrounding buildings are not of great distinction. The palace of the Divan has not an interesting exterior; its tower and spire are sometimes, mistakenly, floodlit, and make a very poor effect if seen from the Golden Horn below. But the three rooms of the Divan are attractively decorated in the Turkish-baroque of the early eighteenth century; in the domed hall of the Divan, or *Kubbealti*, a small oriel window projects high above the seat of the Grand Vizir – from this vantage point the Sultan could follow the proceedings of the Divan, without anyone knowing if he were present or not. A faience museum and an arms museum are accommodated in adjacent rooms, on this, the left side of the court; and the harem is behind.

On the right side of the court are the kitchen buildings, twenty domed chambers in two parallel rows of ten, built by the great architect Sinan; their enormously solid outside walls face the Marmara. There were here separate kitchens for the Sultan, for the Harem, for the Chief White Eunuch and for others, also rooms for the kitchen staff, pantries, coffee-rooms and dormitories. The great chimneys on the Marmara side are perhaps a later addition.

In the early seventeenth century, we learn, two hundred head of mutton were daily consumed in the Seraglio, one hundred head of lamb or kid, forty of veal (of which the eunuchs were particularly fond), thirty to fifty brace of geese and between one and two hundred of poultry. Sheep and goats came from Angora, turkeys from Gallipoli (hence its name, from γαλόπουλο – a young turkey), chickens from Broussa.

Later in the century the accounts mention vast quantities of rice and vermicelli, and of honey, sugar, pepper, cloves, nutmegs, ginger, saffron, ice, oil, vinegar, lemon juice and amber. Dates, plums and aubergines came from Egypt; honey from Roumania, and a better sort from Crete; oil from Messenia, but that for the Sultan from Crete; cheese from Italy; pomegranates from Broussa and ice and snow from Mount Olympus above it, brought by eighty files of mules.

Part of the kitchens has been turned into a porcelain museum, and may easily be visited.

By the Divan tower, a carriage gate gives entrance to the harem. This was partially transferred from the palace on the third hill by Süleyman the Magnificent, probably between 1541 and 1545. The immediate cause may have been a fire in the Eski Saray in 1540-41; the underlying cause was the ambition of Roxelana. She was originally a Russian slave girl (hence her name Roxelana – Russelanie) or Khösem, once, perhaps, the property of the renegade Greek page Ibrahim, the companion of Süleyman's youth, the sharer of his bed and board, and later his Grand Vizir. At first she held the subordinate position in Süleyman's harem of second Kadin; the first Kadin (a favourite concubine made free on the birth of a child and acquiring something of the position of an 'unmarried wife') was Bosfor Sultan, otherwise known as Gulbehar, 'Flower of Spring'. In 1526 there was a fight between two Kadins; the Flower of Spring scored a physical victory, pulling the Russian girl's hair and scratching her face, but Roxelana scored a much more important moral victory. She refused to appear until she could show an undisfigured face, and by this strategic retirement triumphed, and made Süleyman her slave. In 1533 Hafiza, the Sultan Validé, that is the Sultan's mother, the first Lady in the harem, died; in the same year the first Kadin went into virtual exile in Magnesia, where her son Prince Mustafa was governor. In 1536 Ibrahim was murdered, for no particular reason; most probably Roxelana was jealous of his influence with the Sultan. Rustem Pasha, her son-in-law, husband of her daughter Mihrimah, succeeded him as Grand Vizir. With Rustem's aid Roxelana was able to induce Süleyman to order the strangling of Prince Mustafa in 1543, which secured the succession of her own family. The move to the Seraglio was a further consolidation of her power, which was complete when she became Süleyman's legal wife. Roxelana reigned so absolutely over her husband that he promoted no more Kadins, and even married off some of his more attractive women. Though she predeceased him, dying in 1558, and never held the coveted position of Validé, her personal ascendancy was sufficient without it.

Roxelana had come with her own slaves and eunuchs, leaving the rest of the harem on the third hill. Her son Selim II brought his favourite Kadin, Nuru Banu Sultan, to the Seraglio, with fifty ladies attending on her, and their attendants. When Murad III, her son, succeeded in 1574, Nuru Banu Sultan, now the Validé, was permitted to stay on, which she did until her death in 1583. Henceforth the Validé remained, and ruled in the Seraglio; and the Palace of Tears, the dower-house for the harems of deceased sultans, was moved from Adrianople to the Eski Saray. By the end of Murad III's reign, there were eleven to twelve hundred women in the Seraglio.

The carriage gate was built by Murad III: here the ladies of the harem entered the carriages that took them for occasional excursions, or visits to the Eski Saray. From a small open courtyard one enters the quarters of the black eunuchs. A high corridor is flanked by three storeys of cells; at the end is a great fire-place by which the whole building is centrally heated. The youngest eunuchs slept in the top storey, and descended with seniority. The tiny cells, relatively few, seem to be inadequate accommodation for the large number of eunuchs that served in the harem, but some of them were always absent on duty, nor have oriental people any objection to overcrowding. The eunuchs had also a common-room, and a room for making coffee.

It is not known when the Black Eunuchs first became the guard of the harem, supplanting White Eunuchs in this office; it has been suggested that this was one of Roxelana's innovations. This was a step on the road to decadence and towards the total corruption of Turkish court-life. The civilized, educated, White Eunuchs, a heritage of Byzantium, were replaced by coarse and uneducated savages, to whom greater powers were continually being assigned. During the hundred and fifty years when the harem, usually in the person of the Validé, ruled the Sultan, and thus the Ottoman Empire, the Chief Black Eunuch, or *Kizlar Agha*, her Prime Minister, had one of the first places in the kingdom.

While the White Eunuchs were partially castrated, having their testicles only removed or crushed, complete castration by the removal of both penis and testicles was inflicted by the Turks on those who guarded their women; they had observed that coitus is not impossible after partial castration. Juvenal and Martial tell us that Roman women even preferred eunuchs for their lovers, for they provided the same pleasure, without any risk of pregnancy; and Burton, who had spoken familiarly with a eunuch's wife, was able to adorn the *Arabian Nights* with a note on the loves of eunuchs who were by no means like the angels in Heaven, but much more like the angels in Milton.

Not content with total castration, the rules of the Seraglio demanded a periodical medical inspection of the Black Eunuchs, in case a miracle of nature had restored to them their severed parts; and, emasculated as they were, the Sultan's jealousy preferred that the ugliest possible should guard his women, even as in modern times females of the most repellent appearance are chosen as servants in boys' schools, or in the colleges of the ancient universities. The dangers of the operation have been greatly exaggerated, though there was considerable mortality, particularly among boys who had reached puberty before submitting to it; so also have been exaggerated the miseries of the eunuch's state, and the corruption of his character. The Black Eunuchs, indeed, had seldom chosen their state for ambitious reasons, as had some of their White colleagues, and many of them may have felt they owed society a grudge because of their mutilation; we hear of eunuchs' sulkiness and arrogance and spitefulness. On the other hand, positions of power and influence were open to them, and they were spared military service; we are also told of their generosity and simplicity, their neatness, their love of music, and of children and animals, and of the great charm of their society. Some western travellers, indeed, admit to an irrational shrinking from them, but this seems to be due to no more than prejudice, or to a kind of sexual snobbery. Flaubert, however, did not mind the Black Eunuchs of Constantinople at all, though he found a White Eunuch a disagreeable sight.

The Black Eunuchs acted as ushers to the young princes, while they still remained in the harem, which they did until they were about eleven years old. Their *hodja* or tutor was ushered into their schoolroom in the Black Eunuchs' quarters, and ushered out again after school hours, without setting eyes on the harem women. The schoolroom upstairs is an enchanting place, but the painted pattern and the faience must have made plentiful distractions for young eyes; little X-shaped desks for the Koran still reveal the purpose of the room, and there is a faience chimney-piece. The *Kizlar Agha's* suite, which is hard by, has also very great charm.

The courtyard of the Sultan Valide and the small rooms assigned to her are the heart of the harem, the centre of its life; this is where an ambitious Turkish woman most hoped to arrive, for the position of first Kadin was nothing to that of the Queen-Mother. The Turks reasoned that a man might take as many wives as he pleased, and dispose of them as he pleased, but even the Sultan could only have one mother. The Valide's apartments are therefore of the greatest associational interest, but they have been done up to suit the taste of late eighteenth-century Valides, and are not in themselves remarkable. The decoration is Turkish rococo; Italianate Adrianople woodwork and poorish frescoes, with rather crude landscape. The *salon* is early-nineteenth-century, and not without charm.

It is now probably impossible to penetrate into the vast labyrinth of the hospital, the slaves' quarters, and the apartments of the lesser members of the harem. The best authority[1] was himself frequently impeded by fallen masonry, and could often only stand in the doorway of a room whose floor had collapsed. Of the many women who lived there, all were, technically, the slaves of the Sultan; the hard work, however, was almost entirely done by negresses, and the other girls had duties that varied with their training.

A white girl, newly acquired, might go through something like the following *cursus honorum*. She would be attached to the court (*oda*) of one of the principal women of the harem, who might herself have bought her; there she would be educated, and trained to make herself useful. If she never caught the Sultan's eye, she might yet make a career for herself; she might reach the head of the *oda* and become one of the members of the Valide's cabinet — Controller, Stewardess, Administrator, Treasurer, Keeper of the Baths, Mistress of the Robes, Keeper of the Jewels, Keeper of the Store-rooms, Reader of the Koran, Chief Coffee-maker — and that is not all. There were opportunities for intrigue, for the use of administrative or executive powers, and for the accumulation of a fortune. Normal love would of course be denied her in this lay-convent, for the Sultan was the only permissible lover. Nevertheless, the emotions were not necessarily starved. 'In the Society of Women,' Sir Paul Ricaut tells us, 'they die with amorous affections one to the other; especially the old women court the young, present them with rich Garments, Jewels, Money, even to their own impoverishment and ruin.' She might, however, be married off by the Sultan, instead of going to end her days in the Eski Saray — or, after she was past child-bearing, she might be allowed to serve as concubine to one of the younger princes, who were not permitted to beget issue.

A girl, however, who had been fortunate enough to attract the Sultan's notice, was at once named *gözde*, or 'in the eye'; she was given a separate apartment, and attendants, and awaited a summons to the royal bed. When she had received this favour, she was known as an *ikbal*. Her visits to the Sultan or, more uncommon events, his visits to her were kept entirely secret. If the Sultan did not care about her, she returned to her former position, but it must be her hope to bear him a male child, when she might be promoted to the position of Kadin; all her hopes would

[1] N. M. Penzer.

then be concentrated on the future reign of her son, which would give her the supreme position of Validé.

Lady Mary Wortley Montagu reports a conversation she had with a widow of Mustafa II: 'She assured me that the story of the Sultan's *throwing a handkerchief* is altogether fabulous; and the manner upon that occasion no other than this: He sends the *Kizlar Agha* (i.e. the Chief Black Eunuch) to signify to the lady the honour he intends her. She is immediately complimented upon it by the others, and led to the bath, where she is perfumed and dressed in the most magnificent and becoming manner. The Emperor precedes his visit by a royal present, and then comes into her apartment: neither is there any such thing as her creeping in at the bed's foot.'

Mr. Penzer thinks that this statement may only be true of Mustafa's practice, and should not be allowed to discredit all the contrary evidence. It has frequently been stated that the concubine first must kiss the coverlet, then creep in at the bed's foot, and work her way up till she is level with her master. George Sandys tells us that the same act of humility is imposed on the husbands of Imperial Ladies: 'But for his Daughters, Sisters and Aunts, they have the *Bassas* given them for their Husbands, the *Sultan* saying thus, *Here, Sister, I give thee this man to thy slave, together with this Dagger, that if he please thee not thou mayst kill him.* Their Husbands come not unto them until they be called: if but for speech only, their shoes which they put off at the door, are there suffered to remain: but if to lye with them, they are laid over the Bed by an Eunuch, a sign for them to approach; who creep in unto them at the Bed's feet.' The throwing of the handkerchief is equally well authenticated and, as Mr. Penzer reminds us, the handkerchief was the normal wrapping for any present until the later introduction of envelopes or cardboard boxes.

Kadins or *ikbals*, like girls who never won the Sultan's attention, might end up in the Eski Saray, or might even marry thence. In the seventeenth century an ex-kadin of Ibrahim's married a Pasha, and after his death profited by her harem training to become the most expensive procuress in Constantinople; from her way of life she was nick-named *la Sultana Sporca*.

For many of the women, in spite of its intrigues, the life of the harem was boring; an occasional brilliant fête was given for them, an occasional excursion was made on the Bosphorus, but their days were monotonous and empty. Boredom more than anything else prompts to foolhardiness; some of them were foolhardy, and ended in the Bosphorus. The Chief Black Eunuch turned the condemned women over to the head gardener, who saw them placed in sacks weighted with stones. Gardeners, accompanied by a eunuch, rowed out in a small boat, towing a smaller one in which the women were placed, and capsized the smaller boat opposite Seraglio Point. Sometimes there were mass drownings; Ibrahim drowned his whole harem in order to have a change. Penzer records the horrible story of a diver, sent down after a wreck off Seraglio Point: 'Almost immediately he signalled to be drawn up again, and explained in a voice quaking with terror that at the bottom of the sea was a great number of bowing sacks, each containing the dead body of a woman standing upright on the weighted end and swaying slowly to and fro with the current.'

The Selamlik or 'place of greeting', the men's part of the palace, is now difficult to distinguish from the harem, through which it is entered. The women were sometimes admitted to entertainments in the big Throne Room, and here they greeted the new sovereign before he went to Eyüp for his ceremonial girding with the sword. It is a fine room with a noble dome, the work of Sinan, but the eighteenth-century decoration is rather clumsy. Adjoining this are two exquisite vestibules, one with a fountain, and the other distinguished by a huge chimneypiece, both with faience of great beauty. This spot was the scene of the strangling of Murad III's brothers on his accession, though he had with tears pleaded for their lives. Here the Validé Koesem, grandmother of Mehmet IV, met a horrible death. 'She was in a moment dispoiled of her Garments,' says Ricaut. 'Her Furs were torn off into small pieces; and being stript of her Rings, Bracelets, Garters and other things, she was left naked without a Rag to cover her ... The Queen, though she were by this time besides her Senses, and worn out with Age, being above eighty years old, and without Teeth; yet she with her Gums onely did bite the thumb of his left hand, which by chance came into her mouth, so hard that he could not deliver himself untill with the haft of his Poinard he struck her on the forehead near her right eye.' She was then strangled, blood pouring from her nose and ears; the eunuchs and the palace pages perpetrated this crime, fearing that she was plotting against them with the Janissaries.

Parallel with the Throne Room is the great domed bedroom of Murad III with its big chimneypiece and two huge divans. Round the chimneypiece are superb blue faience panels, with a design of almond blossom, and everywhere is a lovely border of tomato-red tiles; the very best work of the Iznik factories is to be seen in this lovely room, and in the even more lovely vestibule through which it is entered. This is a strangely shaped room, for its dome is pierced by the shaft of a chimney; it has a most noble wall of faience, the best, perhaps, in Constantinople, and a very grand stalactite door into the bedroom, which recalls the fine Seljuk-influenced portals of the mosque of Bayazit II. Nowhere is the light more propitious for faience than in these beautiful rooms, where it filters in through stained-glass windows, or through outer rooms.

The Murad III rooms are the most beautiful part of the Selamlik, and perhaps of the whole Seraglio. Mention, however, should be made of the library of Ahmed I, charming with its green and blue tiles, entered through Murad III's bedchamber, and of the elegant, panelled, painted dining-room of Ahmed III, with a looking-glass framed in its marquetry roof.

Across a paved courtyard, a high raised platform behind the Throne Room, the wooden kiosque of Osman III overhangs part of the garden where once the menagerie was kept, into which it has a sudden, deep view. It is a pretty, flimsy structure, lavishly over-decorated in Turkish rococo; its slightness, grace, and silliness all form a strong contrast with the grim outer walls. Here one can feel how hemmed in was the House of Felicity.

I was not able to visit the *Kafes*, or the Princes' prison. On the death of Murad III in 1595, his successor Mehmet III had his nineteen brothers put to death, and had seven of his father's concubines, who were pregnant, drowned in case they gave birth to male issue. On the death of Mehmet III in 1603, his young successor Ahmed I refused to countenance the usual fratricide; the idiocy of his brother Mustafa, and the influence of his tutor were both reasons against it. Henceforth princes were generally locked up in the Selamlik instead of receiving the silken cord. An eighteenth-century traveller, Jean-Claude Flachat, has given an interesting account of it. 'This prison is like a strong citadel. A high wall is built all round it. Osman caused it to be lowered and to have the windows opened. It is entered by two doors carefully guarded by Eunuchs both within and without, each having a double iron railing. The place has a dismal appearance. There is a pretty enough garden, well watered. The Princes have

N

fine apartments and baths in the detached buildings which surround the court. The Eunuchs detailed to their service all live on the ground floor, and there is a large number of them. They spare no pains to mitigate their hard lot, and to make their prison at least endurable ... They have all kinds of masters, and they even encourage them to perfect themselves in all handiworks that are applicable to their rank.'[1] A harem of sterile women was provided for their amusement; if one such, by accident, became pregnant, the child was immediately drowned. Here the princes were shut up, in an existence less interesting than that of the harem women, for no career or progress was open to them, and there was nothing to gain by intrigue. A more stupefying life, or one less suitable as an education for rulership, it would be hard to conceive. Süleyman II came out of it, after thirty-nine years, in 1687; the monster Ibrahim had grown up in it; the hunchback Osman III was fifty years in it, before his accession in 1754; Abdul Hamid I came out of it, after half a life-time, in 1774. The decadence of the later Ottoman empire, and the incapacity of its masters for rule, were largely due to this institution; it is strange that in the Seraglio, founded by so intelligent a prince as Mehmet II, no better alternative could be found to civil war or fratricide.

The Gate into the third court is called *Bab-i-Sa'adat*, the Gate of Felicity: those who lived within, in the House of Felicity, might not go out. Here was the most private part of the palace, and those who were permitted to enter must first kiss the threshold.

At its entrance is the Throne Room or Audience Chamber, an isolated building erected by Ahmed II for the reception of ambassadors; its roof is heavy, but the colonnade surrounding it is elegant. There are panels of faience facing the Gate of Felicity and a pretty fountain. Inside there is a vast treble-bed, the Sultan's divan, a great bronze chimneypiece, and a fountain that is said to have been used to cover, with its sound, any private conversation that the Sultan did not want overheard by curious ears outside.

On the right of the third court was the Palace School: its site is now occupied by the museum galleries, and offices, and the rooms are altered beyond recognition.

It was a school for slave-pages, not a Turk was there: 'The boys were Austrian, Hungarian, Russian, Greek, Italian, Bosnian, Bohemian, and

[1] Cit. N. M. Penzer.

even German and Swiss, as well as Georgian, Circassian, Armenian, and Persian.'[1] The pick of the slave boys, acquired by tribute, capture or purchase, were chosen and trained as pages for the Sultan's court. Such a school had existed at Adrianople, and Mehmet II founded this great school in the Seraglio which was, at its time, the best school in Europe. The curriculum, which allowed a great liberty in the subjects chosen for study, and was designed to reveal promise in the students, is thought to owe something to the *Republic* of Plato. Its aim was to produce the warrior statesman, trained to fill military or civil posts, who should at the same time be a good Moslem, a scholar and a gentleman. Mehmet himself, one of the most cultured men of his age, was largely responsible for the curriculum, which reflected his own fine education; he spoke Arabic, Persian, Greek and (bad) Italian, he was a historian and a student of philosophy, a master of the arts of war, and a superb horseman.

The course of education lasted fourteen years; there were preparatory schools in the palaces of Adrianople and Galata, and a third built by Ibrahim Pasha, the Grand Vizir of Süleyman the Magnificent, as well as two others within the Seraglio itself. The *ich-oglans* or Inside Youths of the higher standard in the Seraglio, numbered about 300 in the time of Mehmet II; their numbers rose to 900 under Murad III.

In time the school had a conservatoire (the Palace choir, blindfold, was sometimes called upon to sing to the women of the harem), two mosques, baths, and a field for archery. There were also vocational schools; nearly every man in Turkey learned a craft, even Sultans; Mehmet II had been gardener, and Selim I and Süleyman I were both goldsmiths. The pages also learnt cookery and falconry, also manicure and shaving and all the offices of the bath; those destined to attend the Sultan on military expeditions must know something of music, for his entertainment, and of washing, for his laundry was their responsibility.

White eunuchs were employed as ushers in the school. 'They look for all the world like mummified old women', says an observer,[2] 'and are, for the most part, very thin and shrivelled. Their duty is to attend upon the Grand Signior when he goes out in State, and also to keep order among the white pages, mostly Christian lads, stolen from their parents, to the number of about 300 to 400 each year. Some of these boys are very good-

---

[1] Cit. N. M. Penzer.
[2] Archives of the Bank of St. George at Genoa, cit. Penzer.

looking, and wear magnificent dresses. Their cheeks are plump, and their painted eyebrows meet. Very strange things are told of them, but these things are common hereabouts, and nobody thinks much about them.' Sir Paul Ricaut tells some of these strange things: 'In their Chambers, though watched by their Eunuchs, they learn a certain language with the motion of their Eyes, their gestures and their Fingers, to express their Amours; and this Passion hath boiled sometimes to that heat, that jealousies and rivalries have broken forth in their Chambers.'[1] If their loves were discovered, the pages were severely beaten, and expelled from the Seraglio.

The white eunuchs had generally been imported from India and the Caucasus, or were prepared for service outside Constantinople; for the Koran forbids castration. Nevertheless, a seventeenth-century description by Ottaviano Bon[2] suggests that the operation was sometimes performed within the Seraglio: 'They choose some of the renegade boys, who are given as presents to the King . . . but are rarely castrated against their will, because the Master of Ceremonies says that they would incur great danger of death. Although aware of this, the youths are tempted by the certainty of becoming in time men of great consequence if they live.' The eunuchs, therefore, were partly recruited from the most courageous and ambitious of the captured or tribute youth; there was one white eunuch to about every ten pages, and the Chief White Eunuch, the confidential agent of the Sultan, was the director of education, one of the most privileged people in the Seraglio. The teachers were visiting professors, mainly from the *Ulema* (the body of learned clerks who, in priestless Islam, correspond most nearly to the secular clergy); in 1612 there were forty teachers for eight to nine hundred boys.

The mosque of the palace school, now a library, stands opposite the school on the left side of the court; behind it is part of the harem and the Selamlik. The northern corner of the court is occupied by the Pavilion of the Holy Mantle. Selim I, after his conquest of Egypt in 1517, brought to Constantinople the relics of the Prophet which had been preserved in Cairo by the titular Caliphs, whose heritage they were. They consisted of the Prophet's Mantle, Staff and Seal and, by some accounts, of his Sword also: a special Pavilion was built for them, and they were entrusted to the

---

[1] *The History of the Present State of the Ottoman Empire.*
[2] Cit. Penzer.

care of the pages of the Royal Bedchamber. No Christian has even claimed to have entered the Pavilion, and our accounts of those relics are, at best, second-hand. The Mantle has been variously described as green, black, white and striped: Dr. Barnette Miller was told by several Palace attendants that it was cream-coloured, and was inclined to believe them.

In the seventeenth century a very curious ritual grew up round these relics, which were venerated in a way that to an orthodox Moslem must have seemed idolatrous. Tavernier tells us that yearly, in Ramazan, the Holy Mantle was dipped in a large gold cauldron, adorned with emeralds and turquoises. The Mantle was then carefully wrung out, and the water in which it had soaked was put up in half-pint bottles of Venetian glass; this infusion was then distributed to the imperial family, and to other notables of Constantinople.

Similarly, on the fourteenth of Ramazan, impressions of the Prophet's seal were made on fifty small pieces of paper: 'The Sultan sends to the Sultanesses, and the Grandees of Constantinople, as also to most of the considerable Bassas of the Empire, to each of them an Impression of the Seal, in a little script of Paper roll'd up and well fastened with silk, and with that, one of those Bottles full of Water', so Tavernier tells us. The recipients must soak the paper in the water, and swallow both; they must not presume to look at the impression of the seal.

The Sacred Standard came into Selim's hands with the other relics from Cairo. He sent it to Damascus, where it was preserved in the Ommayed mosque, whence it headed the yearly pilgrimage to Mecca. Some legends make it the curtain at the entrance of the tent of Ayesha, the Prophet's favourite wife; it is more generally believed to be the turban of Buraydat, who was sent from Mecca with a troop of horse against Mohammed, during the Hegira. He was suddenly converted, fell on his knees, unwound his turban and fixed it to the point of his lance, dedicating himself to the Prophet's service.

The standard was sent by Murad III to the armies in Hungary, and was brought back by Mehmet III in 1595, and deposited in the Pavilion of the Sacred Mantle. Henceforth it was only exhibited at moments of national emergency; its last appearance was in 1915, when a Holy War was declared against the Allied Powers.

The remaining part of the Seraglio is, for the sake of convenience, known as the fourth court, though it is bounded by outer walls only, and is in no real sense a court. Here were the privy gardens, and kiosques erected for their greater enjoyment; the beautiful views of the Marmara, the Bosphorus and the Golden Horn, and the fresher breezes of Seraglio Point, marked out this part of the enclosure as the most suitable for pleasure-grounds.

The pages of the Royal Bedchamber were allowed to spend their break there. Sometimes (more rarely) the whole harem was taken into the gardens for a treat; on such occasions, the pages were cleared out, and all the surrounding windows were closed and barred. Only the back windows of the Treasury and the Hall of the Pantry overlooked this area.

The gardens are now ill-planted, and neglected; little of their former beauty remains. From the time of the conqueror, who planted exotic trees on Seraglio Point, most of the Sultans interested themselves in the gardens. Roses were imported from Adrianople and hyacinths from Aleppo; Mehmet IV was particularly fond of every sort of ranunculus, and had seeds and roots sent him from Syria and from the Aegean islands. The lilacs and carnations were splendid, but above all it is the tulip that we most associate with the Palace gardens.

It was in 1562 that an Amsterdam merchant first brought tulip bulbs from Constantinople to Holland; in the next century an Austrian ambassador to the Porte reintroduced the improved tulip from Holland and it became the favourite flower of Ibrahim. The eighteenth century, during the reigns of Ahmed III and of Mahmud I, was an age of tulipomania, almost of tulipolatry.

Ahmed III had created the office of Master of Flowers; in his diploma, all the subordinate gardeners are enjoined to be 'in his presence all eye, like the narcissus; all ear, like the rose; that they have not ten tongues like the lily . . . let them keep their lips closed, like the rosebud'. His tulip fêtes, at the April full moon, when the gardens were full of marvellous Dutch and Persian tulips, must have been the loveliest scenes the Seraglio ever witnessed. Rows and rows of shelves were arranged with vases of tulips, and tiny lamps of coloured glass, and glass globes filled with liquids of different colours. On the highest shelves were placed cages with singing birds in them. One night the guests were officials, another night the harem held a bazaar at which the Sultan was the sole patron; or there might be a hunt for *bonbons* concealed, like Easter eggs, in the grass. But these fêtes devoured the resources of the empire to such an extent that the revolution,

which deposed Ahmed III, and in which the kiosques by the Sweet Waters
of Europe were destroyed, has been represented as an anti-tulip revolt.

The cult reached its height in the 'tulip reign' of Ahmed III; nevertheless,
Flachat, on the authority of his friend, the Chief Black Eunuch, describes
a lovely fête under Mahmud I. 'The extensive walk in the enclosure
formed by the wooden structures offers to the sight various well-designed
edifices, such as pyramids, towers, and floral bowers set up in different
places . . . The women rush out on all sides, like a swarm of bees settling
on the flowers and stopping continually at the honey they find.' The
Chief Black Eunuch told Flachat that the gaiety of the occasion inspired
them to use all their arts, and that there could never be anywhere so
violent a display of feminine charm, all concentrated on one man: the
Sultan. For many of them it was perhaps a unique occasion, in the whole
year, to seek his favour: an unnoticed virgin might hope to be promoted
to the rank of *gözde*; a *gözde* might become an *ikbal*; an *ikbal* might be
asked back again to the Sultan's bed, with the hope of bearing a son and
becoming a kadin. The Sultan, said the Chief Black Eunuch, threw a handkerchief to the concubine of his choice; a curtain fell in front of his sofa,
leaving him alone with her in a kiosque. At a signal, the Chief Black
Eunuch parted the curtain again, and everyone came up to the kiosque to
congratulate the happy couple.

The kiosques, of which several survive, were often ceremonial in purpose, designed as audience chambers; sometimes they were pleasure-
haunts and summer-houses — such a one was that room built for his siesta
by Bayazit II, cooled by water flowing over its glass dome.

The loveliest building in the Seraglio, perhaps one of the most beautiful
rooms in the world, is the Baghdad Kiosque. It was built by Murad IV,
after his capture of Baghdad in 1638, and modelled on a kiosque which he
had seen there, which seemed to him the most perfect building of its sort.
Its plan is an octagon, imposed on a cross; the central, octagonal, domed
room sends out four lower, transeptal arms, each containing a sofa, under
a flat gold roof. The central dome is rose, patterned in other colours; from
the middle a rose and gold ball depends on a long chain. Up to the spring
of the dome, the walls are covered with faience, except where there are
doors or cupboards of woodwork inlaid with ivory in polygonal designs.
The faience, though the best period of ceramics was already over, is
mostly of good and small design, in blue and white; there are, however, a

few tiles that are too bold in design, and some yellow tiles have been used in the small niches by the sofas. A calligraphic dado of faience runs all round, beneath the sills of the upper windows.

On one of the four oblique sides, between the transepts, there is a tall, canopied, bronze fire-place, the logs were placed in it upright, to make an upward draught and avoid smoke. The handsome silver *mangal*, or charcoal brazier, now in the middle of the room, has only been placed there for its decorative effect. On each of the other three oblique sides there is a door, with a single, stained-glass window above it, and there are two stained-glass windows at the ends of each transept – plain, white glass set with jewelled lumps of bright colour.

Here, if anywhere in Constantinople, is 'the gorgeous east'; and yet, for all its richness of decoration, this lovely room has a tranquillity and restfulness due to perfect taste. At different times it has been a smoking-room, a library, a reception-room, and a prison. Now it is only a show-place, but its colour and life have not left it. It is pleasant to sit on the step of a transept (the sofas are corded off from use), as long as the custodian will suffer you, absorbing the beauty of the blue walls and the rose dome, and the subdued light falling on harmoniously coloured carpets.

A broad arcaded cloister surrounds this room, following its shape; the slender columns have lotus capitals. The outside of the room is tiled down to a ledge below the upper course of windows. Part of the arcade is open and the rest is glazed in. There is a superb view of the Golden Horn, and on one side a charming outlook on a garden; there is a rectangular green tank, overarched by trees, with bronze statuettes of animals standing on the stone rim – a lovely, quiet garden, yet with a sophistication that makes it an appropriate appendage to such a superb work of art as the Baghdad Kiosque.

The broad, overhanging roof, the dome with a lantern, the minaret-shaped chimney of the Baghdad Kiosque all combine to make its exterior rather fussy. The earlier Revan kiosque, also erected by Murad IV, is without a surrounding cloister, and therefore more simple; but the adjacent buildings have been allowed to encroach upon it, and it no longer stands free. This also commemorates Murad IV's victories in Asia, and is said to be copied from a kiosque which struck his fancy at Revan in Transcaucasia.

The kiosque of Mustafa Pasha owes the name of that Grand Vizir to its later restorations: its origin is unknown, but an inscription records that

Ahmed III restored it in 1704. It is sometimes called the sofa room, from its pretty, low sofas in the windows. It was put at Pierre Loti's disposal during his last visit to Constantinople, and is often honoured by his name. It is an enchantingly pretty glass room, in the Turkish-Louis-Quinze style of its later restoration; there is a gold, fretted ceiling, and there are soft, salmon-pink walls, relieved by bands of soft green, and contrasted by a dark blue line just below the ceiling.

From about 1850 the Seraglio ceased to be the royal residence. Abdul Mejid preferred the palace of Beşiktaş; in 1853, he had the new palace of Dolmabahçe built on its site, by the Armenian architect Balian. It is a clumsy affair; the high central block, which contains a vast throne-room, composes badly with the low, straggling wings, and the façade as seen from the Bosphorus is unimpressive, despite the long, marble quay. It was better when imperial architects strove less for exterior effect: 'The Turks are wont to say that they build not to pleasure the sight of those that passe by the waye, but for thier owne commoditie; deridinge the goodlie shewes that our pallacies in Christendome make outwardlie, and that within they are not agreeable to thier minds.'[1] Inside, it is very much more splendid than beautiful; the immense throne-room, with the *trompe l'œil* effects in the dome, has, however, a certain magnificence. There are huge chandeliers of rock crystal, giant candelabra of silver.

'Ah wanna see where Roxane lived,' clamoured an American tourist. 'Ah'm mad about Roxane!'

But her guide, a citizen of the new Turkey, cared nothing for Roxelana (who may have visited the Bosphorus at Beşiktaş), nor even for Abdul Mejid. 'Here coffin Atatürk lie,' he insisted: 'everybody wisitink him three days.' For Dolmabahçe is the residence of presidents of the Turkish republic.

The Topkapu Saray had now become the 'old palace'; it was a 'palace of tears' for the harems of deceased sultans. It began on the process of decay, similar to the decay suffered by the Great Palace of the Byzantine Emperors, which started with the Comnene preference for Blachernae. After the revolution of 1908 the harem was dispersed; the Young Turks, with startling modernity, advertised for the next of kin of the harem women to come and claim them, and telegrams were sent to the Circassian villages of Anatolia, from which they had largely been recruited.

[1] John Sanderson: *Travels in the Levant, 1584-1602* (Hakluyt Soc., 1931).

'In consequence of this, a large number of Circassian mountaineers came in their picturesque garb into Constantinople, and on a certain fixed day they were conducted in a body to the Old Palace of Top-Kapu, where, in the presence of a Turkish Commission, they were ushered into a long hall filled with the ex-Sultan's concubines, cadines and odalisques, all of whom were then allowed to unveil themselves for the occasion. The scene that followed was very touching. Daughters fell into the arms of their fathers whom they had not seen for years. Sisters embraced brothers or cousins, and in some instances relatives met who had never met before, and were only able to establish their relationship by means of long and mutual explanations ... The number of female slaves they liberated was two hundred and thirteen.'[1]

Some girls had died, or had been killed by Abdul Hamid, others were taken away to share his exile in Salonica; others were drafted into other harems. Many women were left unclaimed, and lived on for a while at the Topkapu Saray, until accommodation was found for them elsewhere; the Seraglio was then gradually thrown open as a museum.

[1] Francis McCullagh: *The Fall of Abd-ul-Hamid* (London, 1910).

CHAPTER IX

THE THREE SEAS

The Bosphorus

THE Thracian Bosporos of the Ancients was so named, Ox-ford, from the wanderings of Io, the paramour of Zeus, in her guise of a heifer. This strait, some eighteen miles long, divides Europe from Asia, and connects the Black Sea with the Marmara. It twists and turns, narrows to less than half a mile in breadth at Kandilli, and between the two Turkish fortresses; opening out wide at Beykoz and Büyükdere, and at its exit into the Black Sea. The currents are strong, uncertain and dangerous; the sweet waters of the great Russian rivers flow into it, out of the Black Sea, and it is far less salt than the Mediterranean. The Byzantines called it the strait, *stenon*, and the Turks have translated this name as Boghaz.

The place of embarkation for all water-traffic is underneath the Galata Bridge, that thoroughfare so romantically described by travellers as the beginning of this century. 'Its thousands of passengers in every strange garb, its Persian carriages, its Arab steeds bearing alert officers, its beggars, mollahs, white-turbaned and whitecoated tolltakers' – all, all are gone, and their descendants, in European reach-me-down suits, are hardly distinguishable from the crowd that flows daily over London Bridge.

The boat sails out of the Golden Horn, leaving on the north the dingy quays of Horaçköy; on the south is Seraglio Point, but this is not perhaps the best view of it. A tower, called that of Leander, marks a little island off the coast of Asia; the story of Hero and Leander, however, is traditionally placed in the Dardanelles. It is better to associate this tower rather with the sultan's daughter who was imprisoned here for safety, because it had been foretold that she would die of a snake-bite; and so she did, for the snake entered her prison in a basket of grapes, which she bought from a passing boat, and hauled up to her window.

From Kabatas a car-ferry crosses to Asia, a solemn, slow, black object, with lights in its four corners at night; it has always seemed to me a vast hearse, or a great floating catafalque, and indeed it must often be transporting the dead to one or other of the Asian cemeteries. Then, after the elaborate water-front of the Dolmabahçe Palace, is Beşiktaş, the station for the ferry-boats that take the living across to Scutari.

Scutari (Üsküdar) was first named Chrysopolis, from the grave (so it was said) of Chryses, son of Chryseis and Agamemnon; it was little more than a suburb of Chalcedon. The corps of the *Scutari* had then barracks there, and gave their name to the place, and to the imperial palace of *Scoutarion*. After the Turkish conquest it became important as the bridgehead into Asia; from here the sacred caravan departed yearly to Mecca, and here the caravans from the East unloaded their merchandise. Mosques and palaces were built in Scutari; even without disembarking one can see the beautiful fountain of Ahmed III, and the mosque that Sinan built for Princess Mihrimah, on a raised platform behind it.

Today Scutari is tumble-down and quaint; it has been ravaged by fire, and its commercial importance has been stolen by Haydar Pasha, the railhead, on the Marmara. Behind it is a vast city of the dead; the cemeteries of Scutari were often preferred, because they were at least in the same continent as Mecca and Jerusalem, the holy cities of Islam. Here is a great part of that forest of cypresses and tombstones that seems to encircle the city, the male graves marked with a turban or fez, at the top of the tall steles, the female graves by bunches of flowers. The cemeteries have a bad reputation as places of furtive love-making, and are sometimes associated with the origins of life, as well as with its end.

Travellers who, unlike myself, have been able to read them, have often delighted to collect curious or touching epitaphs. Here are two that are pleasant.

On a young man:

Harvested by death in the flower of my age, I leave a beloved father and mother weeping for me. My consolation is that here below I gave myself to the study of belles-lettres, for I have the hope to become the nightingale of Paradise.

On a girl:

The bird of my heart has flown from its cage, to take its place in the gardens of Paradise. Going it has left an eternal wound in my soul. It was decreed by Fate that my daughter should only live thirteen years. She was gifted with all the qualities of a budding flower, and death has taken all from her mother in taking her away. Heaven! Is it just that her nest should be of stone?

Behind Scutari is the hill of Çamlica, higher than most of the low hills of the Bosphorus; perhaps it is the most splendid of all the famous view-points round Constantinople. From the high plateau there is an eastern view into a great, peaceful Bithynian valley; from here, as from every-where, Bithynia seems a noble beginning to Asia, and Thrace, in compari-son, a dull scrag-end of Europe. The Princes' Islands, that lovely orna-ment to the Marmara, are seen through a gap in the coastal hills; then Scutari, with its cypresses and minarets. Across the sea, the low Thracian coast disappears towards the south-east; the whole triangle of Stamboul is revealed, and most of the land walls behind it; then comes the Golden Horn, dividing it from Pera, and then wooded hills on hills, going back towards the Balkans; northwards the Bosphorus, hidden by the hill at Kandilli, and by other hills towards the north, gleams below like a series of lakes. It is the most complete panorama of the city and its setting.

The lower Bosphorus is a much over-rated channel. Its banks are lush with vegetation, and suburban with building. The traditional wooden country house of the Bosphorus, the *yali*, is now the exception; more European-looking buildings contribute to the ribbon-development along this water-way. Nor does the *yali*, inoffensive though it is, much add to the beauty of the water-side; raised on piles, or on a brick or stone sub-structure, the house is of wood, and very much resembles a large and rather grand Swiss chalet, a melancholy style of domestic architecture.

It is not possible to agree with Byron (who seems to be speaking of exteriors) when he writes:

> Each villa on the Bosphorus looks a screen
> New painted, or a pretty opera-scene.

Inside, the low, spacious rooms are often very pretty; large windows look on to the glittering water, and fill the house with a strange, aqueous light. If the walls are coloured in the delicate pastel shades, or the soft red of old Turkey, and if there are low sofas and good rugs, each interior may have great charm. But it is a frail kind of charm, like that of a doll's house. When the last light has faded behind Rumeli Hisar (and on the European side the hour of damp and darkness is, of course, much earlier), you are left, you feel, in a frail, wooden summer-house by a dark and melancholy stream. There are no other houses that are so pretty, and yet such undesirable residences.

Now passenger-boats serve these shores; generally your boat hugs either the European or the Asiatic coast, crossing, perhaps, only twice or three times in the course of the journey. A boy clatters round with a tray of glasses, intoning 'tea, tea, coffee, tea'; a man offers sandwiches in a basket. There are tramp-steamers going to or from the Black Sea ports, and one or two caiques, but these are now uncommon. The traffic of the Bosphorus has lost its romance as much as that of the Galata bridge. And yet, at one time, every *yali* had its caique, tethered at its water-steps, 'the most elegant of boats, the prettiest works of man's hands, after the minarets, that we see at Constantinople', said the English traveller, Charles MacFarlane, at the beginning of the nineteenth century. Lady Hester Stanhope, and her physician and historian, seem to have been almost as delighted with the watermen: 'Their shirts, of a texture like Chinese crape, are open to the bosom; so that their muscular forms and brawny arms are seen to great advantage. They wear a red cloth skull-cap and white balloon trousers; the feet and legs are naked.'

Most impressive were the imperial caiques. John Sanderson, at the end of the sixteenth century, describes them as 'most ritch and bewetifull to behould, the poupe all ivory, ebonie, or of seahorsse teeth, mother of pearle and goulde, sett with all manner of pretiouse stones'. When the Grand Turk goes on the water, 'to rowe him he hath eighty chosen men, two and two at an ower, twenty owers one aside, all in white shirts and redd capps, who often in thier rowinge barke like doggs. The reason I know not, except it be when they heare him talke (to the Bustangiebassi, who sits at the rudder) that they dare not harken to his talk'. Purchas repeats the story of the oarsmen barking: 'I have often heard them upon the water. Now and then between times many of them say *Bough*, bough-wahe, bough, boughwahe etc., and then pull some few strokes and tut againe.'

It is, perhaps, some small consolation for vanished beauty that one no longer has the horror of encountering a basket floating by containing the severed head of an unfaithful wife. An English governess in the middle of the nineteenth century, Miss Emmeline Lott, used to be embarrassed frequently by such sights, as she walked by the Bosphorus with her charge,

little Prince Ibrahim; it was difficult to explain to the boy what the poor
ladies had done to have their heads cut off. Miss Lott was employed by
the khedivial family, who occupied a palace at Bebek in the summer. She
has also a pleasant story of how the Grand Eunuch wished to be dressed
like the Prince Consort, in order to attend the Validé Princess on a visit
to the Sultan; he wished, however, to have the Garter mantle in red. The
English governess had to interpret his wishes to his tailor.

Sometimes, however, the execution was done by drowning. Trenery
records a drowning witnessed by a foreign visitor (c. 1854). 'A stifled
shriek rose upon the quiet air. It had not died away when he heard a dull,
heavy splash. A woman confined in a sack, that was fastened round her
neck, was flung from the caique into the Bosphorus . . . There the poor
young creature still floated; her eyes were closed, her long hair was spread
out upon the dark waves. She did not sink immediately, and the officers
in the caique were pushing her under by their oars.' She had been the
favourite wife of an elderly merchant, and had been given her choice of
poison, the bowstring or drowning. Such executions were uncommon
by that date.

The unfaithful wives probably first fell into temptation by the Sweet
Waters of Asia. After Kandilli, with its big *yalis* and its overhanging hill,
the small Sweet Waters enter the Bosphorus; here there is a very pretty
little rococo palace, reconstructed by the Sultana Validé of the time, in
1815. There is a handsome fountain here, and behind it a meadow much
frequented by picnic parties. On the other side of the meadow the great
Sweet Waters flow in — the stream called Aretae in Byzantine times, a
name also given to a village in that valley.

At one time the Sweet Waters of Asia were a favourite picnic place for
Ottoman society. Caiques went up the stream to shady spots under
spreading plane trees, or ladies drove in carriages to the river-head, where
slaves spread carpets on the grass, with a great display of gold and silver
plate. 'The women keep on one side of a long alley winding along the
bank of the stream,' wrote Madame Kibrizli-Mehmet Pasha,[1] 'the men on
the other, but the intervening space is small, and readily available for
purposes of flirtation. The gentlemen throw flowers, or little compli-
mentary notes, to the ladies; and the latter, if respectable, content themselves with acknowledging the attention by the gift of a flower.'

[1] *Thirty Years in the Harem* (London, 1872).

Not that the language of flowers was always so innocent. An English traveller reports a long silent conversation by the Sweet Waters.

'Flowers she already has; he purchases a bunch also, and, with the free-and-easy air of a gentleman and a coxcomb, flings himself upon the grass opposite the araba. Here he amuses himself with picking, sorting, inhaling the perfume, and admiring the flowers, as it seems to her black guards. In reality, he and the lady are conversing.
"Am I not pretty?" and she holds up a white lotus.
He holds up a flower of Paradise.
"You are lovelier than the houries in Korkham." [Paradise.]
"Do you love to look upon me?" asked by presenting a blush-rose.
"As the tiger-lily loves to gaze upon its own shadow."
"Can you love me?" and she shows a daffodil.
"As the daisy loves the sun!" and he turns towards her the flower in question.
"Would you die for my sake?" and she pulls a rosebud in two parts.
"I would submit my neck to the bowstring, without a murmur"; and he pulls off the head of a yellow geranium, or a violet . . .
She takes a sunflower, and holds it by the side of the jasmine.
"Meet me tonight, at twilight"; now a lily is quickly added; "by the fountain"; a grape tendril or a moss-rose; "in the kiosque" . . . then a lavender-bud; "there is nothing to fear". But a white rose is "be as careful as you can".'

Lady Mary Wortley Montagu obtained as a curiosity a Turkish love-letter in much the same style, consisting of an assortment of objects in a box; the interpretation was written in verse.

Pearl	—	Fairest of the young
Clove	—	You are as slender as the clove!
		You are an unblown rose!
		I have long loved you, and you have not known it.
Jonquil	—	Have pity on my passion.
Paper	—	I faint every hour!
Pear	—	Give me some hope.
Soap	—	I am sick with love.
Coal	—	May I die, and all my years be yours!

Facing, above: TOPKAPU PALACE.
below: TOPKAPU PALACE, INTERIOR.

A rose	—	May you be pleased, and your sorrows mine!
A straw	—	Suffer me to be your slave.
Cloth	—	Your price is not to be found.
Cinnamon	—	But my fortune is yours.
A match	—	I burn, I burn! my flame consumes me.
Gold Thread	—	Don't turn away your face from me!
Hair	—	Crown of my head.
Grape	—	My two eyes.
Gold Wire	—	I die – come quickly.
P.S.		
Pepper	—	Send me an answer.

Now all the grace and danger is gone; the name of the Sweet Waters of Asia is all that is left of their romance. Life has moved to the smaller Sweet Waters; there is a bathing establishment at the mouth, and a fair-ground in the meadow. There are cafés where bourgeois picnic-parties can bring their luncheons and eat them, for the price of a *consommation* – lemonade or 'visinade' (syrup of black cherries). Old trousered beggar-women replace the ladies and their black eunuchs; odd little jaunting-cars replace the smart carriages. I have sometimes taken my own luncheon there, and have sat gazing across towards Mehmet II's splendid castle, Rumeli Hisar, on the European shore; I do not think I should have felt so comfortable there in the great days of the Sweet Waters, but of course they are more entertaining to read about.

At the Sweet Waters of Asia, the horses of the imperial stud were grazed. When they went to grass, they used to pass through Constantinople at night, to avoid the evil eye, or else they would be hidden by their accoutrements from the glance of envy. Bulgarians walked in the middle of the cortège, playing upon pipes.

The great Sweet Waters now consist of a muddy stream; caiques are laid up on the bank. Over the bridge is the village of Anadolu Hisar, built in the Asiatic fortress. The village, and the remains of the castle, are very attractive: the road passes through the middle of the *enceinte*, there are two towers above, on the landward side, and two towers on sea level; a small public garden has been made inside the walls. This castle was built by Bayazit I at the end of the fourteenth century.

The European shore is more built over with scholastic establishments

o

Facing, above: HOUSES BUILT INTO THE WALLS AND
          FUNDAMENTS OF THE OLD PALACES.
  below: ORTAKÖY MOSQUE ON THE BOSPHORUS
          AT DEFTERDAR POINT.

and with casinos; this is very natural, for communications with the capital are far more rapid, though there is now a project under consideration for making a bridge across the Bosphorus at Kandilli. It is there that Mandrocles of Samos made a bridge for Darius; he hung up a votive picture of the passage of the Persian army into Europe in the temple of Hera in Samos.

Bebek, on a bay opposite Kandilli, is sad, suburban and melancholy, with a touch of vanished grandeur. Rumeli Hisar, on a promontory, is very much more agreeable.

The castle, built by Mehmet II, is magnificent. Two handsome towers face each other across a dip in the hills; walls descend to connect them, and other walls zigzag downhill to unite them with towers by the sea. There is a little hamlet inside the *enceinte*, with the broken minaret of a mosque. Byzantine capitals lie about, and at the entrance there are two fine Byzantine columns; the great church of St. Michael at Anaplous, and other Byzantine buildings, were pillaged for materials by Mehmet's labourers. The story that the fortress was designed in the shape of the Kufic letter M, the initial of the Prophet and of the Sultan, is apocryphal; the architect has simply profited by the natural contours for defensive purposes. The former name of this site was Phoneus (killer) from the violence of the Bosphorus at this point. The fortress always looks splendid from the water, and from the Asiatic shore; while from Rumeli Hisar the less imposing Asian fortress is extremely pretty, with the village clustering round its towers.

Above Rumeli Hisar is the valley of Baltalimani, by some identified with the place where Darius entered Thrace; opposite is Kanlica, with its handsome *yalis*, a place famous for the excellence of its yoghourt. On the European shore there is a small gulf at Istinye, with various vessels in dock. This place was Sosthenion to the Byzantines, a corruption of Leosthenion, for it owed its name to Leosthenes of Megara, a companion of Byzas, founder of Byzantium. Here the Argonauts raised a temple in honour of a winged genius who had succoured them, and Constantine appropriately consecrated a church on the same site to the Archangel Michael. Here the Stylite, St. Daniel, practised for many years on top of his pillar.

After Yeniköy (a literal translation of the Byzantine Neapolis) the Bosphorus turns due west till Tarabya (Therapia); there it opens out, and there is a right-angled turn northwards. Tarabya, a favourite summer resort, and the site of several embassies, figures very largely in fiction and in memoirs concerned with the last years of the Turkish empire.

An early-nineteenth-century traveller writes romantically of the classical associations of this spot and of its surroundings: 'There tradition had placed the palace of King Phineas; the summit of that mountain was occupied by Jupiter Urius; along that silver current did the intrepid Argonauts pass, to encounter the terrors of an unknown and inhospitable element; on that promontory did Phryxus offer sacrifice to the Gods; here Medea uttered her incantations; from yonder pinnacle the ambitious Darius Hydaspes first contemplated the savage coast of Thrace, and the mazes of the Cyanean rocks; beneath yonder grove reposed the giant limbs of Amycus King of Bithynia, "The Og of Bashan" in Grecian poetry.'[1]

Argonautic geography is very difficult and extremely involved. Lemprière hedges, in his brief account: 'From Cyzicum they visited Bebrycia, otherwise called Bithynia, where Pollux accepted the challenge of Amycus King of the country in the combat of the cestus, and slew him. They were driven from Bebrycia by a storm, to Salmydessa, on the coast of Thrace, where they delivered Phineus King of the place, from the persecution of the harpies. Phineus directed their course through the Cyanean rocks or the Symplegades, and they safely entered the Euxine sea.' Mr. Robert Graves, in his brilliant and careful reconstruction of the story of the Argonauts,[2] places King Amycus, the giant wrestler, somewhere on the Marmara: some legends, however, bury him under the Mont du géant on the upper Bosphorus. Out of his grave grew the insane laurel, a branch of which caused strife. The blind Phineus, and the harpies that fouled his table, are generally placed on the Bosphorus; some authorities put him in Thrace, others in Bithynia.

On the Bithynian coast, north-east of Tarabya, is Beykoz, a big village beneath the hill of Jupiter Urius, once noted for its glass factory; it turned out a prettyish, oriental version of Venetian glass. At Büyükdere, where the channel turns northwards, there is the outlet of the valley called Kalos Agros in Byzantine times, which leads to the forest of Belgrade, the chief ornament of the Thracian side of the Bosphorus.

The upper Bosphorus, above Büyükdere, is very much more pleasant

---

[1] Adam Neale: *Travels* (1818).   [2] *The Golden Fleece* (London, 1944).

than the shut-in, melancholy lower stream, enclosed by built-over hills, overgrown with lush vegetation, with its damp and muzzy atmosphere. From Büyükdere there is a wider view; the open sea, the Euxine, can be seen. On the Asiatic side at last there is some bare earth exposed to view, uncovered by trees or houses. There are some passable cliffs; here they may even be called fine, and the hills rise to a more appreciable height. At Anadolu Kavagi the fine Genoese castle, later taken over by the Turks, is finely situated on a hill-top; there is a pleasant, homely, wooden village below, with lovely coloured nets and boats lying on the shore. At this village (poplar of Asia), and at the opposite Rumeli Kavagi (poplar of Europe), foreigners are not allowed to disembark. Just before it a chain of floating buoys stretches across the Bosphorus. These two are the last ports served by the passenger steamers.

It is, however, possible to go to the Black Sea overland; on the Thracian side you can go by car through the forest of Belgrade, and very pleasant it must be. The bus journey to Chile, through Bithynia, should only be undertaken by people with great powers of endurance; it is, however, worth a good deal of discomfort. From Scutari it is two-and-a-half-hours' journey, in an overcrowded bus, and on bad roads. If it is possible to see out of the window, you note, almost at once, that roll and rise in the Bithynian landscape which is sadly absent from eastern Thrace. The road goes through a plain, golden with maize and sunflowers, but bracken-covered hills are never far away. On the return journey I noticed the sunflowers sullenly turning their backs on the setting sun, perhaps in their unseemly haste to greet the rising sun next day. Later the road follows a long and narrow valley and then emerges in a sad country of dunes; on one such, Chile is built. It is a dull, brown, wooden, red-tiled town, Calpe to the ancients; here, down at the port, the Argonauts offered a sacrifice to Apollo on their outward journey, and near here Xenophon and the ten thousand won a victory over the Bithynians. Looking down from the village, you see a great curve of dunes and sand and a prettyish little archipelago of rocks. The Euxine for miles and miles was shining and sparkling, as if it were not black at all, or at all inhospitable to seamen. Chile is valuable as one of the places to which you can go to breathe; the shut-in muzziness of Constantinople and the Bosphorus forces you to seek real mountain or sea. Any little port of north Devon is probably more beautiful and interesting.

The entrance from the Bosphorus to the Black Sea is guarded by the islets called by the ancients the Cyanean rocks, or the 'Blue rocks'; they were also called the Symplegades, from the belief that they were constantly clashing together: 'The waves of the sea,' says Lemprière, 'which continually break against them with a violent noise, fill the air with a darkening foam, and render the passage extremely dangerous. The ancients supposed that these islands floated, and even sometimes united to crush vessels into pieces when they passed through the straits. This tradition arose from their appearing, like all other objects, to draw nearer when navigators approached them.' Byron also has offered a description:

> The wind swept down the Euxine, and the wave
> Broke foaming o'er the blue Symplegades;
> 'Tis a grand sight from off 'the Giant's Grave'
> To watch the progress of those rolling seas
> Between the Bosphorus, as they lash and lave
> Europe and Asia, you being quite at ease:
> There's not a sea the passenger e'er pukes in,
> Turns up more dangerous breakers than the Euxine.

Of the passage of the Argonauts there is more than one story. The Clashing Rocks were charmed by the song of Orpheus, or safely negotiated by aid of a heron sent by the goddess Athena. In Apollonius Rhodius the story is almost reminiscent of the dove set loose by Noah.

> Euphemus loos'd the bird of pinions light;
> With heads uprais'd the sailors mark her flight,
> And wait the event with mingled hope and dread,
> As through the pass on airy plumes she sped,
> Then furious rushing through the dark profound,
> The rocks together crash'd with horrid sound . . .
> Safe through the closing rocks the turtle springs
> But shorn of plumage from her tail and wings.

Byron brags in a letter to his friend Drury of having clambered up the Cyanean rocks at the cost of a good deal of effort; he admits that it was not worth while.

The Golden Horn

The Golden Horn is an arm of the sea, some seven miles long; the

Byzantines called it Keras or Horn from its form like that of a stag's horn. Chrysokeras, or Golden Horn, is a name more rarely bestowed; it was earned by its infinite value as a safe harbour, and perhaps, more picturesquely, by its shimmering gold appearance in the evening. The Turks, prosaically and incorrectly, call it Haliç, or canal. This arm of the sea, flowing into the Bosphorus where it joins the sea of Marmara, is the northeast boundary of Stamboul, and divides it from Galata and Pera.

Though an infinitely more attractive water-way than the Bosphorus, its shores are far more squalid. 'All the filth and rubbish of both towns are constantly flung into it — custom-houses, barracks, storehouses, the dockyard, all there are placed on the borders of it — whole dunghills are swept into it.' So wrote Elizabeth, Lady Craven (1789), and the process has gone on uninterruptedly since her day.

At night, suffering from the 'spleen of Pera' by which nearly all travellers seem to have been infected — for in the summer in that intolerable suburb (where, nevertheless, travellers nearly always find they have to stay), it is too stuffy to remain indoors, and too damp to remain out-of-doors — it is a consolation to watch the waxing moon over the Golden Horn from some overhanging terrace or to watch the waning moon over the Bosphorus from the gardens at Taxim. Both water-ways are then lovely.

But while the day-time Bosphorus, as much (that is) as you can see of it from Pera, is not impressive, has only the prettiness that we are apt uncritically to attribute to any water view from the midst of a town, and must depend on its shipping for charm, the Golden Horn is always magnificent because of the superb outline of Stamboul behind it.

The best view-point is the most obvious, the tower of Galata. This medieval Genoese construction, once called the tower of Christ, and surmounted by the cross of Genoa, is used nowadays by fire-watchers, who are always needed in this city where so many wooden quarters still survive. It is the only building that lends any distinction to the view of Pera and Galata from Stamboul.

From the top of this tower you see Seraglio Point to the best advantage, for from this height it can be seen as a point: the Marmara appears behind it. There is the spire of the Serail amid its trees, St. Irene, St. Sophia, and the mosque of Ahmed with all its minarets. The mosques of Nuruosmaniye and Bayazit are seen on either side of the valley now filled by the covered bazaars. In the forefront, as it were on a terrace overlooking the water, the Süleymaniye is grandly poised. Farther back, the gap between the third and fourth hills is nobly bridged by the arches of the aqueduct of Valens, damaged by invasions and by earthquakes, so often restored both by emperors and by sultans, and still keeping its character as one of the most ancient and splendid monuments of Constantinople. Beyond the aqueduct, the fourth hill is marked by the Conqueror's mosque, the fifth hill by that of Selim I, the sixth by that of Mihrimah. That princess here, and in Scutari, chose splendid sites for her mosques; it is fabled that she built them with the sale of the jewels off one slipper, which is more reasonably explained as half her 'slipper-money', i.e. her pin-money.

Nobler even than the view across from Haydar Pasha, this splendid prospect entitles Constantinople to the praise of having the most magnificent skyline of any city in the world; and this skyline, seen in whole or in part from every point on the Golden Horn, makes that dirty and slummy and stagnant channel infinitely more distinguished than the clean, swift-flowing, tidy and residential Bosphorus.

But indeed there is another side to it, as most discerning travellers have observed. The sixteenth-century William Lithgow says: 'Truly I may say of Constantinople, as I said once of the world, in the Lamentado of my second pilgrimage:

> A painted whore, the mask of deadly sin,
> Sweet fair without, and stinking foul within.

For indeed outwardly it hath the fairest show; and inwardly, the streets being narrow, and most part covered, the filthiest and most deformed building in the world.'

Aaron Hill (1709) concurs: 'The ravish'd Traveller believes himself approaching a Place no less agreeable, than was the fam'd *Elyzium* of the ancient Poets. But nothing can be possibly a greater Disappointment than I found at Entrance; all those bright and golden Glories, which had tempted at a Distance Lost their Beauties in a nearer view; and I, instead of an expected Heaven, was amaz'd to find a *Hell* of darkness; narrow Streets, with dirty Causeways on each broken side, and Windows hanging over, almost meeting in a dark conjunction.'

Two nineteenth-century travellers echo him. John Galt (1812) says: 'The superb distant prospect of Constantinople only serves to render more acute the disappointment, which arises from its interior wretchedness.' While Clarke (1810) is even more eloquent: 'After what has been said of the exterior magnificence of this wonderful city, the Reader is perhaps ill prepared for a view of the interior; the horror, the wretchedness, and filth of which are not to be conceived. Its streets are narrow, dark, ill paved, and at the same time full of holes and ordure. In the most abominable alleys of London, or Paris, there is nothing so disgusting. They more resemble the interior of common sewers than public streets.' Much the same might truthfully be said today.

Only the distant prospect pleases; almost the whole length of the Golden Horn has squalid shores. The mouth, lovely as you sail in from Asia in the evening when the water is golden, and always adorned by the beautiful pyramid of Yeni Cami, is impressive enough to make you ignore the dreariness of the railway station on the Stamboul side, and of the grim warehouses and quays of Tophane. There is a moment when the great mosque of Süleyman almost looks as if it were sitting on the Galata bridge.

Under the Galata bridge is the quay for the drab little steamers that serve the Golden Horn. The gloom of Galata on one side, the sordidness of the fish-market on the other, occupy the unlovely shores between the two bridges; nevertheless, it is an instructive journey, you learn better the position of various monuments, such as the mosque of Rustem Pasha.

At the new Atatürk bridge the well-restored mosque of Azap Kapu, in its emplacement, is slightly reminiscent of a London city church near a bridge. The boat puts in on the northern side, at the gloomy dockyards of Kasim Pasha; this would be the place to alight for the walk to the delightful mosque of Piyale Pasha, some half an hour inland.

Unlike the Bosphorus boats, the Golden Horn boat plies from side to side. Something, not very much, of the walls of Byzantium can be made out. At the Phanar there is a pleasant, water-side garden, but that venerable Greek quarter, apart from the Patriarchate, has now completely lost its character, and is a jumble of undistinguished Turkish streets, with only here and there a fine house-front; the Greeks are gone to Pera. The one notable Hellenic touch is unfortunate; the impertinent red-brick tower of the seminary is almost the sole serious blemish to the sky-line of Stamboul.

There follows, near the water-side, the Bulgarian church, a metal and Gothic construction capable of dismemberment and of transportation into some museum of bad taste, where it ought to be; its gates are shut and padlocked, and it has the peculiar pathos, blent with horror, that only really foul architecture can suffer in decay. It deserves to be more famous and more frequently visited than it is. Here is the rather unpleasant Jewish quarter of Balat, and on the other side of the water is the very unpleasant Jewish suburb of Hasköy. Above Hasköy is Okmeydan, formerly the Sultan's archery-ground.

The last port within the walls is that of Ayvan Saray whose name, 'The Great Palace', commemorates the site of Blachernae; there is hardly anywhere in the city more horrible and pitiful than this site of the imperial wharf, with its mud, evil smells, and nightmare warehouses, its mangy cats and mangy curs; here is one of the places most sanctified by associations, and once so full of vanished beauty, the home of Our Lady's girdle, the great Palladium of the 'God-guarded city'. Sadly one echoes the modern Greek epigrammatist who wrote:

> Mud, dogs, and porters, more's the pity,
> Are the sole produce of the city.

The suburbs that follow are little less horrifying: factories on the south-west, slaughterhouses on the north-east, and the prevailing, characteristic and most nauseating smell of Constantinople, that of tanneries; hereabouts Justinian bridged the Golden Horn, and Mehmet II also built a bridge.

All the way, the sky-line has been the reward for the journey, and the end is profoundly satisfying. The last stop is at Eyüp, a holy spot, and a favourite place of burial for sultans and viziers. This place is sanctified by the grave of Eyüp, a companion of the Prophet, and a Moslem saint, who died in front of Byzantium in the Saracen siege of 672. His relics were discovered, rather conveniently, it must be admitted, during the siege of 1453; one is reminded of the almost equally convenient discovery of the bones of Basil the Bulgar-slayer at the Hebdomon, by Michael VIII, the returning Greek emperor.

You walk through a street of tombs, almost like one of the dead cities of Cairo; some are solid, handsome buildings, others are simply domed canopies sheltering two or three graves. The mosque, founded by the conqueror, but since rebuilt and restored, is clean, dignified and peaceful; this, I think, is usually the case with great Moslem sanctuaries. Nothing can exceed the devout gravity of the Dome of the Rock in Jerusalem, or of the lovely tomb of Imam el Shafy in Cairo. It is much to be wished that

Christian holy places had the same simple tranquillity; only a vigorous cleansing of the temples, perhaps only an iconoclastic movement, could give such quiet to Lourdes or to Lisieux.

The only noise is the not unreligious boisterousness of the birds: *et enim passer invenit sibi domum, et turtur nidum sibi ubi ponat pullos suos.* There is in fact a pigeoncote in the outer courtyard, and pigeons coo and fly and tumble all over it; as outside the mosque of Bayazit, it is a pious as well as an entertaining act to feed them, and pedlars sell saucers or little tin lids full of corn or millet. The birds waddle round your feet, expecting a largess. Behind, there are large trees, from which the quacking of storks mingles with the cooing of the doves.

The western wall of the inner courtyard conceals the tomb of Eyüp Ensari; it is coated with rather a jumble of tiles, eighteenth-century faience from Tekfur Saray, but it is uncommonly pretty. Christians may not go inside,[1] but through a small window you may peep into a beautiful, mysterious, blue-tiled tomb-chamber. Lamps hang outside, and there are generally people praying, and, as usual where Christians are admitted at all to an Islamic holy place, there is no discourtesy or fanatic hostility shown to members of another religion; one feels nothing of the fear that the Jews inspire at the Weeping Wall.

Behind the mosque of Eyüp there is a path uphill through the cemeteries; on the hill-top is a small café called after Pierre Loti. This is as charming a place as one can well go to in the neighbourhood of Constantinople, a little before the hour of sunset; a very famous view-point.

On your left are the head of the Golden Horn and the entrance of the Sweet Waters of Europe; these are now even more destitute of their former glory than the Sweet Waters of Asia. Here the Sultans had a palace, already dilapidated in the time of the French traveller Pertusier (1815); it faced a marble tank, and there were charming kiosques in the grounds, and small wooden bridges over the Sweet Waters.

The north-east side of the Golden Horn is an outline not to be compared with that of Stamboul, as seen from Pera; but from the terrace of Pierre Loti's café the hills are pleasant enough, the slaughterhouses at their feet cannot be smelt for what they are, and Pera and Galata compose round the Tower of Galata into a better group than might be expected. The Golden Horn lies, at the right hour, golden below you. You can see

[1] This prohibition no longer exists.

the Serail, St. Sophia, the mosques of Süleyman and Selim, and, best of all, the city walls ascending from the Golden Horn up to their highest point, the mosque of Mihrimah. Outside the Adrianople Gate is a hill-side cemetery, covered with dark cypresses. From this point all the first six hills of Constantinople are visible. It is always difficult to be sure if one has seen the seventh, for it is marked by no domes or minarets; its principal monument is, on the contrary, a depression, the open cistern of Mocius. Then the light fades off domes, minarets and walls, and the waters darken.

Eyüp was the coronation mosque of the Sultans, for here was performed the solemn vesting with the sword, a ceremony corresponding to the anointing and crowning of Christian monarchs. It was also a shrine regularly visited by the court, and the English traveller, Charles Mac-Farlane (1828), describes imperial devotions here which yield little in splendour to the Byzantine ceremonies recorded by Constantine Porphyrogenitus: 'The long *Kachambas*, brilliant with gold and silk, and propelled by thirteen pairs of oars, rapidly approached, and in its train six other barges scarcely less magnificent. The Sultan was seated within a gilt bellice. On the quay, where he landed, was a horse richly caparisoned, with housings of velvet, a gold bit and bridle set with jewels, and broad Turkish strings of massy gold. He mounted; and followed by his splendid household officers and other dignitaries, rode to the mosque, which was only a few paces from the Water's Edge, in all the pomp of oriental etiquette.'

At Eyüp there is a well for divination, where Joseph plays the part of St. Anthony and tells where lost things are. The tomb of Mehmet II's horse is also here, with its power of giving strength to crippled children. The well was at one time visited by Christians, under the mistaken belief that the Eyüp here commemorated was Job; there is, however, no reason to think that there was ever a Byzantine sanctuary on this spot.

The Marmara

You sail out again from the Galata bridge, you circle Seraglio Point, with its gardens, and, sailing into the Marmara, you have the best view of the sea walls as far as the lighthouse.

On the Asiatic shore is the huge Selimiye barracks, and, nearby, the site of Florence Nightingale's hospital. Here that courageous, single-minded and rather unpleasant woman, so tender to humanity at large, so inhumane to individuals, landed on 4 November, 1854.

'Oh, Miss Nightingale,' said one of the party, as they gazed from the deck at the huge Barrack Hospital that was their destination, 'when we land, don't let there be any red tape delays, let us get straight to nursing the poor fellows!' Miss Nightingale, exhausted by sea-sickness, replied with even more than her usual asperity: 'The strongest will be wanted at the wash-tub!' That night the British ambassador was able to write: 'Miss Nightingale and her brigade of nurses are actually established at Scutari under the same roof with the gallant and suffering objects of their compassion.' He hoped that 'much comfort may be derived by the sick and wounded from that attractive source'.

Her recent biographer[1] has drawn a vivid picture of the discomforts to which she came: narrow quarters, a scant water-supply, a total lack of equipment, hostility from the doctors, and all the Byzantine red-tape delays of which the British Army was capable. Bad for the nurses, the conditions of the hospital were probably worse for the patients than those of any modern concentration camp have been for their inmates – a nightmare of dirt and horror. The building was densely overcrowded, the floors were an inch deep in liquid filth, the blankets crawled with vermin. Against all this, Florence Nightingale had to contend, against the apathy of Lord Stratford, the ambassador, and against an unwanted detachment of drunken hired nurses, and of squabbling nuns, brought without her consent by the *exaltée* Mary Stanley who was jealously in love with her. But for her extraordinary pertinacity and powers of work the hospital must have collapsed altogether during that terrible winter: by the spring she had triumphed, and two hundred men from one transport could be properly received, bathed, put into clean clothes and beds, and given suitable food.

Trenery and his sister visited Miss Nightingale's hospital; this romantic traveller has nothing to say of its first horrors. There is a rather improbable portrait of a drummer-boy, wounded at Balaclava: 'I looked upon his soft, white bosom, heaving with all the gentlest and kindliest emotions of the human heart . . . upon that holy soul which revealed itself through the pellucid deeps of his heavenly eyes.' He also much admired 'the quiet dead', of which there were such hecatombs until Miss Nightingale's life-saving activities had borne fruit: 'We looked through the mists of tears on their sweet, sad, long faces: and never did one reverence our English

[1] Cecil Woodham-Smith: *Florence Nightingale* (London, 1950).

faces at their worth until now, that we could compare them after death, with those of Russians, Osmanlis, French and Algerians.'[1]

Hard by is the Crimean cemetery, the kind of 'garden by the sea' dear to English sentiment; it is entered through the football ground of the Selimiye barracks. Here, among the scabious and long grass, a few table-tombs commemorate the Crimean dead; these have generally been erected by their sorrowing sisters. One can imagine them, the gallant, whiskered young officers whom John Leech drew, feasting off plum pudding out of a hamper amid the Russian snows; then carried in the crowded and squalid misery of a transport down the Black Sea and the Bosphorus, to die soothed by Florence Nightingale's presence, and then to present sweet, sad, long, dead faces to Trenery's gaze.

The majority have no memorial apart from the grey obelisk erected by Queen Victoria and her people in 1857: this symbol, probably chosen to avoid the offence to Moslem eyes that any more Christian monument might have caused, is supported by four mourning Pre-Raphaelite angels, apparently wearing thick, grey, Guards great-coats, each carrying a wreath and a palm.

A tree-shaded path (commanding a view of the gas-works) leads on to the new English cemetery, within sound of the rumble of the railway station at Haydar Pasha. It is another 'garden by the sea', and prettily planted. Oleanders weep over Anglo-Levantine families, Whittalls, Barkers, La Fontaines; these have all placed comforting inscriptions over their graves, intended, so it would seem, to give comfort rather to the dead. 'It is not for long now, dear', is the sentiment; I wonder if this is greatly comforting to the living as the years pass. There are here the cemeteries of the two last wars.

In the fading light I searched in vain for the grave of an acquaintance; I owed him, I felt, this small act of piety, and a De Profundis, for he had bored me, and I had shown it. Perhaps no one has bothered to mark his grave, and I am his only visitor; that is a sad thought, too sad, I am afraid, to be untrue.

The railway station, the terminus of the Taurus express, the gate to Asia, is not unlike a great London terminus on a smaller scale. Then comes the bay of Kadiköy, the ancient Chalcedon; perhaps those Megarians who founded it were not so blind as Delphi would have them, for neglecting

[1] *The City of the Crescent* (London, 1855).

the advantages of Byzantium and the Golden Horn. The Asiatic promontory, with its Phoenician settlement, was no doubt easier to occupy than a promontory of the fierce Thracians. It was defensible; and to this day many people much prefer its climate, and have chosen to live there, crossing daily to their work in Stamboul or Pera. A tunny fishery, like Byzantium, sometimes it was its rival but more often suffered the same fate as the younger foundation. Its chief claim to fame is that it was the seat of the fourth General Council of the Church, which in 451 issued the vitally important definition: 'We confess one Jesus, Lord, only Son, whom we acknowledge *in two Natures.*' By this definition Monophysitism was condemned, and Egypt was lost to the yet undivided Church.

Modern Constantinople, like ancient Byzantium, stretches out its suburbs, colonies and settlements both on the Asiatic and the Thracian coasts. But after two calls on the Asiatic shore, the boat goes straight ahead for the islands. 'Kizil Adalar', the red islands to the Turks, from the colour of the earth, the 'Princes' islands' to everyone else, though only the big island of Prinkipo had that title during the Byzantine period.

The islands, lovely and almost Greek when seen from afar, are the great adornment of the Marmara: beautiful whether you see them as dim, blue shapes from the first hill of Constantinople, or from the hill of Çamlica, or from an aeroplane, flying to Broussa. Near, from the sea, they are (as islands so often are) rather disappointing; the low brush or tree-covered hills lack the beauty of the distant, blue outlines, and they are too green and lush to be really Greek. But the deck of a boat is not usually the best place from which to see islands; like other islands, these have beauties which they are only prepared to yield up to people who will give themselves the trouble to land.

They are charming; even when the Marmara has been green during your journey, it seems to turn azure when you look down on it through their pine trees. A vital air breathes here that never visits Constantinople or the Bosphorus; it is the best antidote that I know to 'the spleen of Pera' which, indeed, would be insupportable but for the relief of an occasional visit to Halki or to Prinkipo. They might easily, one feels, be near somewhere much more pleasant than Constantinople. The only Byzantine existence one can imagine as tolerable would have been as an exile on one of these islands; provided that one was allowed to keep one's eyes, castration would be a small price to pay.

The two larger islands are tourists' paradises, and yet empty of foreign tourists. Their amenities, their air of being holiday places, so happily contrast with the unwelcoming character of Constantinople. Prinkipo (Turkish: Büyük Ada) abounds in this kind of charm; its steep, gay little town mounts abruptly from the sea. Little yellow carriages, brightly painted inside, are ready to take you for 'the long round' or 'the short round'; they have stiff, fringed awnings that protect you from the sun. It is such a stiff, fringed awning that shades the hotel omnibus at Aswan; that, I must confess, is the reason that (by a kind of Proustian association) I feel such a peculiar bliss at Prinkipo. The green Nile is absent, as are the graceful, black Nubians in their *galabiehs*, and the golden sand of the Arabian desert. But there is the same sensation of coming, suddenly, into a better and dryer climate; hotels and villas have the same atmosphere of holiday, and their gardens also blaze with flowers; the purple, papery bougainvillaea is as ubiquitous here as in Aswan in the spring, trailing over white walls or pergolas.

Halki (Heybeli Ada) is less brilliantly cheerful; it has a quieter charm, and even greater beauty. A French Byzantinologist who, like most people, hated Pera, enjoyed frequent escapes to this island where 'the most delightful paths, under sweet-smelling pines and silver olives, opposite view-points changing with every pace, go up and down, round wild and solitary little bays, true Thebaids in this Paradise of nature, where the Marmara sleeps so calmly under a sky of fire, that it seems a mirror of gold'.[1]

This island is chiefly famous for the convent of the Mother of God, founded by Maria, wife of John VIII, and reconstructed in the seventeenth century by a Greek drogman, or grand-interpreter to the Porte. It has undergone further vicissitudes, became a commercial school in the nineteenth century, and now is a naval school. Tombs of seventeenth- and eighteenth-century patriarchs are here, and that of Sir Edward Barton, Elizabeth I's ambassador to the Porte, who died in Halki of a chest affection in 1597.

Halki, so pleasantly shaded, is the best island for the middle of the day; the afternoon view across to Bithynia is of great beauty. The great, red-purple mountain, with the pudding-basin hill near the shore in front of it, has an almost Aegean nobility. Later in the day, it is better to go on to

[1] Adapted from Gustave Schlumberger: *Les Îles des Princes*.

Prinkipo; here, sitting on the water-front, you can watch the sun set on the neck that joins the two hills of Halki; and the mauve evening of Bithynia attains its most beautiful moment when lights come out and twinkle all over the pudding-basin hill, before the colour has altogether faded from the great mountain behind it.

These islands are much more cosmopolitan than Constantinople, and more noticeably Greek-speaking; and so it has always been. Grelot speaks of them as a place of debauch for Turks, who feared to drink at home. 'Though the Turks rarely drink Wine, yet they love to take their full swinge when they can get a private convenience, not believing that they have so much as tasted it, unless they can feel the effects of it in their heads or their stomachs three days after. To this purpose away they go to these Islands, inhabited only by Christian *Greeks*, with a design to bouze it about briskly, and when they are got drunk, they commit all the disorders that their inflam'd heads can devise. They swear at the poor *Greeks*, beat 'em, and seize for their own proper use (as Lords of the Mannour) whatsoever they have a mind to.'

The boat sails on from Prinkipo to Yalova, nearly an hour-and-a-half's journey. From this little village buses take you the two miles up to the Spa, an admirable drive, already a foretaste of the beauties of Bithynia. At the Spa there is a hotel, and there are bath establishments, in a well-planted park tightly enclosed in a valley. The wooded hills that surround it, if rather Swiss, are noble Swiss scenery; while the Marmara is like a Swiss lake from which mist has concealed all that is high or grand in the surroundings. The baths here, used in pre-Christian times, had a great vogue in the epoch of Justinian; Theodora came here, and lodged her suite in tents, as Henrietta Maria did eleven centuries later at Tunbridge Wells. Nor did the Turks disdain this spa, though it was not fitted up as a modern watering-place till 1928.

Facing, above: THE BOSPHORUS.
below: DOLMABAHÇE PALACE.

CHAPTER X

FLYING FROM ISTANBUL

THE hymns of other travellers to the beauty of Constantinople linger in one's ears. Tournefort said that human language was powerless in front of it; Gautier could not believe that what he saw was real; Pouqueville thought himself in another world; a German visitor said that the most beautiful illusions of youth, the dreams of first love, were poor and insipid compared with the delicious sensation he felt at the first sight of these charmed shores. Kinglake, as often, was lyrical: 'Even if we don't take a part in the chaunt about "Mosques and Minarets", we can still yield praises to Stamboul. We can chaunt about the harbour; we can say and sing that nowhere else does the sea come so home to a city; there are no pebble shores – no sand bars – no slimy river beds – no black canals – no locks nor docks to divide the very heart of the place from the deep waters; if being in the noisiest part of Stamboul, you would stroll to the quiet side of the way amidst those cypresses opposite, you will cross the fathomless Bosphorus; if you would go from your hotel to the Bazaars, you must pass by the bright blue pathway of the Golden Horn, that can carry a thousand sail of the line. You are accustomed to the gondolas that glide among the palaces of St. Mark, but here at Stamboul it is a hundred-and-twenty-gun-ship that meets you in the street. Venice strains out from the steadfast land, and in old times would send forth the chief of the state to woo and wed the reluctant sea; but the stormy bride of the Doge is the bowing slave of the Sultan – she comes to his feet with the treasures of the world – she bears him from palace to palace – by some unfailing witch-craft, she entices the breezes to follow her, and fan the pale cheek of her lord – she lifts his armed navies to the very gates of his garden – she watches the walls of his serail – she stifles the intrigues of his Ministers – she quiets the scandals of his court – she extinguishes his rivals, and hushes his naughty wives all one by one, so vast are the wonders of the deep!'

Reading such passages, even re-reading the previous pages of this book,

227   P

Facing, above: THE VIEW OF HEYBELI ADA FROM BÜYÜK ADA.
    below: THE EYÜP CEMETERY AND THE GOLDEN HORN.

I feel, what perhaps I did not always feel at the time, how privileged I was, at the bidding of a generous publisher, to be able to learn to know this wonderful city in some detail. Day after day it was my only duty to wander from monument to monument, sitting in quiet courts with oriental patience (for I had all the time in the world), waiting for the door to open on the cool beauty of marble and tiles within and, once inside, sitting cross-legged on the thick-carpeted floor, my feet relieved of their shoes. Or I might take a boat on the Bosphorus – a waiter went by with a tray of glasses, clinking them and intoning: 'çay, çay, kahve, çay', while I looked out at those fabled shores – or I might walk along the grand sweep of walls, between the Marble Tower and the Golden Horn, or make yet another visit to St. Sophia, which every time has some further secret to give up. I might (when I could get in) watch the patient work of restoration on the Kariye mosaics, or lose myself in the maze of the Covered Bazaars. I often spent the last moments of daylight at some famous viewpoint, particularly at Pierre Loti's enchanting café, with its splendid panorama of the walls and of the Golden Horn.

But travellers to Constantinople belong to two schools of thought, and I belong to both of them: there are those who deeply admire the wonderful city, and those who are continuously unhappy there. The last is a personal reaction, but reasons can be found for it.

The first reason is physical, the damp that rises from the three seas; on summer evenings, when the heat makes it intolerable to sit indoors, the damp makes it intolerable to sit out-of-doors, whether one suffers the miasma of the Golden Horn as one watches the waxing moon over Stamboul from the Rue des Petits Champs or thereabouts, or the miasma of the Bosphorus as one watches the waning moon over Asia from Taxim or one of the garden-restaurants below it. Only the islands are free from this, and they are far away. Another physical trial is the wind that blows down from the Black Sea and, swirling round street-corners, puffs finely powdered dung in your face.

The second reason is spiritual: the profound melancholy of a city that has died twice. Through the ages, even when the city was only decaying, travellers have felt this. The lyrical Kinglake speaks of 'the dreary monuments of past power and splendour'. A city totally dead, like Delos or Jerash, need not be sad; a small town that has lost its importance and become 'quaint', a port from which the sea has receded, a spa where no one drinks the waters any more, a small market town by-passed by the road of progress may be havens for the spirit. Constantinople is too thickly populated to be regarded as a ruin, and too big to have become 'quaint'. Its sadness is there all the time: *fuit*. Cemeteries surround it, and it is full of images of death. I measured the passing of time by observing black-edged notices of the 'forty days' mind' appearing posted on the walls, with the names of people whose funerals I had earlier seen announced in the same place. No doubt it matters very little where one dies, but Constantinople is one of the very few places that I have felt I must, at all costs, leave alive; other people have told me that they have felt much the same thing.

The third reason is more personal: the sub-Greek world, places like Constantinople and Alexandria that have been and still partly are Greek, fill me with an unbearable nostalgia for real Greece, for the clarity of Attica and of the Aegean. There should be a word that is exact, and yet can be used in a slightly derogatory way, bearing the same relation to 'Greek' that 'British' bears to 'English'. The answer to: 'What do they know of England, that only England know?' is: 'Everything that matters.' A similar judgment might be made about Greece and the Greek world of the dispersion. To a nostalgic Philhellene, Cairo is more agreeable than Alexandria, and Broussa than Constantinople.

The fourth reason, which almost every traveller has found cogent, is the peculiar hatefulness of Pera. That is where one is almost condemned to live, where one must return every evening, with a sinking heart, after long hours among the monuments of Stamboul. Whirled dangerously in a taxi, frequently threatened with head-on collisions, or grinding more securely in a tram, one scales the steep hill under the Dark Tower. '*This city builds a horror in my brain. . . .*'

'The spleen of Pera' must have been an even greater affliction in the days when Christians could not safely visit Stamboul except with the escort of a janissary, a 'Christian pig-keeper'.

(Aaron Hill speaks pleasantly of this custom, and of the tact with which janissaries would obey the call to prayer, while taking *Giaours* round Stamboul. 'When a Janissary whom you hire to guard you up and down the city, hears the Notice which is giv'n 'em from their Steeples, he will turn about *Stand still*, and beckon with his Hand, to tell his *Charge* he must have Patience for a while, When taking out his *Handkerchief* he spreads it on the Ground, sits *cross-leg* thereupon, and says his Prayers, tho' in the *open Market*; Which having ended, he leaps briskly up, *Salutes* the Person whom he undertakes to Convoy, and renews his journey with the *mild Expression* of *Ghell Johnum Ghell*; or Come *Dear* follow me.')

The spleen, the vapours, accidie then had all day to work their havoc upon the visitor. Now the day need only begin and end there. But each day does not end with sleep; 'the nightingale of Athens', or some other musical attraction, seems to go on all night in the garden-restaurants, and, long after midnight, men come with pickaxes and attack the cobbled streets, only ceasing from their labour when the trams begin to grind again. Nightly, for I do not know how long, the cobbles under my window were taken up and laid down again. The first day I congratulated myself on the thought that the workmen must now move farther down the street: not a bit of it. Was it sheer inefficiency, I wondered; had they left their tools buried by mistake, was it a ritual, or a hunt for buried treasure? After a while I wondered if it were calculated cruelty.

All day, and much of the night, trams grind noisily up the steep streets, almost sweeping you off the narrow pavements. The architecture is unrelievedly hideous. The signs in neon lighting strike a peculiar and personal chill into my heart; for Turkish (which I do not know) bears such a marked likeness to Finnish (which I do not know either). I could almost fancy myself in Helsinki, which would be worse. One day the radio in my taxi played 'Mandatemi un poco di Milano', and I almost wept with nostalgia for a place that I have only been through in a train.

At night, when Stamboul is a dark necropolis, Pera is dimly lighted enough, except in the Taxim Square and the Grande Rue de Péra; here the pavement is broader, and down sweep the ugly, unfriendly faces, four in a row. It is almost a comfort to find how unimportant politics really are in personal relations: in hostile Egypt, almost anyone would be kindly and helpful to a stranger; in friendly Turkey a stiff, proud xenophobia seems to be endemic; nor, in this once cosmopolitan city, where ten languages were spoken in Lady Mary Wortley Montagu's household, does anyone seem to speak anything but Turkish.

'Habit remembered', I have read, 'is happiness', so I tried to order my day by habits: breakfast in a Greek confectioner's, dinner in a White Russian restaurant which was pleasant before the war – now the courtyard is built-over, and it is stifling – an evening sitting on a terrace overlooking the Golden Horn, drinking light Turkish beer. 'The nightingale of Athens', or someone else, sang:

On an evening when it rained. . . .

And I tried to read Boswell or the Brontës, saving up *Villette* as a treat and as a refuge, in case 'the Spleen of Pera' became more than I could bear.

Nevertheless, Pera is very easy to get out of. There can be few cities so large and complicated as Constantinople that are so easy to find one's way about in, and where the communications, though disagreeable, are so good. The three seas that wash the city are all thoroughfares; from the suburb of Beşiktaş, near the tomb of Barbarossa, one can take the ferry to Scutari, or a Bosphorus steamer. Bosphorus travel is a little complicated, needs some working out, for steamers generally hug either the European or the Asiatic shore, only crossing once or twice. And from the Galata bridge there are ferries to other Asiatic suburbs, boats to the islands, and the Golden Horn boat.

By land, there is a network of trams, and at many tram-stops there is a most useful map posted. The traveller who has, as he should have, M. Mamboury's invaluable guide-book, can easily find the *points de repère* from which the monuments are to be sought: the square of Eminönü, the mosque of Sultan Ahmed, the square of Bayazit, the mosque of Fatih, Aksaray, the Adrianople Gate, or Yedikule and the Seven Towers. With a map, there is little that is hard to find; and, if you are lost in some distant purlieus of the city, soon there will appear a dolmuş '(stuffed)' taxi, in which you can take a seat, and it will bring you back to some centre, or to Pera. But the excellence of the communications does not mean that the conscientious visitor will be spared much climbing of the weary seven hills, or much wading in evil-smelling filth by the side of the Marmara and the Golden Horn; and the cobbles tear the shoes and tire out the feet.

And though sleep in Constantinople is too often short and disturbed, food is rather good. Not only in famous restaurants such as Abdullah's, in the Grande Rue de Péra, where you can eat Circassian lamb and other delicious oriental dishes; or Pandeli's, in the Fish market, or the restaurants of Prinkipo where the langouste, or the swordfish grilled on skewers (with bay leaves between the pieces) are beyond praise, but even in quite humble eating-places you can, if you order judiciously, eat very well indeed. Often under the shady trees near the Covered Bazaars I have had a simple and admirable luncheon: a cold green pepper stuffed with a pilaff to which dill, currants and pine-nut kernels have been added, followed by a yellow yoghourt from Kanlica, as good as Cornish cream. There I have sat, watching the coffins come out of the mosque of Bayazit, or the pigeons picking at grain and millet in the square. It is also pleasant and cool to have luncheon in the restaurant from which you can look down into the bustle of the Egyptian bazaar, while you eat your *shish kebab*. As any sort of lump of meat is a *kebab*, and an Irish stew could be correctly so described, it is as well to learn the different names from a phrase-book, to avoid disappointment: a *shish kebab* is skewered and grilled, with onion or tomato between the pieces. Everywhere fish is good, and fruit delicious.

Sandys, perhaps English in his tastes, unduly despised Turkish food. 'Their most ordinary food is pillaw, that is, Rice which hath beene sod with the fat of Mutton. Pottage they use of sundry kinds, egges fried in honey, tansies (or something like them), pasties of sundry ingredients: the little flesh which they eate is cut into gobbets, and either sod, or rosted in a fournace. But I think there is more in *London* spent in one day then is in this City in twenty. Fish they have in indifferent quantitie. But the commons do commonly feed on herbes, fruits, roots, onions, garlicke, a beastly kind of compressed cheese that lyeth in a lumpe; hodgpodges made of flower, milke, and honey, etc. so that they live for little or nothing, considering their fare and the plenty of all things . . . Their usual drink is pure water, yet have they sundry sherbets (so call they the confections which they infuse into it) some made of sugar and lemons, some of violets and the like. . . .'

In the markets, and elsewhere, the cake-shops often provide the only oriental note, particularly among the groceries and haberdashery and neon lighting of the Egyptian bazaar. The basis of Turkish confectionery is honey, nuts and papery pastry; it is only for people with a very sweet tooth, but it looks nice. There are *kadayifs*, a sort of shredded wheat, soaked in honey and sprinkled with nuts; *revani*, sponge cake soaked in honey or syrup; *baklava*, a spiced nut cake between layers of pastry, and *börek* (which I very much dislike), lumps of custard enclosed in pastry.

All over the city are stalls or shops for soft drinks; they look a little like miniature chemists' shops with their big bottles, green bottles of lemonade, red of visinade, yellow of orangeade, or of an apricot drink, white bottles of *ayran* (whipped yoghourt) – every bottle stoppered with a large lemon. Sometimes there are brown bottles of tamarind, which I find very nasty; but I have seldom gone to bed in Constantinople, to face another night of grinding trams and of pickaxes, without a final glass of *ayran*.

Another compensation of the city is that, though so unlike Oxford, it is 'branchy between towers'. The Moslem love of gardens has produced here nothing so beautiful as the riverside gardens of Cairo, but the shady walks of the garden below the Serail are attractive in themselves, not only because they conceal the column of the Goths, and part of an ancient cistern, and offer the modern amenity of a bathing-place. Here there is a splendid view of the entry of the Bosphorus, and the ships anchored in it. Even the simple, little garden of the Phanar, where caiques bob up and down at the edge of the Golden Horn, lingers gratefully in the memory, though one looks across into squalor on the other side.

The first court of the Serail, too big to be felt as a court, is green and leafy; a breeze comes from the Marmara, and from this hill-top there is a good view of Scutari and the islands. Here, temporarily weary of sight-seeing, one can sit down to rest on one of the old cannons round St. Irene. The Hippodrome, round the corner, is also a pleasant if rather formal public garden, with pollarded acacias down either side.

Any distant view shows the branchiness of the city. As well as public gardens and deliberately planted avenues, there are the old 'sunk gardens' that fill the Byzantine open cisterns: those of Aetius, Aspar, Mocius and others. Some of the burnt quarters of the city have been allowed to become rural and, as in late Byzantine times, the enclosure of the walls is no longer fully built over; there are orchards, and villages among them, within the Theodosian walls – they stretch most of the way up from the Silivri Gate to Topkapu. Everywhere there are unexpected market gardens; they fill most of the site of Blachernae. But the market gardens and the 'hollow gardens' of the cisterns are dusty and dreary, though in early spring their blossom and fresh greenness must lend a grace to very ungracious parts of Constantinople. (Judging from the charming post-cards on sale at photographers' shops, the city is always white either with fruit-blossom or with snow; I am very glad that I have never seen it in the latter aspect.)

As well as market gardens, Constantinople has a great number of vegetable and fruit markets. These have great charm; wandering among them when the sun is low, one feels something of the gentleness and graciousness of the East. Courgettes and aubergines are displayed geometrically, though not with quite the sense of design that I have noticed in Syria and the Lebanon. Black and red cherries are decoratively wreathed round the scale on which they are weighed. All kinds of rice, lentils, dried peas or beans or pine-nut kernels are becomingly displayed. There are tall pottles of strawberries, and huge, cart-wheel-size, flat baskets of red or white mulberries, decorated with little bunches of sweet peas. At night they are sometimes carried by, as on a bier, by two men, and lighted with a small lamp.

There must be a cat to every two inhabitants of the city, and an even higher proportion of pigeons. Everywhere the creatures swarm – it is sinful to kill them. The pigeons are much better fed, because it is more amusing to feed them, as well as being a meritorious act. The Eastern hatred of taking animal life is extremely shocking to some English people, whose love for animals finds its most natural expression in 'putting them to sleep'; but anyone who has loved an animal must feel gratitude for the way an Eastern vet will fight for its life, long after it would have been condemned in England. On the other hand, when animals are not wanted, they are horribly left to die. Some thirty years ago, when Constantinople was intolerably dog-ridden, the dogs of the city were collected, over a period of three weeks or a month, and marooned on the waterless island of Oxyaea. The Marmara resounded with their howling, and those who sailed near saw new arrivals being set upon by the others, who tore them to bits and drank their blood. Such a purge had taken place before, in the seventeenth century. The cats are never such a nuisance or such a danger, and their lives are more secure. Nevertheless, I was slightly unnerved by a sight I saw one evening. I was returning from the square of Bayazit to Pera in a *dolmus* taxi; one of the other passengers was an old woman carrying a big bag. When we reached Taxim, she got down, and let the cat out of the bag, with a cynical laugh.

Apart from the fruit and vegetable stalls, markets and bazaars are disappointing. As in the Mousky in Cairo, there is little that is worth looking at except rugs and embroideries from Persia. Travellers in the past have uttered similar complaints: 'Ask for a Turkish carpet,' said Clarke, the collector of manuscripts, 'you are told you must send for it to Smyrna; for

Greek wines — to the Archipelago; for a Turkish sabre — to Damascus; for the sort of stone expressly denominated *turquoise* — they know not what you mean; for red leather — they import it themselves from Russia or from Africa.' The Covered Bazaars are pleasant enough for a morning's walk, but the importunity of the vendors much exceeds that which you meet in Cairo, and the wares are inferior. One section smells intolerably of hides, like so many parts of Constantinople. And cheap tailors, and haberdashers' shops abound, and diminish the small romance that is left. A shop with the splendid name of 'Trebizond Bazaar' sells reach-me-down suits.

With the secularization and Europeanization of dress, life is ugly; the Turks are not a beautiful people, and needed the dignity that Eastern dress gave to them. And yet I have sometimes seen signs that the East is not entirely forgotten; I have seen them dance. One day, looking over the courtyard wall of the Süleymaniye into the sunk street beneath, I saw a piper and a drummer. Boys were dancing in a line — even two little girls standing apart, even a small brother and sister perched up on an unharnessed cart, even fowls (tethered by one leg to the wall), all seemed to be caught up by the wild rhythm. It was something like a Greek *syrtos*, but far more lively. Then they formed up, as for 'oranges and lemons', and danced with a hauling-in movement, as if they were drawing in a fishing line. Another day, in the blazing sun, I saw a builder dancing alone on the roof-top on which he was working. But such gaiety is rare in Istanbul.

Melancholy the city is, for all its splendid exterior: the best skyline in the old world, at least; but within Stamboul there are vast quarters of insignificant ugliness — such stretch all along the tram line out to the gate at Topkapu. Slums are less dense than those of Cairo, but sadder, as slums are worse the farther north one gets. Southern dirt is burnt up at once by the sun, and the most repellent dirt I have ever seen is that of Ostro-Bothnia. To me, as to most dwellers in the Byzantine or Ottoman empires, Constantinople is a cold, northern city; with heartbreak I would climb its slippery, almost perpendicular hills, whose gutters flowed with urine, or I would slosh down the filthy streets of Ayvan Saray or of Galata. Unburnt slums are largely wood-built, black and depressing, and inviting future fires; these also recalled Finland to me. In the burnt quarters there were often just piles of stone, or new brick buildings had just gone up, and gaped through windowless apertures, or there were hideous concrete blocks. It is a place where there has been no pretence of good building for more than a hundred years.

The art of Constantinople is, more than that of any other place, an escape. It is not the worse for that; it is an escape from the hideous architecture of the modern town, its pickaxe-torn and tram-tormented streets, its filthy foreshores, its stinking tanneries, its ugly faces, and its misery. These were not at all my business, and I had no compunction for escaping them as much as I could; I wish I could have escaped them altogether. But I have more warmth of feeling for the Arabian monuments of Cairo, in whose cool splendour one rests from the noise and heat of the day, not escaping the life of the modern town, to which they organically belong, but refreshing oneself for a return to it. Prayer there is still vital, while in Constantinople it is tepid, outside the holy place of Eyüp. A religious monument grows very cold, with the decay of the faith to which it owed its significance; and now that the Cross and the Crescent have learned to live side by side, dreading a common enemy, it does not seem right for Christians to rejoice in the decline of Islam, which is only another gain to infidelity over Deism. It is more conducive to cheerfulness to sit in such a building as the lovely Baghdad Kiosque, where there is only the fall of a decadent empire to remember.

All over the town were photographs of the celebrations of the fifth centenary of the Fall; from every other shop, it seemed, the handsome melancholy face of Mehmet II looked from the window, in more or less crude reproductions of Gentile Bellini's portrait – the face that Proust chose for Bloch. It also appeared on the top of boxes of cigarettes. One could not help wondering how the Greeks would really like to have this city, object of so many prayers and vows and legends of reconquest, now that the Turks hardly seem to value it any more.

No serious person, of course, wishes the poor kingdom of Greece to be burdened with the defence of the Dardanelles and the Bosphorus. No one who is not a visionary fails to be content that Greece has a strong and friendly power between her and the Black Sea. But, in the abstract, apart from all other considerations, would one like Constantinople to be Greek? It would of course be a more pleasant place, if it were.

I am too Philhellenic to wish it; to me it is Hellas that makes Hellenes, more than blood or tradition. Bavarian families who have come to Greece with Otto can now be regarded as perfectly Greek. And this scrag-end of Europe, this sad, misty Eastern Thrace, an outpost of the Hellenic world, is not Hellas, any more than Aden is England. The Byzantine empire, with its Asiatic rulers and its Roman heritage, never managed to be so Greek as modern Greece, never had so living a Greek language. It would be sad indeed to see a city with the brilliant light and the sparkling climate of Athens turn into a second capital, while life moved from the Aegean to the Bosphorus. Though it might be gratifying to see St. Sophia and SS. Sergius and Bacchus in Christian hands, it would be very unbecoming if they became an object of dispute between the churches. Moreover, such gratification would be outweighed by the even more rapid decay of the Islamic monuments. We are used to St. Sophia being a museum, and SS. Sergius and Bacchus being a mosque; it would be more horrifying to see Rustem Pasha turned into a café or the Süleymaniye into a bath. (I can think of hardly any instance of a mosque being turned into a church, except where it has originally been built as a church.)

There is no use in wishing to turn back the pages of history, the city has seen the fall of two empires, and now it is moribund. It must always be an inhabited site; it must be important to Turkey that no one else should have it; it is important to all lovers of beauty that its monuments should be preserved, though more and more they may come to seem 'the dreary monuments of past power and splendour'. It is a place to visit and not to live in, for it is a place that life is deserting; though it has given new hope to refugees from the Balkans, who have found shelter there, most of them plan to go on further to the west.

Sunset is, appropriately, its finest hour — between the heat of the day and the damp of the night. All my memories of that hour are grateful, whether I have passed it at the great view-points of Çamlica or Eyüp, the tower of Galata, or above the Adrianople Gate or, even more happily, have watched Asia turn from purple to blue, sitting on the water-front of Prinkipo. Even the early Bosphorus sunsets, behind Rumeli Hisar, have a melancholy beauty, watched from the deck of a steamer or from a *yali* on the Asiatic shore. And even the most rapid of tourists is likely to have a cherished memory of the boat-filled mouth of the Bosphorus turning dark, as one sits on the balcony of the Park Hotel. The muezzin leans from a neighbouring minaret, and gives the sunset call to prayer, gently and civilly addressing the apéritif drinkers. 'God is great, if I may say so', he seems to cry. It is a pity that Christianity, except in the measured beat of the *Angelus*, does not use a call to prayer; church bells are vaguer in their message. It would be delightful and edifying to hear from a London steeple: 'Dearly beloved brethren, the Scripture moveth us in sundry places. . . .'

The sunset hour is not long enough; too soon the waters darken, and the damp and noise of the night follow.

I left one day at dawn; my fellow-travellers had been all round the Mediterranean, and were exchanging impressions of hotels in Casablanca and Tel-Aviv; some of them, tired with the rapid round, thought they would leave out Athens. They had been whisked round Constantinople in the comfortable buses of a travel agency; I am not sure that they had not chosen the best way of seeing the place.

We drove down the familiar way — a last glance over the Golden Horn from the heights of Pera, a last shuddering look at the Dark Tower of Galata. We went up the Atatürk Boulevard, below the little domes of the Pantocrator, passed beneath the aqueduct of Valens, saw again the hideous mosque at Aksaray, that looks as if it were modelled in lard. We drove through the ugly quarters that stretch out towards Topkapu, slums of dark wooden houses or concrete blocks. I gave a backward glance at the land walls, so venerable and so tragic, and then we went on towards the airport, through quiet, green, Metrolandish country.

Extraordinary city — dove-haunted, tram-grating, hide-stinking, tomb-ringed, sea-surrounded. So splendid, and so squalid; so immortal, and so dead. One of the most beautiful cities in the world, one of the most interesting, and one of the most unpleasant. A city that can exercise such fascination, that can inspire an almost superstitious fear but (in me, at least) cannot wake an atom of love.

With no sorrow, but with some compunction for not having learned to come closer to it, I left it to fly over the Marmara, that salt lake that is so nearly Mediterranean. We crossed a corner of Anatolia, and there was the Aegean again — and Greece began at Mitylene, with its two deep gulfs. Here was a brightness of colour, a briskness and freshness of atmosphere unknown in the three enclosed seas of Constantinople. Soon Scyros, burial place of Theseus and of Rupert Brooke, was seen in the north, and then we were over Euboea, and the warm, red earth of Attica. Behind western hills was Megara from which, so long ago, Byzas and his companions set forth to found their city on the Golden Horn, opposite to Chalcedon 'the city of the blind'.

★

These pages were written before the fire, which destroyed a large part of the Covered Bazaars, and before the lamentable occurrences on 6 September, 1955, when Greek establishments were attacked, and Greek churches violated.

APPENDICES

APPENDIX A

A TABLE OF THE PRINCIPAL MONUMENTS, GROUPED ACCORDING TO THEIR LOCATION

North of the Golden Horn
Mosque of Piyale Pasha
Tower of Galata
Mosque of Azapkapu
Fountain of Tophane
Mosque of Kiliç Ali Pasha
Palace of Dolmabahçe
Palace of Yildiz

Eminönü Square
Egyptian Bazaar
Yeni Validé Mosque (Yeni Cami)
Mosque of Ruştem Pasha

The First Hill, and its slopes
St. Sophia
Fountain of Ahmed III
St. Irene
The Seraglio
The Museums
The Çinili Kiosque
The Basilican Cistern
The Hippodrome (remains and the monuments of the Spina)
The Great Palace (mosaic pavement)
Mosque of Sokullu Mehmet Pasha
SS. Sergius and Bacchus (Kuçuk Aya Sofya)
Sea Walls of the Marmara
Mosque of Ahmed I

The Second Hill, and its slopes
The Burnt Column
Nuruosmaniye Mosque
The Covered Bazaar

The Third Hill, and its slopes
Mosque of Bayazit II

Mosque of Laleli
Mosque of Shehzade
Mirelaion (Bodrum Cami)
Akataleptos (Kalender Cami)
Aqueduct of Valens
Mosque of Süleyman the Magnificent, and tombs
St. Theodore (?) (Kilise Cami)

The Fourth Hill, and its slopes
Mosque of the Conqueror (Fatih)
Pantocrator (Molla Zeyrek Cami)
Pantepoptes (Eski Imaret Cami)

The Fifth Hill, and its slopes
Mosque of Selim I, and tombs
Pammacaristos (Fetihye Cami)
St. John the Baptist in Trullo
Mouchliotissa
Patriarchal church of the Phanar
St. Theodosia (Gül Cami)

The Sixth Hill, and its slopes
Mosque of Mihrimah
Adrianople Gate
Tekfur Saray
St. Saviour in Chora (Kariye Cami)

The Seventh Hill, and its slopes
St. Andrew in Crisei (Koca Mustafa Pasha mesdjit)
Mosque of Hekimoğlu Ali Pasha
Mosque of Ramazan
St. John of the Studium (Imrahor Cami)
Castle of the Seven Towers

Extra-mural
The land walls
Tekiedj Ibrahim Agha
Mosque of Eyüp

Scutari
Mosque of Mihrimah (Büyük Cami)
Eski Validé Mosque
Yeni Validé Mosque
Çinili Mosque

APPENDIX B

TABLE OF RULERS OF CONSTANTINOPLE

East Roman Emperors
St. Constantine I, the Great, d. 337
Constantius II, 337-61
Julian the Apostate, 361-63
Jovian, 363-64
Valens, 364-78
Theodosius I, the Great, 379-95
Arcadius, 395-408
Theodosius II, 408-50
Marcian, 450-57
Leo I, 457-74
Leo II, 474
Zeno, 474-91
Anastasius I, 491-518
Justin I, 518-27
Justinian I, 527-65
Justin II, 565-78
Tiberius II, 578-82
Maurice, 582-602
Phocas, 602-10
Heraclius, 610-41
{ Constantine II, d. 641
{ Heracleonas, overthrown, 641
Constans II, 641-68
Constantine IV, 668-85
Justinian II, 685-95
Leontius, 695-98
Tiberius III, Apsinarus, 698-705
Justinian II (restored), 705-11
Bardanes, 711-13
Anastasius II, 713-16
Theodosius III, 716-17
Leo III, the Isaurian, 717-41
Constantine V, Copronymus, 740-75
Leo IV, 775-80
Constantine VI, 780-97

Irene, 797-802
Nicephorus I, 802-11
Stauracius, 811
Michael I, Rhangabes, 811-13
Leo V, the Armenian, 813-20
Michael II, the Amorian, 820-29
Theophilus, 829-42
Michael III, 842-67
Basil I, the Macedonian, 867-86
{ Leo VI, the Wise, 886-912
{ Alexander, 886-913
Constantine VII, Porphyrogenitus, 912-59
Romanus I, Lecapenus, 919-44
· Romanus II,[1] 959-63
{ Basil II, the Bulgar-slayer, 963-1025
{ Constantine VIII, 963-1028
{ Nicephorus II, Phocas, 963-69
John I, Zimisces, 969-76
Romanus III, Argyrus, 1028-34
Michael IV, the Paphlagonian, 1034-41
Michael V, 1041-42
Zoë and Theodora, 1042
Constantine IX, Monomachos, 1042-55
Theodora (restored), 1055-56
Michael VI, Stratioticus, 1056-57
Isaac I, Comnenus, 1057-59
Constantine X, Ducas, 1059-67
Romanus IV, Diogenes, 1067-71
Michael VII, Ducas, 1071-78
Nicephorus III, Botaniates, 1078-81
Alexius I, Comnenus, 1081-1118
John II, Comnenus, 1118-43
Manuel I, Comnenus, 1143-80
Alexius II, Comnenus, 1180-83

[1] Some historians here insert Stephanus and Constantine VIII, sons of Romanus I; hence inconsistencies in the enumeration of the Constantines.

Andronicus I, Comnenus, 1183-85
Isaac II, Angelus, 1185-95
Alexius III, Angelus, 1195-1203
Isaac II, Angelus (restored) ⎫
Alexius IV, Angelus   ⎬ 1203-04
Alexius V, Ducas, Murtzuphlus, 1204

Latin Emperors
Baldwin I, 1204-05
Henry, 1205-16
Peter, 1217-19
Robert, 1219-28
John of Brienne, 1228-37
Baldwin II, 1237-61

Emperors in Nicaea
Theodore I, Lascaris, 1204-22
John III, Ducas Valtatzes, 1222-54
Theodore II, Lascaris, 1254-58
John IV, Lascaris, 1258-61
Michael VIII, Palaeologus, 1259-82

The Restored Empire
Michael VIII, Palaeologus, 1261-82
⎧ Andronicus II, Palaeologus, 1282-
⎨ 1328
⎩ Michael IX, Palaeologus, 1293-1320
Andronicus III, Palaeologus, 1328-41
⎰ John V, Palaeologus, 1341-76
⎱ John VI, Cantacuzene, 1341-54
Andronicus IV, Palaeologus, 1376-79
John V, Palaeologus (restored), 1379-91
John VII, Palaeologus, 1390
Manuel II, Palaeologus, 1391-1425

John VIII, Palaeologus, 1425-48
Constantine XI, Palaeologus, Dragases,
   1448-53

Turkish Sultans
Mehmet II, the Conqueror, 1451-81
Bayazit II, the Mystic, 1481-1512
Selim I, the Great, 1512-20
Süleyman I, the Magnificent, 1520-66
Selim II, the Sot, 1566-74
Murad III, 1574-95
Mehmet III, 1595-1603
Ahmed I, 1603-17
Mustafa I ⎱ 1617-(1618)
Osman II ⎰ 1623
Murad IV, 1623-40
Ibrahim, 1640-49
Mehmet IV, 1649-87
Süleyman II, 1687-91
Ahmed II, 1691-95
Mustafa II, 1695-1703
Ahmed III, 1703-30
Mahmud I, 1730-54
Osman III, 1754-57
Mustafa III, 1757-74
Abdul Hamid I, 1774-89
Selim III, 1789-1807
Mustafa IV, 1807-08
Mahmud II, the Reformer, 1808-39
Abdul Mejid, 1839-61
Abdul Aziz, 1861-76
Murad V, 1876   ⎫
Abdul Hamid II, 1876-1909 ⎬
Mehmet V, 1909-17
Mehmet VI, 1917-22

INDEX

INDEX OF NAMES

INDEX OF PLACES

[1] It is very important to avoid confusion between the two Cannon gates, at opposite ends of Stamboul. The Topkapu Strait takes its name from that by the Marmara.